D1710244

THE 12-HOUR FILM EXPERT

THE 12-HOUR FILM EXPERT

Everything You Need to Know about Movies

Noah Charney and James Charney

ROWMAN & LITTLEFIELD
Lanham • Boulder • New York • London

Published by Rowman & Littlefield
An imprint of The Rowman & Littlefield Publishing Group, Inc.
4501 Forbes Boulevard, Suite 200, Lanham, Maryland 20706
www.rowman.com

86-90 Paul Street, London EC2A 4NE

British Library Cataloguing in Publication Information Available

Library of Congress Cataloging-in-Publication Data

Names: Charney, Noah, author. | Charney, James, 1946- author.
Title: The 12-hour film expert : everything you need to know about movies /
    Noah Charney and James Charney.
Other titles: Twelve-hour film expert
Description: Lanham : The Rowman & Littlefield Publishing Group, Inc., 2024.
    | Includes bibliographical references and index.
    | Summary: "The 12-Hour Film Expert is for anyone who wants to learn more about film
    and how to truly appreciate what they are watching, but they aren't sure where to begin.
    This book guides its readers through a selection of film masterpieces in a variety of genres,
    from silent films and westerns to dramas and romantic comedies"-- Provided by publisher.
Identifiers: LCCN 2023047801 | ISBN 9781538173428 (cloth) | ISBN 9781538173435 (epub)
Subjects: LCSH: Motion pictures.
Classification: LCC PN1994 .C34336 2024 | DDC 791.43--dc23/eng/20231128
LC record available at https://lccn.loc.gov/2023047801

To our leading ladies, Diane and Urška

CONTENTS

Acknowledgments

Watch the credits of any film and you'll see a seemingly endless list of people, hundreds of them, who were involved in the making of that film. There are Best Boys and Key Grips and First Assistant Directors to go with all the actors, stuntpeople, and special effects teams, down to accountants and caterers. Books from major publishing houses are not dissimilar, and so we would like to thank the Rowman & Littlefield team for their support and enthusiasm, beginning with Charles Harmon, Christen Karniski, and Deni Remsberg.

Our families are endlessly supportive. Thank you, Diane, Eleonora, Izabella, and especially Urška, who designed this book and made this truly a family project.

Noah

I am grateful to my father James for raising me with a love for, and knowledge of, movies. James kept a precious commodity in the pre-streaming, pre-internet days: hundreds of VHS tapes, each containing three movies that he painstakingly recorded from the TV, often skipping the commercials. There was a master list that amounted to nearly one thousand movies, and we worked our way through this list, including all the classics. It was a great way for a child to learn that older, black-and-white films can be just as wonderful (and sometimes more so) than the easy-to-like eye candy of color, quick-cut edit, action-packed movies that are so common today.

James

I am grateful to Noah for many reasons. He is the author of an array of books that make a father proud. And he is a very good son. When I was finishing up with the writing of my first book, which at the time I thought was to be my only book, I felt a bit at sea. The project had kept me happily busy during COVID-19. I enjoyed the writing. I even enjoyed the copyediting, which most people find tedious. Suddenly, I was contemplating having nothing more to do. I asked Noah if he ever had that reaction as he came to the end of a writing project. He told me that he avoided it by always having another project ready to start, or sometimes, even starting it before he had finished the one he was completing. Then, he said, "Why don't we write a book together?" I thought it was a wonderful idea, especially when he came up with the topic . . . movies! I think that offer was a wonderfully sensitive and loving thing to do to help his pop move on to the next thing. Thank you, Noah, for giving me this project for us to do together. You are a wonderful teacher (I have learned a lot about writing and publishing) and a great collaborator, and you made it fun.

Introduction

Like the rest of us, you surely watch a lot of films. But most of us do so as pure entertainment. That's fine—entertainment helps us wind down, relax, and escape into alternative worlds. There's a lot to be said for just lying on the couch, popcorn in hand, and letting yourself go.

But there is a world of people who would like to take their film experience a step further, a step deeper. If this sounds like you (and the fact that you are reading this makes us think it does), this book provides a concise and easy point of entry to understanding movies more deeply.

The 12-Hour Film Expert is formatted into twelve chapters that are divided into periods of film history and genres. It will take around twelve hours to read, but if you finish early, feel free to top it up with some screen time (or just cross out the "12" on the book cover and insert the number of hours you need). The point is to offer all you need to know to level up your screen entertainment and deepen your understanding of how films are made, and how to watch them in a more thoughtful way.

The chapters start with the invention of movies: the discovery of how to make pictures move, and then, how to tell a story with them. That brings us to chapter 2, on the era of silent movies when the techniques of filming and storytelling became increasingly sophisticated and movies became not just a novelty, but popular entertainment. Chapter 3 explores the development of the studio system in Hollywood, and how that system evolved to produce some of the best movies ever made. The following chapters each feature a specific movie "genre."

Westerns, gangster films, comedies, thrillers, horror, musicals, film noir, fantasy—these are all genres, with typical features that the audience can expect from film to film. Genre is a branding mechanism, a shorthand way of telling the audience more or less what to expect.

In the days when moviegoing was a weekly tradition, movies were predictable: different enough to be interesting, but not *too* different.

For a Western, for instance, the audience will know the era in which the story will take place, what the costumes will look like, that there will be horseback riding and gunfights, and the general nature of the story. The genre establishes a bond with the audience: predictable situations and characters, clusters of meaning around stock characters, themes, plot devices, and images. These repetitions bring the pleasures of familiarity to an audience, welcoming them back week after week.

Why not have a system where every movie is unique and filled with unknowns? Well, there is certainly a place for that and some of the greatest films fit no category. But many great films are refined and improved spins on a genre type, and excelling within the genre sometimes creates a new one. *The Godfather* (1972) is a good example. It is a gangster picture, but it took the essence of that genre and elevated it with complex characters, family conflict, an unexpected story, atmosphere, and superior acting. In transcending the genre, it energized it for a new generation.

For each genre that we cover, we will be giving you its history and the key figures and films within it. This book does not seek to be encyclopedic, and so there are genres we don't cover (war, documentary, animation, and costume drama, to name a few)—the goal is to provide an engaging and accessible point of entry. We hope that this will spark your interest and lead to watching many other films than those explored here and reading other great books on film. But we've chosen genres and elements of film that seem most universally applicable and most important to the story of film: its history and "how to watch," for this is really our goal. What is there about each film that makes it a good example of a particular genre? What did the key films do differently that is worth noting? How did they push the envelope and establish new precedents? The result of reading the book—and watching as many of the referenced films as you would like (and we do recommend that you "watch along" with the films we discuss)—is a capsule-sized "course" in film appreciation.

We guide you through a selection of the best movies of each genre and point you to the occasional masterpiece. The Key Films noted at the start of each chapter are all best of breed and are there primarily because they are definitive examples of the genre, the most important ones to watch.

The "Movie Playlists" at the back of the book contain a list of additional recommended viewing: top twelve lists for various genres and directors. The playlists cover good films that are definitely worth watching but are *not* discussed in the text, so our focus in each chapter can be on the key films and others that best convey the essence of each genre. You will get to know these films in depth. You can use them as a lens to enhance your understanding of the many other related films in the playlist and others that you encounter in the future.

So, read this book and it will be the only one you need to get started on film history, technique, and appreciation. It can be a gateway to reading and watching more, or your one-stop source to achieve a level of solid knowledge in a short amount of time.

We hope that reading about the movies will inspire you to watch many of them. Most of these films are easily found on streaming services, for rent or purchase online, or to borrow from your school or public library. We particularly recommend the Criterion Channel and Mubi, streaming services that offer well-curated selections of great films, old and new.

Of course, the best way to see any movie is in a darkened theater with an audience. You have few distractions, the darkness helps you stay focused, the big screen pulls you in, and the audience's reaction can enhance your own. Laughing by yourself at a comedy is nowhere near as satisfying as laughing with others. The gasp of surprise while watching a thriller or finding tears in your eyes during a tender moment in a drama are all the better when shared: strangers in the dark, together. Many universities and town libraries host regular showings of classic movies. Your local movie theater may occasionally feature classic films. If you have the opportunity to see any of these movies that way, grab it. If not, grab the popcorn and curl up at home.

Warning! Spoilers Ahead!

It is not possible to explain why a film belongs to a certain genre without giving away some plot elements: an unexpected development, a surprising revelation about a character's history, a new character arriving in the story to mix things up, even the sudden death of a main character. We have tried to minimize revealing important plot twists. But there will be some spoilers along the way, when we think that referencing plot points is necessary to help explain something important about how the movie works. We do it with the conviction that knowing the spoiler will not lessen your enjoyment of the movie once you see it. In fact, it may increase it, since you will experience the plot development with the new understanding our chapter brings.

Is the popcorn ready yet? Because here we go!

Chapter 1

The Invention of Movies

Key Films

A Trip to the Moon (1902)
The Great Train Robbery (1903)

Movies Don't Actually Move and Silent Movies Weren't Silent

Eadweard Muybridge (1830–1904) had a problem, and not just with figuring out how he'd like to spell his name—he changed it several times, toying with archaic spellings. The Englishman emigrated to the United States at the age of twenty and had some success as a bookseller before a serious head injury sustained in a stagecoach crash changed the course of his life.

Muybridge returned to England to recover and took up photography. He learned the contemporary wet-plate collodion process to develop film in a darkroom immediately after a photograph was taken. This immediacy made photography far more dynamic, replacing the original photography method, daguerreotype, which was complicated to produce and easily damaged. There was pace and excitement to the new process—take a photograph and then, within a day, you can hold it in your hand. Speed and the ability to capture motion stirred Muybridge's imagination.

Technically adept, he tinkered with improving the method of film development and worked on faster shutters for cameras. Both improvements would make it possible to take photos without the subject having to stand or sit still for long exposures, which had been the case with photography to date.

Back on his feet again, Muybridge moved to San Francisco and opened a successful photography business. He soon had contracts with the US government to document Alaska and the Yosemite Valley in California. This led him to meet Leland Stanford and to his big problem.

Stanford was the former governor of California, a senator, and the founder of Stanford University. A rich industrialist, he was also president of the Central and Southern Pacific Railways. Racehorses were his hobby and his passion. He hired Muybridge to document their gaits. He was interested to find out if, when running at a trot or a gallop, all four hooves ever left the ground at the same time. This was not visible to the naked eye, so swiftly did the horses pummel the turf as they raced. But perhaps this relatively new technology, and Muybridge's improvements upon it, could document the answer.

Muybridge's first attempts to photograph this, in 1873, were blurry and inconclusive. But Stanford was intrigued. After some "distractions" in Muybridge's personal life (he killed his wife's lover, shooting him point-blank with a revolver, and was then acquitted for "justifiable homicide"), he returned to tackling the problem—how to clearly photograph a horse in motion. His solution came in 1878, after increasing the sensitivity of the film emulsion, and dramatically improving the speed of the shutter. He laid out a series of twelve cameras along the racetrack, with trip wires set to open each camera shutter in turn.

Testing several horses, he was able to show that indeed all four hooves left the ground when galloping. But what no one had suspected was that the legs were gathered under the torso, and not stretched out, as had been thought and as many paintings depicted. This discovery was a media sensation, covered extensively in the press. It wasn't so much about how horses run as it was a demonstration that this new technology of photography could show something that the normal eye could not see.

Muybridge had silhouettes of the photo images painted onto glass discs and displayed them using a device he invented, the wonderfully named "zoopraxiscope," which created the illusion of motion through a sequence of images. This was the inspiration for Thomas Edison's kinetoscope, a peep-show device for one person to view at a time. The principle will be familiar to anyone who has ever made flipbook animations. Draw a series of images, each one in a slightly different position from the previous, and then flip through the images quickly. Our eyes "read" the image as moving, when in fact our minds are just sewing together a series of still images. This is how early cartoons were made. And Muybridge is credited as the forefather of cinematography for having invented this method for stitching still images together so that we view them as moving.

Supported by the University of Pennsylvania, Muybridge continued to create motion studies of animals, and of people, all with an eye toward scientific study, rather than entertainment. He wrote himself into the history of movies not only through his proto-film technical advances. In 1893, he hired a hall at the Chicago World Columbian Exhibition and projected his motion pictures to a paying public for the first time. Tickets were sold to an audience intrigued to see "moving pictures," which is the original term for what we now call "movies."

Making Movies Move

When we watch a movie, even today, we see a series of still photo images, projected at a steady rate. Your brain does the work, to make the images appear to be moving.

Creating the machinery to show us these images was complicated and not always obvious. Often the sticking point was that the technology had not yet been invented to do what was needed. For instance, Thomas Edison and his employee, William Dickson, working on the kinetoscope, first put the images onto cylinders, which had been used for the first sound machine, the phonograph (the predecessor to the modern record player). But the images were blurry and tiny. Then they tried putting the images onto celluloid, a mixture of chemicals that resulted in a synthetic plastic. This was an improvement since the images on it were far better defined.

But it was not until George Eastman and his colleagues invented flexible celluloid, in 1889, which could be fed through a sprocket system at speed, that they were able to get clear enough images that could be shown in sequence and looked like they were moving. This invention led to film coming in rolls for still photography (Eastman was the founder of Kodak), and reels for projecting film. Edison understood that, for the device to work, each image needed to pause in front of the lamp, light projecting through the image onto a screen, to be seen by the viewer for a split second, before being replaced by the next image. You couldn't just run the images through without stopping. Each image needed to linger for a moment for the eye of the viewer to register it.

Edison's solution was soon bested by the **Maltese-cross gear** which translates a smooth rotating movement into an intermittent one, advancing one frame at a time in front of the lens and the light source. Sprockets in the film roll, which are engaged by gears, made the movement of the roll predictable and smooth.

In the earliest films, the speed past the lens was as slow as twelve frames per second. Though these "movies" did seem to move, because the images changed so slowly, they would appear to flicker. This led to their affectionate nickname, "the flicks," with early viewers suggesting they "go see a flick," if they wanted to go to a cinema.

The later silent movies were projected at sixteen frames per second, and they still did flicker, making the images seem jerky. Near the end of the silent era, the speed was up to twenty. This speed all but eliminated flicker. But the nickname stuck.

What was missing was enough speed to pass the brain's **critical flicker fusion** rate, which scientists determined is fifty images per second. At that speed, all flicker is lost and you see smooth movement from the sequence of nonmoving photos.

The standard speed for motion pictures in a modern projector is twenty-four frames per second, which you would think would be too slow. But the intermittent stop and start of the frame has one more eccentricity. You see each image two or three times in quick succession: once when the frame enters an exposure gate with a double- or triple-blade shutter, and then again, after one or two interruptions caused by the shutter blades before it leaves and is replaced by the next frame. Seeing each frame twice or three times brings it up to (or well above) the fifty-images-per-second threshold that gives us the appearance of continuous, smooth motion.

The Beginnings of an Industry

Thomas Edison didn't invent movies, but he did figure out a way to sell them. The device he and his workers invented to show his films, the kinetoscope, was used in viewing parlors called nickelodeons. You looked into a viewer attached to a large box and one person at a time could see what Edison produced.

It was first demonstrated to the public in 1891 but was still a work in progress. By 1894, nickelodeons in New York, and then Chicago and San Francisco, contained several kinetoscope machines, each with a different short movie. You could watch them, one at a time, for five cents each. It became a very popular form of entertainment.

Edison had constructed a windowless building, called the Black Maria, to make movies at his laboratory in Menlo Park, New Jersey. The building could be rotated and the roof could be opened to take maximum advantage of sunlight. There, his workers started churning out movies. Most of these movies were only a few seconds long (never, at first, more than a minute, since the amount of film that could fit into early cameras was limited), but as long as they moved, people were fascinated. Well, as with so much technology, it was a hit until the public grew accustomed to it, and wanted more.

To meet this demand for content, Edison showed them various five-second films, including "Fred Ott's Sneeze" (1894, in which Fred takes a pinch of snuff and, you guessed it, sneezes), a sexy woman dancing, a dog killing a rat, a cockfight, a muscleman showing off, a clip simply called "Kiss" and, later, among dozens of other curiosities, prizefights. These were all moments created for the movies in his black box studio. In each, the camera stayed in one place and there was no story being told, just a staged incident. By 1908, there were some eight thousand nickelodeon parlors filled with these machines, scattered in the larger cities of the United States.

Edison showed only half-hearted interest in figuring out how to project his images onto a screen so that an audience of more than one at a time could watch. He thought that letting a group of people see one of these movies together would kill his lucrative business.

But things were happening in Europe that showed how wrong he was. European inventors developed projection systems that would soon put the peepshows out of business.

Learning to Tell a Story

Auguste and Louis Lumière saw the kinetoscope in Paris and were inspired. In 1895, they developed what they called the Cinématographe, which could record, develop, and, most importantly, project movie images. Theirs was not the first such system (there is much debate about who invented the first projection system, with claims from the English as well as the French), but it was the first that could record the movie and project it, too. Their first public showing to a paid audience was in December of that year, an event considered the official "invention of the movies" as the art form we have today.

Their movies were fifty-second-long documentary moments, not staged but simply real-life events caught on film: street scenes, workers leaving their factory, someone fishing, and the first "gag"—a boy steps on a garden hose and then jumps off, dousing the gardener with water. Though they toured showing these films and considered their invention's real importance to be historical and scientific, recording different cultures throughout the world, their true interest was in developing color photographs. To date, all photographs and films had been monochrome: grayscale or sepia (brownish). The only exceptions were hand colored, painted after the film had developed.

When George Méliès (1861–1938) tried to buy one of their cameras, they dissuaded him, saying there's no future in making movies for entertainment.

Méliès ignored their advice and began making his own films to show at the Théâtre Robert-Houdin, where he had originally performed as a magician. Méliès's most popular films were at first his "féeries," fairy stories, with fantastic costumes and sets and special effects, most of which he invented. We might call them fantasy today, or even early science fiction.

Méliès devised many camera effects that became standard in movie-making. **Double-exposure** can create ghostly images. The **stopped camera** allows a man to become a woman, or to transform into a caterpillar, or to suddenly vanish, and would also allow a background to suddenly change, and then change again. It simply involved stopping the camera, swapping out one subject for another, and then starting it again, making the change appear sudden. **The dissolve** involves one scene that seems to melt into another. He also experimented with **parallel cross-cutting**, showing simultaneous events happening separately, which generated suspense. For example, we might see a woman kidnapped by the villain, then cut away to the hero racing to her rescue but not there yet, and then back to the woman and the villain. He also created **match cuts**, showing, for instance, a person leaving one room and entering

Figure 1.1 *A Trip to the Moon* (1902, France) aka *Le voyage dans la lune*. Directed by Georges Méliès. Star Film / Edison Manufacturing Company / Photofest © Star Film / Edison Manufacturing Company.

another. These techniques added to the growing language of film, discovering what an audience could understand as a continuation and deepening of the story, and what might confuse them.

At first his movies were just opportunities to show off camera tricks. It was only later that he began to use them as a vehicle to tell stories, usually fanciful ones, many inspired by the hugely popular fantasy novels of Jules Verne. He was one of the first to use storyboards to plan his films. His most famous movie was *A Trip to the Moon* (1902), where a rocket ship, looking like a giant bullet, lands in the eye of the Man in the Moon, an image famous in movie history. The scientist and his friends on this expedition are kidnapped by lunar aliens. They throw the king of the moon-men to the ground, and he disappears in a cloud of smoke (hand colored, as many images were in his films). Then they return to Earth, splashing down in the ocean (actually the water of a fish tank in double exposure). The film was fourteen minutes long and was a sensation both in Europe and in the United States, where pirated copies dominated. Even in its earliest days, an illegal industry of pirated films existed.

Though a brilliant creator, Méliès was a terrible businessman. He went bankrupt and lost control of his library of films. In a fit of pique, he burned many of his negatives while many others were melted down for their silver and celluloid content. The celluloid was turned into items as mundane as the heels for shoes produced by the French military. Fortunately, some two hundred of his films still exist, because paper prints were preserved for copyright in the US Library of Congress.

Silent Movies Weren't Silent

Quite early in their existence, silent films were no longer silent. Projected onto a screen, they would be accompanied by a live pianist or even a small orchestra. The music would be continuous, responding to the action on the screen and improvising on it. Later, production companies would provide sheet music for the pianist to follow, with suggested themes to accompany the ingenue or the hero, a love scene, or a chase. Sometimes there would be added sound effects, again done live for each showing.

Edwin Porter, who worked initially for Edison, pioneered the story film at about the same time as Méliès. His approach was quite different. He was not interested in camera tricks, only in trying to figure out how best to tell his story.

The Life of an American Fireman (1903) shows his first steps in developing the grammar, the language of film. Most early stories were linear, with one event leading to another. There was no sense of drama, all was in the "showing." However, changing camera placements provided for variety. Changing the point of view allowed you to see things from a different angle, a different perspective, and was a way to bring your attention to what the filmmaker wanted you to know. A normal movie sequence would start with the **establishing shot**, showing an entire room or space. The **medium shot** emphasizes people interacting. The **close-up**, often of a face, shows emotion or an object of importance.

At first, almost all the shots in Porter's films were wide establishing shots, one after another. But an early example of the close-up can be found when a fire alarm sounds. Of course, the audience doesn't hear it, as at this point no sound was recorded. But you see it up close, the ringing bell, telling us visually that the alarm is sounding. Then the action and the story begin.

A fireman, seen in an establishing shot, first has a premonition about his wife and child. Then the alarm goes off, and the fire trucks race to a burning house. This becomes a procession, one horse-drawn fire truck after another. The camera position does not change. As a result, it feels repetitive and boring when it could be exciting had he included close-ups, perhaps, of the firemen on the trucks, or cutaways to the burning house and the mother and child trapped there, possibly with the camera moving to follow the action.

The rescue of the mother and child is shown from two points of view, one after another—from inside the burning house and then outside. The idea that the two could be mixed, alternating from one to the other to increase suspense, was not yet in play. There are experiments with editing, "cutting" from the alarm to the fireman responding, for example. **Cutting** refers to the actual technique used with celluloid film: you had to physically cut off a section of film and then paste another section in its place to insert a different camera shot into the roll of film that will be shown as the movie. That new level of sophistication would come in his next project.

The Great Train Robbery (1903) was the first popular "Western," a term for movies that took place in the American West, often involving cowboy heroes. This was a time when train travel was the most modern and exciting mode of transportation, of consistent fascination to the public. The movie shows the train stopping, robbers boarding it, dynamiting a box of valuables, fighting with the engineer, forcing the passengers off, and escaping on the decoupled locomotive. In this movie, Porter shows simultaneous actions by cutting between them: the train robbery, the telegraph operator recovering from being knocked out, and alerting the posse that will chase the robbers. Almost all of the shots are static. The camera is in a fixed position, recording what is happening in front of it. Porter moves the camera three times, panning to follow the action (for instance, as the outlaws jump off the train and run into the woods). He is discovering how to make the story more exciting, more interesting to watch.

The last image in the movie became famous, even though it has nothing to do with the story. In the only close-up in the movie, one of the outlaws looks straight at the audience (breaking the **fourth wall**), points his gun directly at them (or rather, at us, as we collectively are watching it), and fires. This was quite shocking at the time.

Acknowledging that an audience is present watching a movie, or indeed watching a theatrical play or admiring a work of art, goes against what Aristotle described, in ancient Athens, as an audience's "willing suspension of

Figure 1.2 George Barnes (uncredited) as a bandit. The gun pointed directly at the audience caused panic when the movie was first shown. *The Great Train Robbery* (1903). Edison Manufacturing Company / Photofest © Edison Manufacturing Company.

disbelief." The premise was that audiences will enjoy a theatrical performance by switching off their disbelief—the fact that they logically know that they are in a theater watching actors pretend to be characters in a made-up story—to allow themselves the escapist pleasure of immersion in the story. If we attend a play and keep thinking to ourselves "This is all made up, that's an actor pretending, that blood is actually ketchup," then it sucks the fun out of the experience and makes it impossible for us to be moved by, or emotionally involved in, what we see. That was the case in the fourth century BCE and remains so today. The term "breaking the fourth wall" refers to proscenium arch theaters, in which the audience sits in front of the actors and pretends that they are watching something real take place, while the actors are surrounded on three sides by curtains and the backstage. The fourth wall is imaginary, like a glass window the audience looks through to watch the play—or a screen that the audience stares at watching images move across it to tell a story. To "break" the fourth wall is to have an actor turn to the audience, looking directly out at them, shattering the illusion that we are watching something real, reminding us that we, the audience, are there and that what we are seeing is pretend. This was often done intentionally in stage plays throughout history, but this was the first instance in which it was done in a movie. And it was an action that brought the violence of what the audience enjoyed watching—an armed robbery—to them directly, by turning a gun on them and firing. Hot stuff, circa 1903.

This movie, though not inventing anything that hadn't been tried before, had a real impact, combining elements from other films into an exciting adventure. Porter acknowledged that he had learned much from watching the films of Méliès. But *The Great Train Robbery* was the most popular film to date. It was shown for years in vaudeville houses, amusement centers, and nickelodeons throughout the country.

In just ten years, movies had gone from a curiosity ("Fred Ott's Sneeze") to a minor diversion (street scenes, a woman dancing), to telling real stories. Not depending on language their appeal could be international and was.

They were about to enter their golden age.

Chapter 2

The Golden Age of Silent Movies

Key Films

The Gold Rush (1925)
Sunrise, or A Song of Two Humans (1927)

David Wark Griffith (1875–1948) took silent films to another level. He started, as most directors did, making short films. But European films were pointing the way to longer, more complicated stories. A biblical epic from Italy, *Quo Vadis*, was 120 minutes long! So Griffith made his own Bible-themed movie, *Judith of Bethulia* (1914), which was sixty minutes long. The studio he was working for, Biograph, discouraged these longer films; according to the pioneering silent film actress Lillian Gish, they thought that such long movies would "hurt [people's] eyes."[1] This was enough for Griffith to leave Biograph and form his own company.

His next film, nearly three hours long, was his most influential, and most provocative: *The Birth of a Nation* (1915). It showed Southern slavery as benign, with caricatured portraits of Blacks as brutish, and it glorified the Ku Klux Klan as the (white) saviors of the nation. It was controversial at the time, with the NAACP (National Association for the Advancement of Colored People) declaring it racist and trying to stop it from being shown. There were riots in several Northern cities in protest. But it was also incredibly popular and made a lot of money; it cost some $100,000 to make, and it is estimated to have earned over $60 million worldwide; a huge amount.

Griffith used the **iris**—a shape, most often a circle, usually used to close a scene—to instead focus on a character or a situation by isolating it (the iris circle would get bigger to open up into the scene, gradually close as the scene ended one, or narrow the view to emphasize or point to something important). Griffith employed fade-outs for transitions and often showed parallel action in early battle scenes and in the sequence where his star, Lillian Gish, is rescued from a Black mob. Griffith had a Victorian sensibility and was a Southerner, and this story (indeed, all the stories he filmed) reflected that. The Victorian cliché of the "maiden in distress" was central to all his feature films. Gish was one of the first proper Hollywood stars, with an expressive face which Griffith often photographed in extended close-ups. She had a long career lasting into the 1980s.

No expense was spared. Griffith commissioned a full three hours of original music for the film, which was to be played by a live orchestra or piano while the film was screened. The composer excerpted classical pieces, folk, and popular songs, to add to his original music, with a specific musical theme for each character. Richard Wagner's "Ride of the Valkyries" was the glorified leitmotif for the Ku Klux Klan. The theme used for a romantic pairing in the film was published in sheet music as "The Perfect Song" and was the first example of marketing for a film, using the song's popularity played on the radio to sell the movie.

The ugly racism aside (if one can set it aside), *The Birth of a Nation* was so effective in part because it was so well made. It was also important to film history as it was the first full-length film made in Hollywood, California, where D. W. Griffith had moved. He'd chosen it as an ideal location for filming thanks to its reliable weather, and to escape the scrutiny of Edison's Trust (more on this later). Griffith's ability to tell a story on film was a head above that of anyone else at the time. His camera placements, the tracking shots during battle scenes, his use of lighting, and his reliance on close-ups of his actors to convey emotion and what they were thinking were all revolutionary and came to be cinematic staples. The viewer can struggle to separate a hateful person from the art that person creates, but when examining *Birth of a Nation* purely from the perspective of storytelling through the relatively new art of film, the movie was a triumph and a hugely influential work. This is why, though difficult to watch for its repulsive message, it remains a core work to study in film history courses. The film critic Roger Ebert, in an essay from his *Great Movies* series, wrote, "*The Birth of a Nation* is not a bad film because it argues for evil . . . it is a great film that argues for evil. To understand how it does so is to learn a great deal about film, and even something about evil."[2]

Despite the commercial success of *Birth of a Nation*, Griffith was stung by the criticisms that it was racist. He did not consider it racist. His response was an even more complicated movie (and a longer one, at three and a half hours), *Intolerance* (1916). The film told four stories, each one in a different century and presented in parallel, each intending to demonstrate that revolutionary ideas were always persecuted. This was an epic with a cast of thousands (not just hundreds made to look like thousands, as he had used in *Nation*), dressed in lavish period costumes, presented before enormous sets (the set for a sequence in ancient Babylon was three hundred feet high). Each story had its distinctive coloring in the original prints.

The film cost over $300,000, which was not extreme for an epic film at the time. *The Big Parade* (1925), directed by King Vidor and starring John Gilbert, considered one of the greatest war films of all time, cost about the same. But this was Griffith's own money, so it was quite a risk. *Intolerance* proved a failure. Audiences came away confused by the multiple storylines told in parallel, and they didn't seem interested in his implied argument that he and *Birth of a Nation*, like these four historical moments of revolutionary thought condemned, had been wrongfully accused of racism. It was an expensive flop when it came out, though today it is considered a masterpiece of silent cinema and is studied in film courses.

Chastened, Griffith returned to the melodramas he was most comfortable with. He had some success, in large part thanks to Lillian Gish, who became one of the first bankable stars in the movies: an actor the audience would come to see no matter what the film was about. His later films, in their moralistic style, were quickly considered old-fashioned—he had lost his audience. Griffith left the movies in 1931. Though acknowledged by Charlie Chaplin and others as "The Teacher of Us All," he died, alone, in 1948.

The Edison Trust

The birth of the film studio system owes a lot to Thomas Edison—and trying to escape him. Edison was a shrewd businessman. In 1908, he tried to monopolize the budding film industry by bringing patent-violation suits against his competitors. Since he owned (by invention or purchase) patents that covered most of the cameras needed for motion pictures at the time, he threatened to sue producers if they didn't pay him license fees. That threat persuaded all the major film companies in the United States (including Eastman Kodak, which supplied the raw film), and many in Europe, to join his trust. The only exception was Biograph, which owned one central necessary patent (for the Latham film loop, a way of threading the film through the projector to avoid tearing the sprockets) and used that patent to renegotiate with Edison and finally to join the trust on more favorable terms.

From that point, filmmaking and distribution were controlled by an established group, discouraging any new companies from forming. Films could at first only be one reel long, thirteen to seventeen minutes (eventually, they allowed two- and three-reel movies), and could only be rented by cinemas, assuring that only good-quality prints were exhibited. Much of this was beneficial for the young industry, but the limit on the length of films discouraged making longer features, which froze creativity and progress.

Independent filmmakers, who represented about one-quarter of the market in new films, responded first by moving production to Southern California, to get as far away from Edison's New Jersey headquarters as possible, making it difficult for Edison's lawyers to enforce the rules. Hollywood had the additional advantage of being close to the border of Mexico, where an independent production company could run with its equipment if Edison threatened to seize it.

The sun and steady weather of Los Angeles and the range of filming locations made it ideal for making movies. D. W. Griffith made *Intolerance* there, and by 1916 much of the industry had moved there, too.

This en masse move to California put the trust under pressure. Kodak was the first to part ways with the trust and begin to allow independents to purchase raw film. Then Carl Laemmle, future founder of Universal Pictures, attacked the trust in newspapers and created his own film exchange that offered more generous terms to rent a movie to a theater for projection. In 1915, the US government ruled that the Edison Trust was a monopoly, and it was dissolved.

After seven years under Edison's thumb, independent companies could now flourish, and many consolidated, forming fewer, bigger companies that were already based in and around Hollywood, California. Most were run by Jewish businessmen, former store owners, or theater owners who saw profit potential in this new industry. In addition to Laemmle, Adolph Zucker and Jesse Lasky founded Famous Players, and then Paramount Pictures, while Samuel Goldwyn (born Samuel Goldfish) and Louis B. Mayer established Metro-Goldwyn-Mayer, or MGM, two of the powerhouses still in operation today. The Keystone Film Company was home to Mack Sennett, making slapstick comedies, with the famously stumbling, slapstick Keystone Cops, inevitably receiving pies in the face, while also featuring a young Charlie Chaplin. Another major producer, Warner Brothers (Jack, Sam, Albert, and Harry Warner) was founded later, in 1923. United Artists was founded in 1919 by three major stars and one director: Mary Pickford, Douglas Fairbanks Senior, Charlie Chaplin, and D. W. Griffith. With the stars owning their own studio, they had creative and financial control over their films.

The Stars of Silent Film

In 1908, just as Edison was setting up his trust, Carl Laemmle hired actress **Florence Lawrence** from Biograph—one of the competing studios. She had been known as "The Biograph Girl." She was very popular, but film companies then tried to keep their actors anonymous to better control them—often the public would not know their names. Laemmle offered Lawrence to have her name in the credits, realizing that a favorite actor could sell a film. So she left Biograph and joined Famous Pictures, boosting the studio's bottom line. This was the beginning of the **star system**, with other stars soon to follow.

Charlie Chaplin (1889–1977) looms large in the history of movies. Born in poverty in London, he began a career in music halls as a comedian, joined a company that brought him to the United States, and was recruited by Mack Sennet's Keystone Studios in 1914. In only his second film, he created his character "the Tramp." As he described it in his autobiography: "I wanted everything to be a contradiction: the pants baggy, the coat tight, the hat small and the shoes large. . . . I added a small mustache which, I reasoned, would add age without hiding my expression. I had no idea of the character. But the moment I was dressed, the clothes and the makeup made me feel the person he was. I began to know him, and by the time I walked on stage he was fully born."[3]

The single-reel film that introduced The Tramp was *Kid Auto Races at Venice* (1914). To save money, Sennet often used public events as the setting for his short films—sending a crew to improvise a story around what was happening. In this one, Chaplin, as the Tramp, is a spectator who constantly gets in the way of the cameraman filming a go-cart race.

Chaplin made a point of learning every aspect of moviemaking and kept asking to direct his own films. Sennet finally relented when Chaplin offered to pay if it didn't do well. The movie was *Caught in the Rain* (1914) and it was very successful. From then on, he directed all his films—about one a week. His style was different from the other frantic low comedies from Keystone— slower, calmer, with pantomime that was as graceful as it was funny.

When, at the end of the year, with Chaplin's fame rising, Sennet refused to pay him the $1,000 per week he demanded, Chaplin left for Essanay Studios, which gave him a $10,000 bonus. He formed one of the first stock companies of regulars (actors and crew on long-term contracts with a single studio) and made one hit after another—always as the Tramp. The character gradually evolved, becoming more romantic. In *The Tramp* and *The Bank* (1915), he added a touch of pathos to the story, moments of longing and disappointment, and in the latter, the story ended sadly—something that had not been done in a comedy before.

Incredibly productive, churning out film after film, Chaplin became a worldwide phenomenon: the first international film star. Demanding more time to make films of better quality, he changed studios again and again, each time making more money for fewer films. But the movies got better and better—more sophisticated stories, with drama mixed with comedy.

He joined with Mary Pickford, W. F. Griffith, and Douglas Fairbanks to form United Artists, a studio that gave each of them full control of their output. With this freedom, Chaplin made his longest film to date, *The Kid* (1921), costarring four-year-old Jackie Coogan.

An unwed mother leaves her infant in a car with a note asking whoever finds him to care for him with love. The Tramp finds the baby and tries to give him away, with no luck. Meanwhile, the car is stolen and when the mother, having changed her mind, looks for the car and sees it gone, she faints. Meanwhile, the Tramp has taken the child home. They become a family. Five years later, they are also a grifter team: the Kid throws stones at a window and then the Tramp shows up offering to repair it. The mother has become a wealthy actress forever looking for her child, whom she often passes in the street, unknowing. When the child falls ill and the doctor comes, he discovers that the Tramp is not the father and threatens to put the child in an orphanage. They run away, fugitives. The doctor tells the mother of a note he found—the note she wrote and left with the baby years before. The Kid is found and taken away—reunited with the mother he never knew. The Tramp frantically searches for him, returning to their home. He falls asleep in the doorway and is awakened by a policeman who takes him to a mansion— where he is greeted by the mother and the Kid, who jumps into his arms. All is well.

The plot was sentimental but told with tenderness and humor. The audience swerved from big belly laughs to tears. This combination of emotions produced by a single film was a leap in sophistication. It was immediately considered a masterpiece. If producing, directing, and starring weren't enough, Chaplin even wrote the music, which was played by a live orchestra. It premiered at Carnegie Hall as a benefit for homeless children—combining a philanthropic good deed with a stroke of promotional genius—and it was a major hit. Little Jackie Coogan became the first child star.

Our favorite Chaplin film is **The Gold Rush** (1925). It was meant to be an epic comedy, the story of a prospector looking for gold and love in the

Figure 2.1 Charlie Chaplin. *The Gold Rush* © Charles Chaplin. Screenshot captured by authors.

Klondike Mountains. The film contains a scene that became part of the cultural oxygen, a moment that many will be familiar with even if they haven't seen the entire film. Classic movies are scattered with such moments that then become cultural touchstones, reference points that transcend the genre of film or even the viewership of the film in which the moment appears. *The Gold Rush* provides perhaps the earliest such moment.

Hungry, Chaplin delicately prepares a meal out of his shoe, treating his shoelaces like spaghetti, and the shoe leather and nails that bind the shoe together like turkey with all the trimmings. It is quietly and touchingly funny. We know how hungry his partner, Big Jim, is because he hallucinates that the Tramp has turned into a delicious-looking chicken and starts chasing him. Never before had a special effect been used for comedy. In another scene, Charlie's dance with the bread rolls is a classic too, funny and sweet and sad. *The Gold Rush* was full of such important firsts that resonated with viewers.

Chaplin's next great film defied the new technology of sound. *City Lights* (1930) was made as a silent film, though at a time when every new film was a **talkie**. The only concession to the new age was that Chaplin was able to attach a musical soundtrack that he composed, thus shifting the musical aspect of the film from a live orchestra or piano in each theater to a special track baked into the film itself.

Buster Keaton (1885–1966) was the other comic genius of the silent era. His career was more problematic because he was not the businessman that Chaplin was and was not able to retain control the way Chaplin did. Still, the movies he made are classics—and are often funnier, more creative, and more modern than Chaplin's.

Chaplin had his one character—the Tramp—who changed in small ways but was essentially static. Chaplin's stories were sentimental and touching. Keaton was always inventing new gags and new ways to tell a story. He was very physical and acrobatic and created dangerous stunts for himself to perform. Though he played different characters, he was always the "Great Stone Face," his nickname: seeming without emotion, deadpan, no matter what was happening. His lack of reaction was the kicker to the gag.

Like Chaplin, he directed and starred in all his films. Though he often used someone else's scripts, almost all the gags were his. Film critic Roger Ebert said, of the period from 1920 to 1929 when Keaton made film after film, that it proved him to be the "greatest actor-director in the history of movies."[4]

Though, like Chaplin, he got his start making one-reel short comedies, many of which are brilliant, Keaton's greatest films were full-length. In *Sherlock, Jr* (1924), he plays a movie projectionist who spends his time at work studying a book on how to become a detective. While showing a movie about the theft of a pearl necklace, he falls asleep and dreams that he is in the movie. He appears to approach the screen and walk *into* it, joining the story. At several points, Keaton is kicked out of the film and climbs back in, and the scenes behind him change but Buster remains there, wherever it is—the effect is surreal, wonderfully weird, and funny.

The movie plays with the idea of movies. While what makes the movie fun is simple, largely slapstick comedy, the concept is quite highbrow. A movie about a movie projector who walks into and out of a movie sounds like a postmodernist act of conceptual art and was truly revolutionary at the time.

The climax of *Steamboat Bill* (1928) is one of the most famous moments in silent comedy history. Our hero is in the hospital when a hurricane hits. The walls of the hospital are blown away. As he walks through town, the entire front of a building collapses on him. He is saved because there is an open window exactly where he is standing. He did this stunt himself, with no special effects, and the building facade weighed more than a ton. The markers for the safe place to stand for the gag to work were just a pair of nails. Afterward, he just walks off, and then is blown into the air, clinging to trees and landing finally in the water. This is another of those iconic film moments, like Chaplin eating his shoe, that is familiar to so many people, whether or not they've seen the film in which it occurs.

Harold Lloyd completes the trio of the top comics in the silent film world. His comedy often involved stunts but they were less elaborate (and less punishing) than Keaton's. They also tend to be less funny. But he was very popular. *Safety Last!* (1923) and *Grandma's Boy* (1922) were early hits.

Other genres were developing during this time, and you can see from film to film the discovery of new possibilities, of new ways to convey action, feeling, and story. But also, some themes and structures would be repeated because they were popular and had an audience. They would come to be called "genres." These include the Western, the Swashbuckling Adventure, the Sentimental Drama, and more. Early instances of them developed templates for formulae that would be followed, with usually basic variations in plot and character. This period laid the foundations for genre films to come.

Comic actors were not the only stars of the silent era. **Rudolph Valentino** was the epitome of the romantic action hero, an Italian professional dancer whose persona in film was that of a romantic playboy. He made his mark in *The Four Horsemen of the Apocalypse* (1921). Then he played the title role in the hit film, *The Sheik* (1921), forever defining himself as the "Latin lover." He took his work seriously and tried to make the Arab sheik both dignified and sympathetic, even as he seduced the women around him. He followed this with *Blood and Sand* (1922), in which he played a bullfighter, confirming his image and his enormous appeal. He then joined the United Artists, where he was able to have full control over his pictures.

Women craved him, while men found him not manly enough, too much of a dandy. When he died tragically young, of a perforated ulcer at the age of thirty-one, more than one hundred thousand people lined the streets of New York for his funeral and there were riots as fans tried to get into the funeral parlor. Several suicides were even reported—fans were that distraught over the death of their favorite. This marked the beginning of celebrity culture and the worship of movie stars that has only escalated since, particularly with the advent of social media, allowing fans to feel that they have a more personal, intimate window into the lives of the stars they adore.

Mary Pickford exemplified the Victorian ideals of womanhood. She was referred to as "America's sweetheart," the "girl with the golden curls," and she was among the first stars, an actor who people recognized, knew by name, and looked forward to seeing in picture after picture. She started working for Griffith, then moved to Biograph, and then to Adolf Zukor's Famous Players studio. For *Hearts Adrift* (1914), her name was featured above the title, and with her next picture, *Tess of the Storm Country* (1914), she became the most popular actress in America. Her renown matched Chaplin's worldwide. Sometimes she played a child, in such films as *Rebecca of Sunnybrook Farm* (1917), and *Poor Little Rich Girl* (1917). She could pull this off because she was so small (under five feet tall). In all, she was in fifty-two films, retiring shortly after films became "talkies."

Her marriage to Douglas Fairbanks was called "the marriage of the century." They were considered Hollywood royalty. For years, when Pickford would enter a room at a private party, everyone would stand.

Early on, she took control of her career. As a savvy businesswoman, she was a founder of United Artists (with Douglas Fairbanks, who was her husband at the time). She created the Motion Picture Relief Fund for out-of-work actors and sold Liberty war bonds during World War I, auctioning off one of the curls in her hair for $15,000.

Douglas Fairbanks defined the swashbuckling hero in such films as *The Mark of Zorro* (1920), *Robin Hood* (1922), and *The Thief of Bagdad* (1924). In his earlier films, he had displayed an athleticism and an effusive charm that proved popular. Coupling that with the swordplay and verve of the costume action-dramas, he became a superstar.

The Jazz Age

New modern freedom and energy after World War I were epitomized by the "It Girl" Clara Bow, Theda Bara, who was called "The Vamp," and Joan Crawford, "The Flapper." Their characters were sexy and independent, and the films they made were risqué, suggesting that sex was fun and not something you needed to be married to enjoy. Directors like Cecil B. DeMille, Eric von Stroheim, Ernst Lubitsch, and F. W. Murnau were making sophisticated films about relationships, each director employing his own individual and recognizable style. This was not something that the studio system encouraged, but studios reluctantly supported the individuality of directors if the films were successful. DeMille, for example, became synonymous with colossal scaled epics—audiences would look forward to a new DeMille film, with an idea of the spectacle that awaited them. This was a time when directors began to achieve renown alongside that enjoyed by star actors. A new Chaplin film and a new DeMille film each had their own cachet and built-in audiences, just as today you might look forward to a new film starring Ryan Gosling as much as a new one directed by Quentin Tarantino.

Actors from Europe also made a splash. Pola Negri, from Poland, worked with Lubitsch in such films as *Madame DuBarry*, where she was presented as a European femme fatale. Emil Jannings from Germany won the Best Actor Oscar twice for *The Way of All Flesh* (1927) and *The Last Command* (1928). He returned to Germany when his thick German accent made him unacceptable for American talking pictures. There he made *The Blue Angel* (1930), a talkie with Marlene Dietrich, which was filmed in both English and German. He continued working in Germany during the Nazi era, which ended his international career.

The biggest splash was made by **Greta Garbo**, who arrived in Hollywood in 1925. The actress had been born in Sweden as Greta Gustafson. Her mentor was the director Mauritz Stiller, who shaped her persona (making her lose twenty pounds and changing her name), but he had no success in America. Garbo's first Hollywood film, *Torrent* (1926), introduced a new type of star to critics and audiences: passionate, mysterious, vulnerable, beautiful. She was paired with actor John Gilbert, who became her lover in life. Their love scenes, over the three films they made together, had an intensity and passion that had not been seen before. With Pickford and Fairbanks and Garbo and Gilbert, audiences developed a fascination for real-life celebrity screen couples that has only increased over the decades, as seen recently in the "Brangelina" period, which began with *Mr. and Mrs. Smith*, costarring Brad Pitt and Angelina Jolie, who fell in love while filming. Garbo was a sensation, one of the few silent stars to make a successful transition to talkies.

Expressionism

As Hollywood dominated moviemaking throughout the world, filmmakers in other countries looked to differentiate themselves. After World War I, European studios couldn't match the big budgets of American films, so they sought something original. One solution was the expressionistic style, which had a parallel in the world of fine art. This was an avant-garde movement early in the century, and the film that put it on the map was *The Cabinet of Dr. Caligari* (1920).

Figure 2.2 The shadow of vampire Count Orlok. Max Schreck. *Nosferatu* © Prana Film. Screenshot captured by authors.

In expressionism, shapes are distorted to express emotion: each image is meant to be "graphic art." There is no room for naturalistic reality—it is all expressed in the design. The acting is formal and stiff, with carefully constructed postures, as if each shot were a "tableau vivant" of posed actors and striking scenography. The shapes of rooms are distorted, the makeup and costumes are exaggerated, and there are shadows and evocative silhouettes. *The Cabinet of Dr. Cagliari* shows the world through the eyes of a madman, so the exaggerations make sense. In later films, the stylization was less motivated by the content—it was just there for effect. This period saw movies as a new medium for fine art.

The effect could be mesmerizing, as in the film *Nosferatu* (1922) directed by F. W. Murnau and with the wonderfully named Max Schreck playing the vampire. At its core, this is a horror film, inspired by Bram Stoker's *Dracula*. But it diverted from the novel in many ways (one of the reasons being that it sought to avoid copyright issues). At the end, the heroine, Ellen, sacrifices herself to protect her husband from the Count (whose name is Orlok, not Dracula). As the vampire drinks her blood, the sun rises, and he vanishes in a puff of smoke.

Fritz Lang's *Metropolis* (1927) was one of the last expressionist films. Its scenic design was inspired by art deco, and it is credited with popularizing this style. It is one of the first science fiction films, imagining a dystopian city, with workers laboring underground while the wealthy live in spectacular skyscrapers. The cityscape became famous, supposedly inspired by Lang's first time in New York City, but with interpolated gothic cathedrals, a Tower of Babel (modeled after the Renaissance painting by Pieter Bruegel the Elder), and a robot made to look like the heroine, to fool the workers into rebelling. The story is forgettable, but the images are indelible.

Lang subsequently made the early sound film *M* (1931), starring Peter Lorre as a murderer lurking in the streets of Berlin who whistles "The Hall of the Mountain King" as he preys on children. With long, elegant tracking shots (where the camera moves with the actor), he is hunted by the police and the criminals of the city, despised by both. The use of sound is worth noting here. When you heard the whistling off-screen you knew the killer was nearby. There would be moments of silence then suddenly a noise, ratcheting up the suspense. This thriller is on most lists of the greatest films of all time.

The young **Alfred Hitchcock** (1899–1980) made quite a stir in England with his silent film, *The Lodger: A Story of the London Fog* (1927), based on Jack the Ripper. He had made several movies before but this was his first thriller. Influenced by the German expressionist films he saw while working in Germany on earlier movies, he told the director François Truffaut, in the fascinating series of interviews he did with him about his work, called *Hitchcock/Truffaut,*[5] that he considered this to be his first film, the first one he felt he had mastered. An example of the "Hitchcock touch" that would become iconic and instantly recognizable: the lodger, played by the matinee idol Ivor Novello, is suspected of being the serial killer, and is afraid he may be arrested. The family living below is aware of his agitation. As they look up, the floor of his room above their kitchen becomes transparent, as though it were glass, and you see his feet from below, pacing back and forth. The visual substitutes for the sound of his footsteps.

Hitchcock made his first cameo appearance in this film, in a newsroom. You can catch a glimpse of him in all his films, in a brief, passing appearance that became his signature.

In 2012, the film magazine *Sight and Sound* rated **Sunrise, or A Song of Two Humans** (1927) as the fifth-greatest movie of all time. It won an Academy Award in 1929 (the first year of the awards) as a Unique and Artistic Picture with Janet Gaynor winning Best Actress in a Leading Role.

While on vacation, a woman from the city has an affair with a local farmer. He has a wife and baby, and she is aware that something has changed—he seems preoccupied and upset. The city woman suggests that he drown his wife so he can be free to come with her to the city. He is persuaded by her kisses and embraces, and plans the deed, inviting his wife for a day on the water. When they are well offshore, he threateningly approaches her. She is frightened and cries until he relents. Once on shore, she runs from him, terrified. She boards a tram to get away from him, and he follows.

They are in the city together. She is crying and cannot be calmed. They visit a wedding and join the service. Hearing the vows, he breaks down crying, and she finally begins to trust his regret. They spend the rest of the day enjoying the city. He gets a shave so they can have a celebratory "wedding" picture taken. They go to a circus fair, and he chases an escaped pig before dancing a peasant dance with her, to the delight of the city watchers.

Figure 2.3 George O'Brien as The Man, trying to decide between his wife and the Woman from the City. *Sunrise* © Fox Film Corporation. Screenshot captured by authors.

They are sailing home when they are caught in a thunderstorm, which capsizes the boat. He has tied bulrushes to her back as a float. He manages to get to shore but she doesn't. A search party finds the shreds of the bulrushes, but they don't see her. The man is overwhelmed, thinking she has drowned. The city woman is watching this search, thinking that he has done what she asked him to do to get rid of his wife. When she tries to approach him, he chases her angrily and begins to choke her, only to be interrupted by a cry telling him that his wife has been found and she is alive. He rushes to her. The city woman returns to the city and, as the sun rises, the family has been happily reunited.

What makes this worth watching, and even extraordinarily touching, is how the story is told. This film is late enough in the silent era that there was now a technology (Fox Movietone Sound-on-Film) that could put synchronized sounds with the images. There is no dialogue (only intertitles, often animated, which was unusual), but there is continuous music integral to the storytelling, as well as sound effects—applause, a crowd murmuring or complaining, bells, car motors, thunder, and water. These add a lot to the power of the film.

But the images make it. Tracking shots as we follow him through the woods to meet the city woman, first from behind then from his point of view (POV, as it is abbreviated), as though his eyes are the camera. When the man first contemplates drowning his wife, we see the scene projected behind him. When the city woman tells him of the city, we see images of bright lights, traffic, and flappers dancing. As he watches his wife, who is devoted but worried about his behavior, we see images of him throwing her off a boat—we know what he is thinking. The film uses images to project the interiority of the characters.

Later, in the city, when they have reconciled and she is no longer afraid of him, they embrace, crossing the street. They stop to kiss and cause a traffic jam—we hear horns honking, people complaining—not words, just the sounds, but they are vivid. In that same scene, they walk together, ignoring the cars, which now appear in rear projection. This is a technique common in both silents and early talkies—and sometimes in more modern films. The actors perform in front of a screen onto which a scene is projected, as though they were in it. They may be in a car, for instance—or a mock-up of one—with the images of the landscape speeding past through the windows. These are rear projections. When this filmmaking technique is done well, you hardly notice the mechanism that makes it possible. But it can appear artificial, drawing attention to itself. It feels artificial here, but in a moment you see why. As they continue walking forward into the traffic, the scene changes and they are back at their village in the woods of their youth. Then, a moment later, they are surrounded by cars again. The scene has changed around them. The rear projection allows us to see what they *imagine*, as well as what is happening in the moment. This was a groundbreaking approach.

The camerawork in this film is never flashy, never showing off, but always telling you more. Sometimes there is humor—while taking the "wedding" photo, the couple can't stop themselves from kissing instead of looking properly somber. We see them upside down in the camera, as the photographer decides that this is the shot to get—in effect, the audience steps inside the camera (as cameras work using mirrors to capture the upside-down image of what is seen through the viewfinder). Later, in the photographer's studio, they accidentally knock over a small statue of a woman. They can't find the head, thinking they have broken it, and try to hide that it is missing by putting a tennis ball where the head should be. They don't realize that it never had a head—it is a copy of a headless Greek statue. They hurry off after paying the bill, hoping he won't notice. He notices but finds their attempted fix amusing.

The excitement and energy of the city are conveyed with a spinning wheel, flashing lights, and a long tracking shot of a crowd waiting to get into a fair: visions of a nightclub, a roller coaster, dancing, and even an elephant. We see flappers with their short skirts, bare legs and shoulders, contrasted with the rustic, innocent dress of the man and his wife.

Many small moments ring true. As he is being shaved by a barber, his wife watches a sexy manicurist offer her services. After what has happened, she is understandably concerned, even jealous. We see him, face covered in shaving cream, trying to let his wife know she has nothing to worry about. Finally, he just tells the manicurist to go away. The wife, who has been watching closely, is relieved. You see them counting their pennies at a café, and when they drink a bit too much, she has to find the money in her purse to cover the bill. Nevertheless, they are having the time of their life. But all this is threatened when the storm arises.

This is a film with all cylinders firing, telling a story with feeling and subtlety, using all aspects available in synchronicity: actors, story, sound, image, and film technology. As highly regarded as it is by film critics and scholars, it deserves to be much better known.

Modern Films Influenced by Silent Movies

While talkies arrived and became the norm, numerous modern movies were influenced by them, as well as the occasional new film that opted to be silent for effect.

Any film by Wes Anderson, especially *The Grand Budapest Hotel* (2014) and *Moonrise Kingdom* (2012), tips its hat to the silent film era. His use of formal architectural spaces, a stationary camera, and many silent movie gags borrows and honors the work of Keaton and Chaplin.

Jackie Chan's action comedies are likewise influenced by the comedy stars of the silent era. In *Project A* (1983), Chan combines stunts from Keaton and Chaplin and Lloyd into one three-minute sequence: a house falling around him (*Steamboat Bill*, Keaton), getting caught in the gears of a machine (*Modern Times*, Chaplin), hanging from a clockface (*Safety Last*, Lloyd) and then crashing through a series of awnings that break his fall (*Three Ages*, Keaton).

The first film that comedian Jerry Lewis starred in and directed, *The Bellboy* (1960), is basically a silent film, with Jerry not speaking for fully half of it. The gags would have comfortably fit into any silent comedy, especially Chaplin's.

Rowan Atkinson's TV series and films about Mr. Bean are almost completely silent, physical comedies. Mr. Bean makes some sounds and occasionally speaks, but these are silent movies made modern.

The Mel Brooks comedy, *Silent Movie* (1976), is a parody of, and homage to, the silent film. It's a movie about making a modern silent movie, with Brooks-style "anything for a laugh" sketches, all poking fun at Hollywood. It has a music and sound effects soundtrack, but it is silent in terms of dialogue, with intertitles only, except for one spoken joke—when Marcel Marceau, the famous French mime, shouts "*non!*" when asked whether he will be in the movie. Unlike the silents, many of the jokes require sound effects to work: when Marty Feldman is slapstick bouncing between elevator doors, it's to the sound of a pinball machine.

The Artist (2011) was a phenomenon when it came out. An homage to the silent film, presented in black and white, it had the same 4:3 aspect ratio (screen image size and shape) of old silent movies and used a twenty-two-frames-per-minute film speed to match the films of the 1920s. It is almost completely silent, except for the "non-diegetic" soundtrack (meaning sound that is not part of the world of the movie but which the audience hears, such as music or narration).

The Artist was a big hit and won the Best Actor Oscar (as well as the BAFTA and the Golden Globe) for its French star, Jean Dujardin, as well as the 2012 Oscar for Best Picture and Best Director (Michel Hazanavicius). Dujardin's costar, Bérénice Bejo, won a Best Actress César (the French Oscars).

The story is about the transition from silent movies to sound, from the old faces to the new, with Dujardin playing George Valentin, a swashbuckling leading man, modeled on Douglas Fairbanks.

Valentin's refusal to recognize the new popularity of sound movies ruins his career when he insists on making another silent movie, just as Peppy Miller, a young woman he discovered, begins her rise to fame as a tap dancer in sound films. Years later, she finds him despairing, drunk, and suicidal, destroying the negatives of his films. She lovingly rescues him and his career.

There are montages in silent-movie style (a **montage** is a common editing technique composed of short shots showing a sequence of events over time, often conveyed by dissolves, multiple exposures, or split screens): one summarizing the making of Valentin's last silent movie (we see moments of him acting in different scenes, working on the script, paying the bills, directing), another of newspaper headlines with Valentin dismissing talkies and other headlines showing how increasingly popular they were.

When, after being shown an early trial of sound in movies, he has a nightmare in which he cannot speak, but he can hear the sounds of objects and people around him, we hear them too (an example of diegetic sound is sound within the world of the movie: dialogue, people laughing, sounds from a radio, traffic noises, a phone ringing). This is one of only two moments with sound in the film.

There is an eloquent shot when his film fails, showing an advertisement lying in the rain, ignored, feet stepping on it as people walk by. There are screen wipes, and scene-closing irises, familiar from the silents. There are intertitles, too, but fewer than one would have found in the original silents: just enough to move the story along,

Near the end, Peppy suggests to Valentin that they make a dancing musical together. We hear the sound of tap dancing (diegetic sound, again), then cut to them filming a dance number. And now, in a new world of sound, we hear a director yell "Cut!" as the producer excitedly asks for one more take. Then Valentin says, in a charming French accent, "with pleasure."

Chapter 3
Classic Hollywood

Key Films

Casablanca (1942)
Citizen Kane (1941)

Silent films in the 1920s had reached a high level of accomplishment and artistry, with a visual language and techniques that made it possible for them to be enjoyed and understood throughout the world.

But all of that was about to end, and a new world would open, with the introduction of synchronized sound in 1926. The film that kicked it off was the Warner Brothers feature, *Don Juan*, starring John Barrymore, a famous Shakespearean stage actor. Their sound process, called Vitaphone, used a recorded disc synchronized to the motor of the film projector. It was limited in many ways, impossible to edit, and with discs that were easily damaged, but it allowed for a musical and sound effects soundtrack. This was a whole new ball game.

A year later, Warner's film *The Jazz Singer* (1927) was released, with Al Jolson singing and saying a few words of dialogue, ad-libbing a quote often included in classic Hollywood clips: "You ain't heard nothin' yet." Hearing actors speak was a sensation and spelled the death of silent movies. It also elevated Warner Bros., which had been a second-rank studio, into the big time.

But transitioning to sound was not easy. There were several competing systems for sound and many major studios held back, waiting to see which system would win. In the meantime, they continued to release mostly silent films like *Sunrise* and King Vidor's *The Crowd* (1928) that added sound effects and music but had no spoken dialogue.

Fox's Movietone system became the gold standard, printing the sound directly onto the film and allowing for easier editing and synchronization. By 1930, all the studios, including Warner, were using it. Irving Thalberg, then head of MGM, had called talkies a "passing fancy," but soon realized that all thirty-five MGM silent pictures ready to be released would have to be redone. Audiences wanted sound.

What was immediately lost was the visual fluidity of silent movies: the moving camera, the use of POV, actors interacting naturally with each other. The early sound process was hampered by the limitations of microphones of the day and by how noisy the cameras were, requiring them to be placed in immovable soundproof boxes, lest their whirring be picked up in the audio. Suddenly, the actors were hovering around hidden microphones, unable to move. Swashbuckling Douglas Fairbanks, famous for his sword fights and acrobatics, had to sit down for the dialogue in his first sound film, *Taming of the Shrew* (1929). Being deprived of movement cramped Fairbanks's style, and eventually his swash unbuckled, ending his career.

Other stars of the silents were undone in this new era because of their accent or the sound of their voice, or because, not having a theater background, they couldn't read lines. This opened up opportunities for a new generation of stars, many from the world of theater and vaudeville. James Cagney, who started as a tap dancer, became the ultimate gangster in a series of Warner Bros. movies like *The Public Enemy* (1931), *Angels with Dirty Faces* (1938), and *White Heat* (1949). Archie Leach, who worked under the stage name Cary Grant, was the essence of cool elegance and wit in screwball comedies like *The Awful Truth* (1937), *Bringing Up Baby* (1938), *His Girl Friday* (1940), dramas such as *An Affair to Remember* (1957), and romantic thrillers like Alfred Hitchcock's *Notorious* (1946) and *North by Northwest* (1959). Stalwart, manly Clark Gable became a star in *It Happened One Night* (1931), *Mutiny on the Bounty* (1935), and *Gone with the Wind* (1939). The sexy, smart platinum blonde Jean Harlow became a household name thanks to *Red Dust* (1932) and *Dinner at Eight* (1933). Fast-talking, witty Carole Lombard featured in *My Man Godfrey* (1936) and *To Be or Not to Be* (1942). Exotic Greta Garbo's accent was no impediment in *Camille* (1936) and *Ninotchka* (1939). Barbara Stanwyck starred in *Ball of Fire* (1941) and *Double Indemnity* (1944), while Bette Davis stole the show in *Dark Victory* (1939), *Now, Voyager* (1942), and *All about Eve* (1950). These last two actresses could be anything, from tough dame to clinging vine. That was new. Most actors and actresses specialized in a certain type of role or character, to the point where their personality off-screen melded with their on-screen performances. Actors who could morph into different characters, especially those who could do drama or comedy, dark or light, were rare before this period. Stanwyck and Davis helped to change that. These were actors who acted, not merely performing in multiple films with roughly the same character traits.

It took several years of improvements in camera technology for actors to move again and for the dialogue to get better. Movie studios went on a hiring binge, bringing playwrights and novelists from the East Coast, often turning to anyone who looked like they could write dialogue (with mixed success when their novelistic talents were applied to scripts): William Faulkner (*To Have and Have Not*, 1944; *The Big Sleep*, 1946), Herman J. Mankiewicz (*Dinner at Eight*, 1933; *Citizen Kane*, 1941), and Ben Hecht (*Scarface*, 1932; *Gunga Din*, 1939; *His Girl Friday*, 1940), were enticed by big salaries and Hollywood's warm weather. Mankiewicz got there early and invited his friend Hecht to join him from Chicago, writing "Millions are to be grabbed out here, and your only competition is idiots. Don't let this get around."[1] He wasn't wrong.

By that time, the essence of the studio system was well in place in Hollywood. If we are to understand what defines the Classic Hollywood film, the films of the **Golden Age** (usually considered from about 1930 to 1955), we need to know a bit more about the studios that made them. They each have a fascinating story, but there are many common elements to all.

The Studio System

By the end of the 1920s, there were five major studios in Hollywood and several mini-majors. Almost all of the studios, big and small, had been founded by poor Jewish immigrants from Eastern Europe. Warner Bros. was founded by Jack Warner and his brothers, who came from Poland; Fox, soon to be 20th Century Fox, by William Fox from Hungary; Paramount by Adolph Zukor, also from Germany (he arrived in America with $19 sewn into his pant pocket); RKO (originally Radio-Keith-Orpheum; Keith-Orpheum was a vaudeville theater circuit) by Robert Sarnoff from Minsk, in the Pale of Settlement in Russia (a large area that included several cities, including Białystok, and many villages), in partnership with Joseph Kennedy (the father of the future president John F. Kennedy); and Metro-Goldwyn-Mayer by Louis B. Mayer, also from the Pale of Settlement, one of the shtetl villages where Jews were tolerated, when they weren't being pursued by the czar's Cossacks.

Of the mini-majors, Universal was founded by Carl Laemmle from Germany, while Goldwyn Pictures was established by Samuel Goldwyn (born Goldfish) from Poland. As Jews, they were permanent outsiders in their home countries. They had all fled persecution and lack of opportunity, looking for tolerance and success in the American dream.

The "Dream" proved less than ideal. As Jews, they were not allowed in higher-end professions. There were quotas for admission to college, limiting the number of Jews accepted. Most of the founders never finished high school, as they had to be the breadwinners for their families since many of their fathers could not adjust to the new country and spoke only Yiddish. They'd grown up in tenements, excluded from the better neighborhoods.

Immigrants were obliged to be energetic risk-takers and innovators to establish themselves. Starting out, many began selling what were called "dry goods." Zukor apprenticed with a furrier and, after devising a new clasp for fur stoles, was soon a success on his own, selling them. Goldwyn sold gloves; Louis Selznick, diamonds. Laemmle started working at a clothing manufacturer, creatively modernizing their advertising. Looking to strike out on his own, he bought his first nickelodeon. There is a story about Barney Balaban, who became head of Paramount. He was working as a messenger boy when his mother came home from watching a picture show for the first time and told him, "The people pay money *before* they get the goods. There's money in that business!" Inspired by her comment, he rented his first theater. A few years later, he owned the theater and put in the first balcony in a movie house. Later, he installed "air-conditioning" (a large fan blowing over a big block of ice). The trick worked: people would come in to get out of the heat of summer, making moviegoing a year-round business, whereas it had previously been uncomfortable in warm weather.

There were no Jews making movies then, but these men knew how to show them and how to promote them. They bought up nickelodeons, then theaters. Recognizing that the initial audience was from the lower classes, they upgraded the theaters to make them more attractive to the middle class. They admired high culture, music, art, and literature but, as salesmen, they understood popular culture, too. It was the perfect combination in these early days of the movies.

To keep the customers coming, there had to be a ready supply of films. The Edison Trust had clamped down on who could make them and how. Carl Laemmle imported a movie from France starring the great Sara Bernhardt, a famous French stage actress, thinking that it would bring high culture to the masses. It was a success, but the supply of quality foreign films was not reliable. He was determined to make his own.

Others followed his lead. To do this, and to put as much distance as possible between them and the trust, one by one they shifted their operations to California. Besides providing bright sunny days year-round and a variety of locations to film, Hollywood was a young town and open enough to allow these outsiders room to breathe.

Soon, all of the founders moved there and began creating the studios that would control movies for the next fifty years. Laemmle built Universal City, a 230-acre complex with its own postal code and police force, and facilities for every aspect of moviemaking: enormous hanger-like buildings for the sets, and offices for the writers, editors, costume makers, and executives. Universal made its reputation making classic horror films, such as *Frankenstein* (1931), *The Bride of Frankenstein* (1935), and *Dracula* (1931), but they also made *All Quiet on the Western Front* (1930), one of the best films about World War I. The first film adaptation of a Broadway musical was *Showboat* (1935), the first musical that dealt with a serious subject, in this case, interracial marriage. These were "prestige" pictures. Every studio made a small number every year: movies that might not make much money but would get great reviews and would be well regarded by the "influencers" of the day (newspaper gossip columnists like the rivals Hedda Hopper and Louella Parsons). These two films not only got rave reviews, but they made good money. They demonstrated that people would come to high-culture productions.

Metro-Goldwyn-Mayer was considered the top studio at the time, dubbed as having "more stars than there are in heaven." While that wasn't quite astronomically accurate, they did have an amazing lineup of some of the most popular stars of the era: talented actors with charisma, beauty, and charm whose presence could "open" a movie. It was a time when audiences would flock to the film because of the star, whether or not the story interested them, a habit which continues today. MGM was famous for quality (making more prestige movies than any other studio) thanks to Irving Thalberg, who, as head of production under Mayer, kept close control over every film.

Thalberg had great taste. Before he joined MGM, he'd worked at Universal, where he was responsible for *The Hunchback of Notre Dame* (1923), starring Lon Chaney, who was famous for the elaborate makeup he would create for each film, transforming his appearance. He got the nickname "the man with a thousand faces." When his disfigured face was revealed in *The Phantom of the Opera* (1925), people in the theater fainted. In a good way—it was a big hit.

At MGM, Thalberg took over the supervision of *Ben-Hur* (1925), which was being filmed in Italy, dismissing the writer, director, and the star and restaging the chariot race, at the cost of an extra $300,000—a massive amount at the time. He supervised the editing while recovering from a massive heart attack. It proved worth the effort and investment.

He made *Mutiny on the Bounty* (1935), the Marx Brothers' *A Night at the*

Opera (1935), and *Grand Hotel* (1932), which had a cast of five major stars (including Greta Garbo, John Barrymore, and Joan Crawford), something Thalberg did to counteract falling attendance resulting from the Depression. Usually, movies had one big star to attract the audience, but with money tight this became less of a draw. Pairing up his stars helped turn things around: Myrna Loy and William Powell in the wonderful *Thin Man* comic mysteries; Clark Gable with Jean Harlow in sexy melodramas like *Red Dust* (1932); and Garbo with John Gilbert in *Mata Hari* (1931).

Studios didn't only manufacture movies. They manufactured the stars, too. Thalberg loved to create stars. He wanted his actresses to appear "cool, classy, and beautiful," while his actors should be "worldly and in control." He groomed and made stars of Lon Chaney, Greta Garbo, Clark Gable, Jean Harlow, Joan Crawford, and Marie Dressler.

There was a system he put in place to make a star out of a promising actor. The actor would be hired and signed to an exclusive, long contract, usually five to seven years, with a regular weekly salary. The studio would then take over their lives, often changing their names to make them less ethnic or easier to remember. They'd be taught how to dress, to walk, to behave. They would be given acting, singing, and dancing lessons. They'd change their hair color and create off-screen personas for them, showing them as either tidily domestic or larger-than-life glamorous. Then they'd feed stories to film magazines and newspapers, with invented biographies that smoothed out the rough parts of the actor's true past.

If their off-screen behavior stretched the morality clause of their contract (parties that got out of hand with someone raped or dead, or if caught using drugs, or not effectively hiding their homosexuality), the studios would pay off gossip columnists or promise exclusive (often invented) stories to keep the news out of the papers. If things got too much out of control, they would fire the star. For instance, Fatty Arbuckle was one of the biggest silent movie clowns, in both girth and fame. But when he was accused of raping and killing a showgirl at a party, even though he was acquitted in court, he lost his job and was not allowed to work in Hollywood for years.

Thalberg at MGM was an innovator, introducing story conferences, sneak previews, and scene retakes based on the reaction of the sneak audiences. As a result, MGM had more success during the years of the Depression than any other studio. It was the only one that made a profit every year of that decade. Unfortunately, Thalberg had been born with a congenital heart defect and was always frail. He died of pneumonia at the age of thirty-seven.

Newly hired actors started in small parts. But if they made a good impression, they would get bigger roles, then supporting roles, until, if they were lucky (and good), they might star in a movie. But unless they were the top stars, they had no say in what movies they made. The studio gave them regular employment, and paid them well, as long as they followed orders. Starting salaries might be a few hundred dollars a week, going up to several thousand a week for the bigger stars.

The biggest stars made a fortune. Charlie Chaplin earned $243,000 a week. In 1937, Gary Cooper earned more than $6 million a year. Greta Garbo died with a fortune of $90 million in today's dollars. Cary Grant was worth $130 million. Silent film star Mary Pickford was worth $131 million and she stopped making movies when talkies arrived. But all these actors had to do what they were told. If they rejected a role, they could be suspended with no salary and no other work. Louis Mayer, who was so sentimental it was said that he would cry at a dropped handkerchief, was incredibly tough in negotiations with anyone who challenged him.

The actors and directors were not allowed to work for any other studio unless their studio agreed and was willing to "loan" them out. It was not until the 1940s that a few top stars (James Cagney, Bette Davis, and Olivia De Havilland at Warner Bros.) legally challenged the system and ended the servitude of long contracts.

This empowered actors but marked the beginning of the end of the Golden Age.

As heads of their studios, the founders, referred to as "movie moguls," were driven, demanding, competitive, and often ruthless. But they were also showmen who loved movies and wanted to be admired as much as they wanted to make money. They controlled every aspect of production, supervising the directors, writers, cinematographers, and actors. Most were smart enough to know when they had talent on their hands and they would allow them a good deal of freedom. But if they exceeded the budget or tried anything too "creative," they would be brought to heel.

The studios were factories for moviemaking, churning out hundreds of feature-length movies every year. By the mid-1930s, 75 percent of Americans went to the movies once a week. It had become a ritual. To keep them coming, Hollywood provided them with something new every week. New, but not too different. That's where genre movies came in (the subject of the coming chapters).

Studios didn't only make the movies. They distributed them and owned the theaters that showed them or held tight control of how they were shown in the theaters they didn't own. They built luxurious movie palaces to show off their best films. By 1930, there were seventeen thousand movie theaters in the United States. Eighty million people went to the movies every week.

To get the A-list stars and movies from a studio, most independent theaters had to accept the B movies that the studio made with lesser-known actors. Many of these B movies are now considered as good or better than the A movies of the time, but the theaters then had no choice. They also had to buy newsreels, cartoons, and other short films that the studios insisted on including in every package. Ironically, the major studios became every bit as monopolistic as the Edison Trust they had run away from and successfully killed. The only difference is that they were competing with each other, and with the minis and independent companies that also populated Hollywood.

To run a factory, you need templates, or standards, for what you are making. That applies to making shoes, cars, toaster ovens, or movies. Those standards for movies became the rules of the Classic Hollywood era.

The Golden Era Rules

Because so many films were made in the 1930s (at their peak, five hundred a year), audiences could expect a certain similarity in story and style within genres. This made it easy for them to look forward to the next picture. But for the movie to be interesting, it had to be different enough, with sufficient variation to allow for surprise and the delight of discovery. The more creative writers and directors gloried in managing these constraints.

The essence of the Classic Hollywood style is to make the techniques invisible while they are used to pull you into the story. Editing and camerawork must never distract from the narrative but only enhance it, making it clearer and more urgent. If your editing or lighting or performance in a movie called attention to itself and pulled the viewer out of the story, you might be called by the producer or the head of the studio and ordered to change it. Overexuberant creativity was seen as "showing off" and was strongly discouraged. The creative team could bring their craft and artistry to play as long as it didn't violate these basic standards.

There were several narrative rules to follow, and many can be seen in films today.

Each movie is usually divided into three acts comprising the central story. Act One: We are introduced to the protagonist, the main character;

and a problem or situation is defined. Act Two: The protagonist actively tries to solve the problem, often with unexpected difficulties getting in the way. Act Three: The protagonist succeeds; or, if he or she doesn't, there is still some final resolution that we can understand.

There is often a secondary narrative that intertwines with the first. For instance, in *The Wizard of Oz* (1939), Dorothy is comfortable at home in Kansas (which we see in black and white) but wishes to experience a wider world. This is her first problem. A tornado then lifts her and her house and drops them in the magical world of Oz which, in a wonderful reveal, is a fantasy realm in full Technicolor. She is bewildered and wants to go home—this is her second problem. Following the yellow brick road, she befriends the Scarecrow, the Cowardly Lion, and the Tin Man, each of whom has his own story and problem to solve, each one a secondary narrative. There is an antagonist, the Wicked Witch of the West, who wants to stop her, taking vengeance for Dorothy's house having landed on her sister, the Wicked Witch of the East. She also wants to get her hands on her sister's magic "ruby slippers" that Dorothy is wearing. Dorothy and her friends seek help from the Wizard of Oz, only to learn that he is a phony. They must actively fight the Witch themselves. They kill the Wicked Witch and become heroes. Dorothy has seen a wider world (problem one solved) but still wants to solve the second problem—returning home. Then she is told that she always had the way home, but she needed to discover it herself—a life lesson. She needs only to click her heels together and say, "There's no place like home," and the magic slippers will do the rest. She wakes up in her bed in Kansas, once again in black and white, realizing that, indeed, "there's no place like home." A comforting myth for Dorothy and the audience who loved this movie.

In classic Hollywood movies, nothing happens by chance. Everything is there for a reason, usually related to the actions of the main character. The story is linear, told from event to event in ordinary time. The only exception is the occasional flashback, illustrating a particular moment in the past that tells us more about the present (for instance Rick and Ilsa's days in Paris in the 1942 movie *Casablanca*, which we will be discussing later). This is called **continuity editing**: telling the story clearly so the audience can follow it and become fully absorbed in the world of the film.

Several editing techniques make this work. The **180-degree rule** keeps the audience oriented within the spaces of the story. An imaginary line drawn between characters requires that the camera stay on one side of that line. It can move but not cross the line. This is especially important when two characters are talking, and you cut between them. You must always be looking over the same shoulder of each; otherwise, it looks like they are jumping in space.

Another rule, called the **thirty-degree rule**, says that if you do move the camera, for instance, to get closer, you must change the placement by at least thirty degrees to make it clear that you are simply getting closer. If you keep the camera in the same position, then the new angle looks like a jump cut: it startles instead of simply allowing you to get closer to the action to, for example, show emotion. You don't want to startle the audience—unless, of course, you intend to startle them (as in a horror movie).

Most films will open with a wide shot or series of shots that establish where the action takes place. This is followed by a medium shot, to introduce the main players and show their immediate world (an apartment, an office, or Rick's Place, the nightclub in *Casablanca*). Finally, we zoom in for close-ups, for emotion or emphasis, now that the audience knows "where they are." Watch the opening minute or so of almost every Golden Era film and you'll spot this formula in action.

In classic films, the actors are kept in focus while the backgrounds are blurred. This makes it easier to see them and not be distracted. There is a frontality to most shots: actors essentially face the audience (by facing the camera) rather than each other (rarely will you see someone's back to the camera), even when they are in profile or engaged in conversation. This replicates stage plays, in which the actors "cheat" toward the audience so they can be more easily seen. Most classic-era movies assumed that the audience wanted to be guided through the story and used camera focus to do that. Variations on these rules would come, but in later films, after the Golden Era. It remains useful to understand this standard to recognize the innovations of filmmakers who intentionally diverged from it.

Lighting and the placement of shadows also serve to help tell the story, conveying atmosphere and emotion. Cinematographers were expected to deliver mood and drama, but most importantly, ensure the stars looked good.

In *Casablanca*, Ingrid Bergman, playing Ilsa, is unsure of Rick's reaction (Rick is played by Humphrey Bogart) to her returning to his café in the Moroccan city of Casablanca during World War II. That uncertainty and doubt is underlined by her face often being in half-shadow, or her frequently standing in the dark. As the mood becomes more somber, so does the lighting, with rooms darkening, pierced only with isolated points of light. Key lights (small, focused spotlights) bring out expression: the lights in Ilsa's eyes let us see her tears. Bergman was convinced that only her left profile was attractive. To accommodate this, in all her films, cameramen tried to only film her from that side.

Screenplays in Classic Hollywood had to tell a story that the audience could follow, but with enough surprises to keep them happily off-balance. The dialogue moves the story along but in the best films, it is smart, often witty, and frequently quotable. There were also scripted directions that guided the actors. In *Dinner at Eight* (1933), based on a play by George S. Kaufman and Edna Ferber, with a screenplay by Herman Mankiewicz and Donald Ogden Stewart, Marie Dressler is an elderly matron chatting with Jean Harlow, the trophy wife of a businessman. Harlow looks like the clichéd "dumb blonde," poured into her evening dress. She says to Dressler, "I was reading a book the other day," and Dressler does a double take. It's a scripted moment that is as funny as any line one could write. Harlow continues, "It's a funny kind of a book. You know the guy says that machinery is going to take the place of every profession." Dressler looks her up and down, "Oh, my dear, that is something you need *never* worry about." The acting and the line readings, as well as the dialogue, epitomize the best of the era. Smart, funny, and advancing character and story. These were also the rules of playwriting: dialogue should either advance the plot, deepen our understanding of the character, or provoke an effect in the audience (like a laugh or a moment of pathos). There should be nothing in a script that is just thrown in, filling space. Everything is there with a purpose.

In the 1950s, several French enthusiasts of classic American films, especially André Bazin and François Truffaut, promoted the idea that the director was the sole author of these films (the French word *auteur*), with themes and a style that could be traced in each of their works. The director was the grand master—everyone else was there as part of their bottega, to support them in realizing their artistic vision. Though it may be true for some directors, such as John Ford, Alfred Hitchcock, Howard Hawks, and Frank Capra, who fought for more control over their projects, most of the directors in Hollywood were journeymen craftsmen who were assigned their films and did the best job they could to honor them.

The Hollywood system turned out so many great films because they had people at the top of their profession in every department of moviemaking—not just the director, but the producer, the actors, screenwriters, cinematographers, editors, and set, costume, and lighting designers. For most films of this era, you can't legitimately credit the director alone for the look and style of the movie. Too many people contributed. What is remarkable is how seamless the final movie so often was, despite the many "chefs" working on the "soup."

And what movies they made! Consider 1939, the year that produced a particularly remarkable array of movies that are considered classics today: *The Wizard of Oz, Gone with the Wind, Stagecoach, Mr. Smith Goes to Washington, Wuthering Heights, Ninotchka, Goodbye Mr. Chips, The Women, Young Mr. Lincoln, Only Angels Have Wings*, and *The Roaring Twenties*.

Casablanca (1942)

Casablanca is the most-watched film from the Golden Age and the most popular, displaying what was best in the classic Hollywood system. Many call it the most romantic movie ever made, and many lists name it the best film ever, period. It won the 1942 Academy Award for Best Picture. Michael Curtiz won Best Director, and the Epstein brothers, Julius and Philip, and Howard Koch won for Best Adapted Screenplay. The song "As Time Goes By," performed in the movie by Dooley Wilson (who, by the way, was a drummer and couldn't play the piano—he was acting when he played it on-screen) immediately conjures up images from the film for anyone who has seen it, conveying the romantic longing that is the essence of the story.

This Warner Bros film stars Humphrey Bogart who, in 1999, was ranked the greatest male star of American cinema by the American Film Institute. He was an icon, with his trench coat and fedora; posters from this movie decorated many a college dorm room. He had made an impression playing tough guys for years, first in secondary parts and then, with *The Maltese Falcon* in 1941, as a leading man. This movie made him a romantic hero and the highest-paid actor in Hollywood.

Ingrid Bergman was one of the most in-demand actresses of the time. The producer of *Casablanca*, Hal Wallis, arranged for her to be loaned to Warner Bros. for this picture from David O. Selznick, with whom she was under contract for his various production companies. Wallis should be credited more than he is for the success of this movie. He made every decision about casting and crew and contributed the iconic final line: "I think this is the beginning of a beautiful friendship." Bergman and Bogart have wonderful on-screen chemistry: you could certainly believe they were in love. But Bergman said in an interview that off-screen Bogart was very reserved, even cold, "Though I kissed him, I never knew him."[2] That's acting.

Bogart and Bergman are supported by an extraordinary cast who help define the world of the story. Many of the actors were refugees, putting distance between themselves and Hitler. Paul Henreid, an Austrian Jew, had the unenviable task of playing Victor Lazlo, Ilsa's husband, whose stalwart freedom fighter, as a one-note character, is simply less interesting than Bogart's Rick. Our sympathies are with Rick, who is struggling to find a way for patriotism and love to coexist. We see that Ilsa admires Lazlo (look at her watching him when he inspires the nightclub to sing the "Marseillaise" against the German guests at Rick's Café Américain singing "Watch on the Rhine"), but that she loves Rick.

Conrad Veidt, playing the Nazi Major Strasser, played the somnambulist, Cesare, in the German expressionist silent classic, *The Cabinet of Dr. Caligari* (1920). He had escaped Germany when the Nazis came to power, in part because his wife was Jewish. The Hungarian actor Peter Lorre plays Ugati. He starred in Fritz Lang's early talkie *M* (1931), playing the child murderer, and later, after escaping Nazi Germany, he was the villain in Hitchcock's first version of *The Man Who Knew Too Much* (1934). He specialized in creepy, with his odd insinuating accent and manner, bringing color to whatever film he was in. Lorre was coupled with jolly sinister Sidney Greenstreet, who plays Ferrari, the club owner who is Rick's professional rival in Casablanca, in two other films with Bogart, *The Maltese Falcon* (1941) and *Passage to Marseille* (1944).

Claude Rains was a British actor with a richly distinctive voice. He made his mark mostly unseen in the Universal horror movie, *The Invisible Man* (1933). Here, he is a corrupt but engaging policeman, Captain Louis Renault, who sees the sentimentalist behind the cynical isolationist facade of Bogart's Rick. It may be his most memorable role in what was a long career. In Hitchcock's *Notorious* (1946), he played Ingrid Bergman's Nazi husband.

S. Z. Sakall, another Hungarian who left Germany with the rise of Hitler, was a favorite actor playing lovable, excitable characters in musicals and comedies in the 1930s. Nicknamed "Cuddles," he was the waiter in *Casablanca*, bringing necessary moments of humor to the story. The crowd scenes in the market and at the tables of Rick's Café Américain were populated with other actors who were refugees from the war. They bring an immediacy and urgency to their moments in the film.

If a movie has a couple of memorable lines in it, it is doing well. What makes *Casablanca* so extraordinary is that not only is the dialogue sharp, defining the characters and moving the plot, but almost every scene has a line or two that is memorable and known even by people who have never seen the movie: "Round up the usual suspects," "Here's looking at you, kid," "Play it, Sam," "Of all the gin joints in all the towns in all the world, she walks into mine." Some scenes are so engaging that fans quote them whole.

The best screenplays imply as much as they say. Robert McKee's book on the art of the screenplay, *Story* (1998), teaches that every scene has a text, what the characters say, and a subtext, the thoughts, feelings, and desires that are felt, but not said. These layers give characters and situations depth and make them seem more interesting, more real. If the subtext is stated explicitly, it comes across as hollow and false and, finally, uninteresting. The movement within scenes is often when the conscious desires, what is said or done, and the unconscious wishes, the subtext, clash, driving actions more than any one thing characters may say. A good experiment you can try while watching a film is to imagine what the subtext is when text is delivered. The success of saying one thing but conveying an unspoken meaning that the audience can "read" is the mark of the union of great writing, acting, and direction.

There is a crucial scene in *Casablanca* that is worth looking at closely. It's a lesson in how to tell a story.

Figure 3.1 "Of all the gin joints, in all the towns, in all the world, she walks into mine." Ingrid Bergman and Humphrey Bogart. *Casablanca* © Warner Bros. Screenshot captured by authors.

Rick has confronted Ilsa, his former lover who had abandoned him in Paris just as the Germans invaded the city earlier in the war. The night after this confrontation, she shows up at his nightclub with the freedom fighter Victor Lazlo on her arm. Rick gets drunk, feeling sorry for himself ("Of all the gin joints . . . she walks into mine") and when she comes to try to explain herself, he accuses her of being an unfaithful whore. The next day he runs into her at a market. He feels bad about how he acted and he wants her back in his life. We don't yet know what she wants, or why she left him in Paris.

Actors, directors, and screenwriters talk about breaking scenes into **beats**, moments in the text and the subtext indicating what the character wants to happen, or pointing to shifts in the relationship.

Rick approaches Ilsa and she seems to ignore him (beat). He apologizes for last night, she says it doesn't matter, rejecting his offer of peace (beat). He makes an excuse, "it was the bourbon." She still will not make eye contact and acts like she would like him to go away (beat). Rick changes tack, and asks her why she came back. Was it to explain why she ran away in Paris? She responds with a short, "yes," which is the first positive thing she has said. And she doesn't walk away (beat . . . they keep coming).

He asks her to tell him now, and she says she doesn't think she will. There is a push-pull happening here, with each wanting something different, but both, we will discover, are still in love. He says he thinks he is entitled to know. Trying to sound light, he says, "After all, I paid for an extra train ticket." It's the wrong thing to say. Now angry, for the first time she opens up. She tells him what she saw of him last night told her that he was no longer the Rick she knew in Paris: "[that Rick], I knew he would understand." She tries to say goodbye and end the conversation. Rick ignores that and keeps asking, suggesting his best guess about why she "ran out" on him: that hiding and running throughout the war would be too hard. She says, "You can believe that if you want to." She has every right to be angry at this because, we will discover, it is so wrong. He tells her that things are different now and invites her to return that night. She looks away and down. His invitation is almost a sexual proposition and she is blushing, hiding it from him. Then, angry, for the first time she tells him bluntly that Lazlo is her husband, and he was when they were in Paris, but she had thought he was dead. She walks off. Rick is devastated.

Reading this may seem rather ordinary. What is missing is the acting and the director's choices about when and how to show their expressions. It makes all the difference. The "beats" help the actors with their line readings, indicating the changes of purpose and attitude they need to convey from moment to moment. Here, they are working with a screenplay that has texture and depth, emotions spoken and unsaid, that make us feel for the characters and want to know more.

That night, Ilsa does return, explains all and they reconcile, in another scene as subtle and nuanced as this one. Almost every scene in this film has this level of subtlety, with shifting emotional moments and meanings, often covered with smartly straightforward dialogue. It's what makes it a movie you can see again and again, even when you know how it comes out. Even with repeated viewings, it can bring you to tears at the end.

Casablanca follows the standard three-act structure.

Act One: we meet all the characters. We learn that Rick has no interest in the freedom-fighting activities of Lazlo. He is intent on not taking sides for or against the Germans and their allies, Vichy France. When Ugati desperately asks for his help, he does nothing, and watches the Germans take him away. "I stick my neck out for nobody," he says, which might also define the philosophy of Captain Renault, the police chief responsible for appeasing whoever is in charge at the moment. When asked by a German officer what his nationality is, Rick says "I'm a drunkard."

But then he sees Ilsa and discovers she is involved with Lazlo. A flashback shows their romance in Paris, with Rick left standing at the train station, abandoned by her. We see how hurt and damaged he has been and witness his initial anger at her, not knowing why she left him.

Act Two: they meet again and she begs Rick to help Lazlo escape Casablanca so he can continue his resistance work. Rick has letters of transit that can make it happen. These letters are what Hitchcock calls a **McGuffin**— something that drives the plot but isn't at all central to the real story. Ilsa pledges that she will stay with Rick if Lazlo can go free.

Act Three: Rick cuts his ties to Casablanca, sells his club, and plans to betray Lazlo so he can be with Ilsa and leave Casablanca with her. He will set Victor up with the letter of transit so he will be arrested. [Spoiler Alert. Don't read on if you have not seen the movie.]

Can we be rooting for a love affair based on this level of deception? Earlier, we have seen Rick help a young Bulgarian couple by arranging for them to win at roulette. And we have seen how he treats Sam, the piano player, and the workers at his club. So how he presents himself (as not caring) doesn't match his actions. These are moments where we see him more attentive to others' needs than he admits to.

Figure 3.2 "Round up the usual suspects." Claude Rains, Paul Henreid, Humphrey Bogart, Ingrid Bergman. *Casablanca* © Warner Bros. Screenshot captured by authors.

But how do we understand his actions now? He is a complicated character, and we really don't know what he will do. At the airport, Rick shoots Major Strasser to stop him from interfering with the plane leaving. Captain Renault watches. There is a pause. He and Rick look at each other and then Renault orders his men. We think he will have them arrest Rick. But instead, he commands: "Major Strasser has been shot. . . . Round up the usual suspects!" Then, he looks at the bottle of Vichy water he is holding and throws it into the wastebasket—a wonderful visual metaphor that needs no dialogue. He and Rick have made a choice. They are now on the same side, as patriots.

Rick then announces that Victor and Ilsa will be getting on that plane. He tells Isla, "Last night we said a great many things. You said I should do the thinking for both of us. . . . Inside of us we both know you belong with Victor, you are part of his work, the thing that keeps him going." She pleads with him, "But what about us?" And he tells her, "We'll always have Paris.

We didn't have . . . we lost it until you came to Casablanca. We got it back last night. . . . Ilsa, I'm no good at being noble but it doesn't take much to see that the problems of three people don't amount to a hill of beans in this crazy world. Someday you will understand that." She looks down, beginning to cry, and he gently raises her head, "Here's looking at you, kid." She and Lazlo then board the plane and it takes off. Rick and Renault walk off into the fog, ending with one of cinema's greatest closing lines, added by the producer, Hal Wallis, after filming had finished, "Louis, this could be the beginning of a beautiful friendship."

If you haven't seen *Casablanca*, do yourself a favor and watch it soon. And if you have seen it, watch it again, to remind yourself just how very good it is.

Citizen Kane (1941)

While *Casablanca* is probably the best-loved of all the Golden Age movies (the most often revived in theaters, and the classic movie most frequently shown on television), *Citizen Kane*, directed by Orson Welles, is certainly the most admired, listed for fifty years on the British *Sight and Sound* poll and others, as the greatest film ever made.

Orson Welles was a wunderkind. In his early twenties, he had already adapted and directed a modern-dress production of Shakespeare's *Julius Caesar* for the Federal Theater Project, as well as directing an all-Black production of *Macbeth*—a powerful statement when racism was still overtly rampant. He created the Mercury Repertory Theater with John Houseman, with successful runs on Broadway. His Mercury Radio Theater of the Air made him famous worldwide in 1938 when he directed and narrated his adaptation of H. G. Wells's novel *War of the Worlds*. He presented the story as a series of very real-sounding news bulletins that managed to create panic across the country, with people thinking that Martians were invading Earth. Welles was twenty-five years old.

This got the attention of Hollywood. In 1939, RKO presented him with what is considered the greatest contract ever offered to a filmmaker: Welles would have full creative control and would produce, write, direct, and star in a movie of his choice, and he would have final cut (this was the biggest concession, since studios were notorious for holding the right to the final edit of a movie, to assure them that the movie met their standards, and was not too long or too experimental to compromise profits). For a first-time moviemaker to have this sort of a deal did not go over well with the old hands of the studio system, the ones who had "paid their dues" to get whatever limited creative control they could.

Welles was taken on a tour of the RKO lot and was introduced to the departments he would learn to work with: special effects, optical printer, matte department (painting backgrounds), editing, makeup, sets, and costumes. Of this, Welles said, "It was the finest train set a boy could ever have!"

He took his freedom seriously, studying classic films to learn how they worked. He supposedly watched John Ford's *Stagecoach* (1939) forty times, deconstructing it to see what made it tick.

What he learned was how things *had* been done. What he brought to Hollywood, whether they wanted it or not, was how differently they *could* be done, paving the way to the modern era.

Welles found his fellow rebel in cinematographer Gregg Toland, an experienced cameraman who loved working with someone not tied to the old way of doing things. Toland had worked with John Ford on *The Long Voyage Home* (1940), which uses several of the camera shots that became identified with *Citizen Kane*: deep focus, extreme contrast of light and shadows (which, in art terms, is called chiaroscuro), and lighting from below instead of from above, which allowed for softer and more realistic effects. Toland was nominated for an Academy Award five times and won for director William Wyler's *Wuthering Heights* (1939). He was the cinematographer on, among many other films, John Ford's *The Grapes of Wrath* (1940), Howard Hawks's *Ball of Fire* (1941), and Wyler's *The Little Foxes* (1941) and *The Best Years of Our Lives* (1946).

Citizen Kane broke many of the classic Hollywood rules, particularly with the use of deep focus. Though this technique had been used before, it had always been for emphasis and was not used routinely. It required special lenses and increased light intensity and was difficult to control. In *Citizen Kane* almost every shot is in deep focus. Everything in the frame is clear, not just the character in the foreground. This allows your eye to wander and discover actions or details that the director is not handing to you with a close-up or a cut. It credits the intelligence, interest, and curiosity of the audience to find what is important.

In addition, Welles and Toland used a roving camera and long takes, following the action, as well as keeping all in focus. The movement served the function of cutting, telling you what is important, what you should be

Figure 3.3 Orson Welles's use of depth of field was revolutionary. Here all the figures are in focus: the adults determining the young boy's future, and the boy, seen through the window playing in the snow. Harry Shannon, Buddy Swan (framed in window), George Coulouris, Agnes Moorehead. *Citizen Kane* (1941). RKO Radio Pictures, Inc. / Photofest © RKO Radio Pictures, Inc.

paying special attention to. The camera moves with the actors which adds an energy and increased sense of involvement to the action. To make this movement work, Welles often had to order furniture that could come apart to allow the camera to pass through it, and then be hurriedly reassembled to be seen in the shot.

A good example is the early scene when we see Kane as a child playing in the snow with his sled. The camera pulls back until we are watching him through a window. Then Agnes Moorehead, as his mother, walks away and the camera stays ahead of her, but we can still see the boy through the window, fully in focus, playing outside. She sits down at a desk (which had to be sectioned, to allow the camera to move, and then reconnected in time for her to sit at it, a complicated action on the set). Meanwhile, set at a diagonal next to her in the foreground are his father and Thatcher, the banker who is being asked to become Kane's guardian (to educate him and protect his inheritance of a gold mine his mother had invested in), and, in the distance, the boy. All are in sharp focus.

This was revolutionary. It was complicated, a single shot continually keeping all in focus, but the effect was not at all showy. You are not aware of the camera movements, but only that you are being immersed in the world of the story.

Welles and Toland used chiaroscuro (enhanced darkness and light) borrowed from the works of Caravaggio and the expressionist films of the silent era. It could convey emotion, ambivalence, and mystery and would become central to the film noir movies that came later.

Figure 3.4 Orson Welles as Charles Foster Kane. Shooting from below makes him seem larger than life. *Citizen Kane* © RKO Radio Pictures Inc. Screenshot captured by authors.

Welles (and Toland) liked low angles, constructing sets on pallets so the camera could be at floor level or below. At that placement, you would naturally see the ceiling in a room. Most movie sets did not have ceilings (the actors were filmed straight on, not looking upward), so you could have the lights and the microphones out of sight above. To create the effect of a ceiling and still be able to light from above and have the microphones there, Toland used a muslin fabric surrounded by detailed wooden moldings to create the illusion of a solid ceiling.

Because so many of Welles's techniques have been copied and built on and are now routine, it is hard to imagine how very extreme they were in 1941. The opening moments of the film immediately tell us we are watching something different, when, after the camera tracks into a lighted window in the grand mansion of Xanadu, we see snow. Then, pulling back, we see a snow globe in someone's hand. Then an extreme closeup of a mouth whispering "Rosebud." Then the globe is dropped and breaks and, through the distorted glass, we see a nurse enter the room. Shooting through the broken glass is a bit of showing off (nobody's perfect). "Rosebud" becomes the MacGuffin of this movie. We will be watching a reporter interview the important people in Kane's life to try to understand the man by finding out why that was the last word he said before he died. At the end, the meaning is revealed (and only we in the audience see it), but whether it explains the man is very much in doubt.

Before Welles realized he could do transitions in the camera, he used the techniques of the stage that were familiar to him. So, many transitions between scenes, or those showing memories, are done by fading out the background by dimming the light, then fading out the foreground the same way, while fading in the new scene by increasing the light. All of this could have been done in camera (by gradually adjusting the aperture, first closing it then opening, so one image fades to black and another emerges into the light) but using stage lighting techniques makes for a distinctive look in this film.

He and Toland used montage beautifully to convey the passage of time and the changes in Kane's relationship with his first wife, Emily. We see them at breakfast, first in a two-shot, close together, talking animatedly and clearly in love, as Kane tells her he will postpone going to work that morning to be with her. Then, a **whip pan** (the camera moves so swiftly it blurs into streaks, telling us a few years have gone by), and now we are in medium close-ups with Emily, his wife, dressed differently, complaining that he kept her waiting while he stayed late at the newspaper. In a separate medium shot, Kane smokes his pipe. Then another whip pan, another few years have passed, and we begin to see their political differences. Kane is criticizing "Uncle John," the president. Then another whip pan, they both look older, and we see Kane sternly insist his wife obey him about keeping an inappropriate present. And another whip pan, his wife starts telling him, "People will think . . ." He interrupts her, and sternly declares, "What I tell them to think." Finally, she is silently reading a rival newspaper, *The Chronicle*, giving him a significant look as he reads his own paper. When the camera pulls back, we see that they are now at opposite ends of a long table. The sixteen-year disintegration of marriage has been defined with almost no dialogue in less than three minutes.

Another area where the movie innovates is with the soundtrack by Bernard Herrmann (this was his first film) and in the overlapping of dialogue and sounds, something carried over from Welles's background in radio. Herrmann was asked to compose complete short musical pieces. The cutting of scenes often followed the rhythm of his music. This was the reverse of how things had normally been done, when the music was added after the film was essentially complete. Herrmann even composed a parody opera aria for Kane's wife Susan to sing (badly) at her operatic debut.

The storytelling is as distinctive as these other effects. We know Kane's story right away, when the film shows us the newsreel "News on the March" after his death. This is the public "life." Revealing the full story this way had never been done, but it helps us follow the confusing timelines to come. A reporter tries to understand that final word, "Rosebud," to try to somehow "know" the man. He interviews Kane's wives, his estranged best friend, his accountant, and Mr. Thatcher, his guardian.

Kane is someone who started from poverty, was suddenly given great wealth, idealistically founded a newspaper, and then gradually became corrupted and lost his way, grandiosely running for public office until scandal (the mistress who would become his next wife) stopped him. He continued to obsessively acquire art and objects he had no place for, losing the love and friendships that mattered until he was alone. As the reporter interviews the people in his life, we see him from different points of view, with occasionally contradictory memories, and with flashbacks within flashbacks. These are sometimes so layered it is hard to keep straight whose memory we are sharing. We are being given a behind-the-scenes view of his very public life, but a view in fragments, like a cubist portrait of the man.

Audiences were used to a linear narrative. Here, they were getting a story in pieces, a jigsaw puzzle to solve, and events having different meanings depending on who tells the story. This was very new and, for some, unsettling. But it paved the way for uncertainty in storytelling: the unreliable narrator, the ambivalent protagonists of film noir, the contradictions and overlapping narratives of Kurosawa's *Rashomon* (1950), Alan Resnais's *Last Year at Marienbad* (1961), Quentin Tarantino's *Pulp Fiction* (1994), Paul Thomas Anderson's *Magnolia* (1999), and Christopher Nolan's *Memento* (2000). *Citizen Kane* laid the foundations for all the masterpieces that broke with the Golden Era rules and reinvented how and what film could be.

There is no doubt that *Citizen Kane* is a masterpiece and a "great film." But is it a good film? Does it entertain or move you, do you feel emotionally involved with the characters? There's a great line from nineteenth-century American humorist Bill Nye: "I've heard that Wagner's music is better than it sounds." Something may be "great" and "important" but may also not be something you love or even enjoy.

We must agree with an early critic, the wonderful Argentine writer Jorge Luis Borges, who, in 1941, called it "a labyrinth with no center" and said that its legacy would be as a film "whose historical value is undeniable, but which no one cares to see again." Well, that prediction has not proved true: *Citizen Kane* is watched and watched again and has influenced generations of filmmakers. Thankfully, while it may not be an "easy" film to watch, it is engaging and does everything an audience would want. It just does it differently and asks more of them, more of their active engagement, than they were used to circa 1941. Critic Pauline Kael's observation in "Raising Kane," her controversial reappraisal of the movie (which appeared as a two-part article in *The New Yorker* in 1971), is close to the mark:

> It is difficult to explain what makes any great work great, and particularly difficult with movies, and maybe more so with *Citizen Kane* than with other great movies, because it isn't a work of special depth or a work of subtle beauty. It is a shallow work, a *shallow* masterpiece.

We find *Citizen Kane* to be a rather cold exercise. It is fascinating (we're certainly never bored), but it doesn't move us as *Casablanca* does. As we imagine Ilsa feels, regarding her husband Lazlo: as much as we admire *Citizen Kane*, we just don't love it.

Chapter 4

The Western

Key Films

Stagecoach (1939)
The Searchers (1956)
Red River (1948)

Our first genre, the Western, is a uniquely American form. Nearly 30 percent of the movies of the 1930s and 1940s were Westerns. It is a "founding story," a mythology, fiction that explains and reinforces the dominant, white, Christian values of American culture, including the biases and prejudices of the society. The movie West is not the real West. Most of the movie conventions of the Western come from nineteenth-century dime novels and the Buffalo Bill Cody Wild West shows in the late 1800s.

For most of its history in the movies, American Indians were simply called "Indians." When describing these Western films, we will use the terms they use. But our values have changed and our willingness to see our history more clearly is conveyed now by calling them "American Indians" or "Native Americans." It's the least we could do. But it does not do justice to understanding the times these earlier films were made to do that here.

Westerns are a particularly robust genre, with standard subtypes: the town that needs rescuing from bandits or the powerful, battles between cattle ranchers and farmers, the building of the transcontinental railroad bringing civilization to the wilderness, settlers versus Indians, the covered wagon and the wagon train, cattle drives, the gold rushes of California and Dakota, range wars, Indian wars, the aftermath of the Civil War (with parallels to more current wars, World War II and Vietnam). And there are typical situations and plots: train and bank robberies, saloon fights, schoolmarms from the East, churchgoing moral committees, robber barons, men on horseback, posses going after outlaws, shoot-outs (both one against one, and a gang against the lone hero), and towns made of clapboard with wooden walkways and dusty streets. You can expect grand empty desert spaces; often, in John Ford Westerns, with the colossal buttes of Monument Valley showing how small humans are in the natural world.

There is the iconic scene: two men face each other, guns ready, and the quicker survives. This is a classic trope of the Western (a **trope** is an image or situation that is considered typical of a particular genre, and indicates to the viewer that this is the sort of film you are watching—here, it is the Western). In this case, we are seeing one of many examples of how the myth overpowers the truth of history. The pistols of the day were notoriously inaccurate, and there was no way even the best gunfighters could shoot with such precision. Quickdraws and fancy twirling of your weapon are another myth. They look fancy but only happen in the movies. Cowboys spent their time herding cattle and were rarely involved in gunplay. Similarly, Indian attacks did happen but nowhere near as often or as brutally as most Western movies show.

A classic hero is the gunslinger who is an outlaw and lives by violence, using those skills to bring law and order to the town (another Western trope that is more myth than history). He uses outlaw methods to fight the outlaws. As a result, the hero can never be fully accepted by the town he helps. He represents the chaos and violence that civilization abhors. So he sacrifices himself for a civilization he can never be fully a part of. This is the central Western story. Like a therapist, he exists to become unnecessary. Thus, we have the classic fade-out of so many Western movies, with the hero, his work done, walking away into the desert, alone.

The Western conveys a cultural mythology of hard work, a yearning for freedom, and rugged individualism. It idealizes an imagined simple universal American past and is frequently a story of Western civilization versus Indians, who are defined as "the savage." The classic Western did not acknowledge, until the revisionist films of the 1960s and after, that essentially the goal of Western progress was to annihilate the Indians because they were in the way and society then could not see that Indians had their own culture worth honoring.

The Silents

The early Western movies re-created Western history, turned it into myth, and prolonged it, with the early silent movies giving jobs to cowboys who were losing their real jobs as the West was "won."

"Buffalo Bill's Wild West Shows" were extremely popular in the late 1800s. He took his version of the history of the West and turned it into a circus, with real Indians and cowboys, rope tricks, fancy riding, and dramatized battles, reenacting the Battle of the Little Bighorn (Custer's Last Stand) but with a happy (for the whites) ending. Buffalo Bill spread the legend of the West and invented many of the clichés of the movie genre to come. In 1882 he took the show to Europe and performed for Queen Victoria.

At that time the film industry was located in the East, using artificial backgrounds to look like the Wild West landscape. Then it moved West with a new real landscape. Working in the desert was difficult; there were real pioneers still being settled, so it was not without complication.

When making B Westerns, sets, costumes, and horses were often reused. Filmed scenes that were expensive—like a stampede, or a flood, or the destruction of a town—were often used in more than one movie. The last great real-life cattle drives were photographed for posterity, to be used in dozens of silent and sound era B movies.

The first Western star in silent movies was Tom Mix. He was a real cowboy who directed and starred in dozens of films, full of stunts and humor. His fellow cowboys loved him. His film fights look quite real, even though in one scene he is battling fifteen men. He liked to fight off-screen, too.

Mix loved to go to parades and store openings, always wearing a white hat. For the fun of it, he would ride a horse into a bar, and declare "Drinks are on me!" Since the producers of Westerns had little money for sets or costumes, his movies were filmed in real Western towns. These real towns looked too unglamorous, too realistic, with people living in sod huts, to allow for the "romance of the West" and the public soon tired of them, and of Tom Mix.

They preferred William S. Hart, a New York stage actor. Hart also wanted his films to look authentic (he used real Indian sign language; badly, but he tried). He toned down the reality and set the classic image of the Western hero: slow to anger, quick with a gun, a man of moral courage. His movie *Hell's Hinges* (1916) has a simple but atypical story, not about control of land (which is at the bottom of most early Westerns), but about control of the spirit of an unruly, godless town. A saloon owner wants to keep religion out of town because it will hurt his business, and Hart plays a gunfighter who wants to keep the law away because it will restrict his freedom to do what he wants. Hart is transformed when he meets a minister's sister. From a quiet beginning the story becomes epic, with the town burning, the people running in terror, and Hart, now wanting to do good, rescuing a woman and her child. It's a remarkably powerful and effective film.

The Covered Wagon (1923) transformed the Western from the B movie category into something substantial and even more popular. It realistically shows Conestoga wagons in the grand open spaces of the prairie. A wagon train with pioneer women and families in the daily business of the search for a better life. We see kettles over open fires, flour out of a barrel, the making of biscuits, and when there is no obvious danger, we see the people enjoying themselves dancing, and sitting quietly around the campfires. The director, James Cruise, as a boy had watched these covered wagons go past his ranch in Utah. The film used the actual wagons from that era, which hadn't been that long ago.

The film used local Indians for the climactic raid on the wagon train. They came as extras with their entire families, providing their own teepees. There was a big snowstorm during the filming and they kept it in the story. It turned out to be one of the most dramatic sequences in the movie.

After the success of *The Covered Wagon*, John Ford made *The Iron Horse* (1924) about the builders of the transcontinental Union Pacific railroad in 1869. It was set around a personal story of the son of the man who first planned the railroad, but died in an Indian raid before he could make it a reality. Filmed on location in Nevada, the farthest away from Hollywood any film had ventured until then, the crew at first lived in a hired circus train, and when that proved flea-ridden, they moved into the sets, fighting the extreme cold and living very much as the characters they were playing had lived sixty years before. Many scenes in the movie were improvised, inspired by interactions among the cast in their downtime. Chinese extras were mostly retired workers from the original railroad. A dog followed the production around and would wander into shots, adding interest, and giving the feeling that you were watching a documentary instead of fiction. This was filmmaking on a grand scale.

Other Westerns with big effects followed. The last of them was *The Winning of Barbara Worth* (1926) based on the real Great Flood of 1906, when Colorado River dams failed and towns were wiped out, forming the lake that exists today called the Salton Sea. Every Western needs a villain, and here it is the speculator who cut costs on building the dam. He is drowned in the flood.

Then came sound. Talkies ended the careers of most of the real cowboys, and for a few years they stopped making outdoor pictures while the studios learned how to record sound.

But the Western would rise again.

The Classic Western: 1930–1960

Sound brought some odd versions of the Western. For instance, the singing cowboy. If you are excited about the possibilities of sound, why limit yourself to the crackling of a campfire and the creaking of a saddle, when you can have a cowboy break into song?

Gene Autry and Roy Rogers had major careers making minor movies that allowed them to stop the action long enough to sing a song or two. Autry was a shrewd businessman and once successful (he started out making serials, with new episodes every Saturday; then B movies which grossed ten times their cost; then in the 1950s, television shows), he bought land in Southern California, as well as radio stations, hotels, and the California Angels baseball team. He became one of the richest men in the state.

Though most of the stories in these Western movies were invented, many were based on real events of the Western past. There were movies based on the lives of famous outlaws like Jesse James, *Jesse James* (1939) with Tyrone Power and Henry Fonda, and *The Assassination of Jesse James by the Coward Robert Ford* (2007) with Brad Pitt; and Billy the Kid, *The Left-Handed Gun* (1958) with Paul Newman, *Billy the Kid* (1941) with Robert Taylor, and *Pat Garrett and Billy the Kid* (1973), directed by Sam Peckinpah. There were no less than six movies made about the gunfight at the OK Corral between the Clanton family and Wyatt Earp and his brothers, Morgan and Virgil. Each film has a different take on the conflict, some favoring the Clantons, most the Earps. They all feature the famous final shoot-out. In John Ford's version, *My Darling Clementine* (1946), starring Henry Fonda, the Earps are the heroes. He adds a fictional character, Clementine, the schoolteacher girlfriend of Doc Holliday, but otherwise sticks close to the facts. In later versions, Wyatt and his brothers are seen as trying to control prostitution in the town of Tombstone, and the Clantons are not evil, but just their rivals.

"American exceptionalism" is an important idea to understand if you want to understand the Westerns of this time. The concept, first pronounced by the historian Frederick Jackson Turner in 1893, was that the United States is unique among countries of the world because of its continuously retreating frontier with European settlers constantly pushing against it, allowing them to challenge notions of social class, inherited wealth, and aristocratic government because the frontier allowed them to create a new version of themselves and civilization. It featured a sense that anyone could become a success, start a new life, or define themselves anew. This is very much the story of the moguls who founded Hollywood. American exceptionalism celebrated the settler as a hero, ignoring details like the people who were already living in this frontier, the Native Americans who were being pushed aside, and others, like Black slaves or, after the Civil War as freedmen, who did not share in that possibility of freedom.

Today it is hard to support these ideas, even as we continue to appreciate the artistry of individual films, but they were central to Western myths for the first decades of the classic era.

John Ford (1894–1973)

Though he made films in many genres, the director John Ford is most associated with the Westerns he made. His *Stagecoach* is the film that Orson Welles chose to watch over and over to learn how to make movies. It made John Wayne (born Marion Morrison) a star. With a screenplay by Dudley Nichols, it also starred Claire Trevor, John Carradine, Thomas Mitchell, Donald Meek, and Andy Devine.

Stagecoach (1939)

Stagecoach is an ensemble piece, very much like *Grand Hotel* (1932), telling stories of strangers traveling together, from different walks of life and social strata. Here, they are on a stagecoach traveling through Apache Indian country with the threat of an imminent raid.

The opening as the stagecoach pulls into town to pick up new passengers introduces the travelers, one by one, and also shows the sort of thing rare before in a Western: the ordinary preparations of the coach for the next stage of the trip: changing the team of six horses, cleaning out the carriage, giving ongoing passengers a chance to freshen up, the driver, announcing the planned stops along the way. And then, soldiers from the cavalry come just before they leave, warning them that Geronimo is on the warpath and offering to ride protection.

Each of the passengers is a type: the upper-class lady, Mrs. Mallory (a cavalry officer's wife); the "distinguished" banker, Gatewood (who we learn early on is fleeing town with stolen money); the gambler, Hatfield (who we will discover is a Southern gentleman); the liquor drummer (salesman) timid Mr. Peacock; Doc Boone, an alcoholic doctor; and Dallas, a prostitute, being run out of town as unacceptable to the upper-class women, the moral police of the town. There is also the sheriff riding shotgun; Buck, the driver, who we

Figure 4.1 Andy Devine, John Wayne as the "Ringo Kid" (the part that made him a star), and Louise Pratt. *Stagecoach* © United Artists. Screenshot captured by authors.

know is considered lower class because he is married to a Mexican; and, after the journey has begun, the outlaw the Ringo Kid, played by John Wayne. He escaped jail and is looking to kill Luke and his brothers, who murdered his father and brother. Ringo is surprised to see the sheriff there, who puts him under arrest. We will discover that the sheriff, too, has a history; he was best friends with Ringo's father and wants Ringo in prison not just to follow the law but to protect Ringo from the men who want to kill him.

The conversations inside the coach do more to establish who these people are. Ringo tells them his real name is Henry, then recognizes Doc Boone as the man who fixed his brother's broken arm years ago. When Doc Boone asks how his brother is, Ringo tells him that he was murdered. Shocked silence. Later, Doc smokes a cigar, and it is clear Mallory is disturbed by the smoke. The gambler Hatfield stands up for her and tells Doc to put the cigar away. Doc gracefully apologizes, mentioning his time in the Union army, only to have Hatfield declare his support for the South. Backs stiffen. It is Ringo who tells them to relax, "the Doc meant no harm." The back-and-forth not only tells us their story but also what kind of people they are.

Abandoned by the cavalry, who are ordered away to chase Geronimo, the stagecoach continues on its own.

Another secret is revealed at the next stop: Mrs. Mallory is pregnant, and we see Doc sober up to help deliver the baby. After watching Dallas with the other woman's new baby, Ringo asks her to settle down with him. She cries, "You don't know anything about me" and he looks at her and says, "I know all I want to know."

When Peacock, the drummer, sees an Apache woman in the hacienda where they are stopping, he cries out in alarm, "a savage." Her Mexican husband happily misunderstands, "Yes, sometimes she is savage, but the Indians don't bother us, I think." The movie is casually making a political point. In a later scene the drummer calms bickering among his fellows by quietly saying, "Let's have some Christian charity, one for the other." One moment he is a racist, the next he is preaching that they all should live together in peace. He is as complicated as the other passengers.

The Indian attack is thrillingly filmed. We see Buck driving the horses hard, the men shooting at the Indians coming at them from all sides. In the coach Doc is treating the drummer after removing an arrow from his chest, the banker getting in the way declaring outrage but being of no help. Doc punches him in the jaw to shut him up. We see the Indians up close, horses charging, and when they are shot, they and their horses collapse violently to the ground. There is a camera placement on the ground level underneath the team of horses at full gallop, and under the Indian horses too (the sort of shot Welles became famous for; here used judiciously, for effect, not to show off, and it increases the intensity of the action). When you tell the story simply, the occasional moments of artistry stand out even more.

Another trope played with and improved: The classic shoot-out. Ford and Nichols, his screenwriter, stretch out the suspense, showing us Luke and his brothers gathering, nervous, breaking a glass in the saloon, startled and ready to shoot when the Doc comes in the door, and then Buck. Onlookers back away, the bartender takes down the mirror, and people leave the main street as the brothers group themselves across it. Then a shadow. We see from behind as Ringo comes forward, alone, with a shotgun and only three bullets. He walks slowly to the right; the film cuts to the brothers, guns drawn walking left; then, Ringo walks toward the camera placed low, and drops to the ground shooting. Cut to Dallas hearing shots, crying out "Ringo." Then we are back inside the saloon, the door opens and there is Luke, who stands there quietly, walks forward two steps, and collapses on the floor, dead. Then, we see Dallas, standing outside, bereft. Hearing footsteps, she looks up—it's Ringo. They embrace each other and the future.

Figure 4.2 Monument Valley, Utah. The siguature setting for many of John Ford's Westerns. *Stagecoach* © United Artists. Screenshot captured by authors.

John Ford was celebrated for the elegant clarity and simplicity of his storytelling and his camerawork. He often cut in camera (limiting his footage to the exact moments he wanted to include) to prevent any changes in the editing room. He was good at balancing moments of truth about the West, filling his world with realistic everyday details while embellishing and polishing the myths. He loved the look of the Western frontier, often featuring the grandeur of Monument Valley (in the Navajo Nation, Arizona). His subject was the American character, or at least the version he admired: the lone individual, dedicated to his community but not regulated by it. He worked on this theme for his entire career, mostly but not exclusively, with Westerns.

The Searchers (1956)

The Searchers, which many consider Ford's masterpiece, is in glorious color, with the vast landscapes of Monument Valley demanding that you see the movie in a theater on a full-size screen. There is a new skepticism with the celebration of the pioneer instinct. Ford begins to acknowledge how morally complex the "winning" of the West was, that it is not the triumphal story so often told. Now he shows us the Indians as victims, fighting to keep their land. Ethan, played by John Wayne, is a violent, even nasty man, who becomes obsessed with searching for years for his niece Debbie, who was captured by Comanche Indians when she was a child.

He had rescued his nephew as a child, a one-eighth Indian, whom his brother adopted, and we see Ethan dismiss and insult the young man, calling him "blanket head." He is a racist and doesn't hide it. Ethan is a tortured soul, not sure whether when he finds Debbie he will bring her home or kill her for being "too Indian" and marrying the Indian warrior Scar. The film makes it clear that Ethan and Scar have much in common; both are violent racists with a nasty streak. Both will scalp their victims without a thought.

Ethan fought on the Confederate side in the Civil War, rode with outlaws, and seems emotionally damaged. He has the skills of a killer, which the community is glad for when he works for their benefit, but which makes them want to shun him afterward. It is suggested that he feels guilty leaving his brother's homestead in search of cattle rustlers only to return and find the farm in flames and his aunt and uncle dead. This conflicted, unpleasant hero is not the hero of the typical Western.

There is an early image, looking over the shoulder of Debbie's mother, that captures the contrast between the idea of home and family, the "civilization" being brought to the West, and the imposing wilderness of the open frontier. This is a tension central to this story.

Figure 4.3 The vastness of the Western landscape. *The Searchers* © Warner Bros. Screenshot captured by authors.

Two scenes exemplify how very different this Western is from what came before. With his friend Martin, Ethan rides into a Native American village destroyed by the cavalry. They see an Indian woman they had known, lying there dead. Martin asks, why did they kill her, as she didn't do anything? Ethan has no answer. Next, we see three Indian chiefs watching sadly as their comrades are herded into a prison cell. We are seeing the world through Indian eyes, and now with a sympathy for what they have lost. It is as though Ford wants to make amends for his earlier one-dimensional portrayals of Native Americans.

The other telling scene is the final one. Ethan has returned Debbie to her family. He seems to have a special relationship with the wife of his brother, as they exchange glances, but with his search over he is at a loss. We see other members of the family walk through the door into the house, but Ethan stops at the threshold, his right arm holding his left almost looking helpless, and then turns and slowly walks into the wilderness. This matches the opening image of the film, which was also through a doorway looking into the desert, with the world of the home seeming so much more secure and inviting. It is a world where he doesn't belong.

Figure 4.4 John Wayne, in silhouette, isolated and alone. *The Searchers* (1956). Warner Bros. / Photofest © Warner Bros.

This movie has been remarkably influential, with images and moments from it showing up in everything from *Taxi Driver* (1976) to the first *Star Wars* (1977).

In 1962, Ford made *The Man Who Shot Liberty Valance*. It is a sort of valedictory, a farewell to the Western genre, with James Stewart and John Wayne (together for the first time) and Andy Devine (Buck in *Stagecoach*), the players most associated with his earlier works. It also starred a newcomer to movies, Lee Marvin, as the psychopathic killer Liberty. It is a movie about the stories we tell about the West, and it has a twist ending that won't be spoiled here. It's summed up in the famous quote from the film: "This is the West, sir. When the legend becomes fact, print the legend." As good as it is, this film comes across as old-fashioned, with Ford too often spelling out his themes instead of showing them. Did we need Jimmy Stewart's character teaching a classroom filled with children and immigrants about democracy? It cuts the momentum of the story.

Ford was not a one-genre man. Among many other films, he also directed, beautifully, *The Grapes of Wrath* (1940) with Henry Fonda; *The Quiet Man* (1952), a romance set in Ireland; and *Mister Roberts* (1955), based on the play, a comedy with Henry Fonda, James Cagney, and Jack Lemmon.

Howard Hawks (1896–1977)

Hawks was a versatile director, making some of the best screwball comedies of the Classic Era, *Twentieth Century* (1934) with a brilliantly hammy performance by John Barrymore; *Bringing Up Baby* (1938) with Cary Grant, Katherine Hepburn, and Baby, a leopard; *His Girl Friday* (1940), again with Grant, paired with Rosalind Russell as fast-talking newspaper reporters and former spouses; and *Ball of Fire* (1941) with Gary Cooper as a shy professor and Barbara Stanwyck as a worldly nightclub singer who hides out from the mob with a group of professors studying American slang (the situation is much funnier than it sounds). He did action pictures like *Scarface* (1932) about Al Capone and starring Paul Muni; *Only Angels Have Wings* (1939) with Grant and Jean Arthur, about daredevil pilots; *Sergeant York* (1941) with Gary Cooper as a celebrated World War I hero; and film noir mysteries, like *The Big Sleep* (1946) with Humphrey Bogart as detective Philip Marlowe and Lauren Bacall, and *To Have and Have Not* (1944) also with Bogart and Bacall, based on a Hemingway story.

Red River (1948)

Hawks shared the territory of the Western with Ford, making two of the most iconic films of the genre, *Red River* (1948) and ten years later, *Rio Bravo* (1959), which was a reaction to the Gary Cooper film, *High Noon* (1952). Directed by Fred Zinnemann and told in real time (a clock ticking away the minutes), *High Noon* is about a sheriff who on the day he gets married (to Grace Kelly) and hangs up his badge learns that a gang of killers will arrive on the noon train who have vowed to take revenge on him for sending their leader to prison. He goes around town asking for help from the people there, and one by one they turn him down. He will have to face these killers alone. Hawks and John Wayne hated the message of this film. *Rio Bravo* is their rebuttal. Wayne is the sheriff who has put the brother of a powerful rancher in jail for murder. The rancher has vowed to spring him and kill the sheriff. Wayne doesn't turn to the townspeople for help doing his job. His only help is a couple of deputies: Dude, an alcoholic played by (of all people) Dean Martin, who turns out to be very good; Stumpy, an old one-legged man; and a young gunman played by Ricky Nelson, a teen pop star of the day. This is a leisurely study of character, which slowly builds to the final confrontation.

Red River is a powerful drama about generational conflict and the changing ways of a West that was no longer so wild. It stars John Wayne as Tom Dunson, in a role that foreshadows his character in *The Searchers*. Tom started out with two cows on his ranch and now fourteen years later, has a herd of ten thousand. Back when he was starting, he found Matt, a young boy, the only survivor of an Indian attack, and he adopted him. That boy is now grown up, has fought in the Civil War, and is played by Montgomery Clift, an actor of the new generation of **Method actors** (who employ a technique in which actors draw from their own personal history to summon up emotions projected in their screen roles, a more naturalistic approach than that of classical actors, trained for the stage) who were beginning to take over Hollywood. Wayne represented the old style and the movie plays on that difference. Tom needs to bring his cattle to market and the nearest is in Missouri, one thousand miles away. An almost impossible distance.

The cattle drive is difficult, and they begin to run out of food for the cowboys, who become sullen and angry. When a few of them try to desert the drive, Tom shoots them. After crossing the Red River, the remaining cowboys try to convince Tom to drive the herd to a closer destination, but he stubbornly refuses and threatens to hang anyone who tries to leave. His son, Matt, stops him and takes over leadership of the drive. Tom is furious and threatens to kill his son. He comes across as a bully who shoots first and asks questions later. He and Matt are too much alike in their stubbornness, but Matt is the better leader, less prone to violent control. A confrontation is inevitable.

This is a Western with many classic moments, built around a cattle drive, the immensity of the desert, and a changing morality as rough justice becomes less acceptable. It adds a father and son who love each other but cannot understand or accept each other's ways. Montgomery Clift is very good as a son whose sensitivity guides him until he has to act and take a stand. And Wayne, too, is good, able to equally show unexpressed affection for his son and Tom's violent nature. Dmitri Tiomkin's musical score is one of the best in any Western movie, never intrusive and conveying layers of emotion and grandeur.

International Westerns

The Western as a genre has been extraordinarily popular throughout the world. Something about the wide-open spaces, the lone hero separated from the community but wanting to be at one with it, the horseback riding and the gunfights, resonated with the legends and histories of other cultures. They borrowed the Western tropes to tell their own stories, and when they were successful, the American Western then borrowed them back.

In Japan, this happened regularly. Akira Kurasawa's first international success, *Rashomon* (1950), was not a Western. But his second was. *The Seven Samurai* (1954) was the story of a "ronin," a renegade samurai warrior in sixteenth-century Japan, who is hired by a small village to protect it from bandits. He gathers a group of fellow ronins to help him, and, in exchange for three meals of rice a day, they go about teaching the villagers how to fight. It is a three-hour epic with a climactic battle against the attacking bandits in pouring rain. Kurasawa created background stories for each ronin (this level of detail had never been done before), making it possible for us to see them as individuals. He also used action techniques that have become common now, such as slow motion for emphasis, and multiple cameras to catch the action from different perspectives and give him more editing choices. Toshiro Mifune, who played the reluctant first ronin, became an international star and made many other films with Kurasawa.

The film was immediately appreciated in the States as building on the Western tradition. It was an **art house** hit. The American actor Yul Brynner acquired the rights to the film and hired John Sturges, the director of *The*

Gunfight at the OK Corral (1957), to direct. Their remake was *The Magnificent Seven* (1960), starring Brynner, Steve McQueen, and Charles Bronson, with Eli Wallach as the head bandit. The story now takes place in the American West and the villagers are being protected from Mexican bandits. It is very good and it, too, was an international hit.

Even as interest in Westerns began to diminish in the States, they remained popular in Europe. The Italian director, Sergio Leone, saw a market for a new kind of Western, one that heightens the standard set pieces, but undercuts the glorifications of the Classic Era. Here we have a hero who is in it for the money or personal revenge, and rarely to bring law and order to the community. Leone decided to adapt Kurasawa's next Japanese western, *Yojimbo* (1961) which also starred Toshiro Mifune. This was played as comedy. Mifune is a ronin who comes to a town being fought over by two rival gangs, and he decides to play them against each other. He offers his services to both and encourages them to destroy each other as a way of ridding the town of their influence.

Leone's film was called *A Fistful of Dollars* (*Per un pugno di dollari*) (1964) and was made in Spain with an Italian crew and a minor American actor named Clint Eastwood. He would become an international star in this film, playing "The Man with No Name" wearing the same poncho and hat in this and two other Leone Westerns, *For a Few Dollars More* (1965) and *The Good, the Bad, and the Ugly* (1966). The story was the same as *Yojimbo*, but there was one problem: Leone had never gotten the rights to the story. Kurasawa sued him and won a monetary reward and the right to distribute the film in Japan, where he changed the name to *The Return of Yojimbo*.

This was the first so-called Spaghetti Western to become an international success. The other two films in the series were even bigger hits. Leone's hero is cynical, out for himself. In *A Fistful of Dollars* when we first see him come to town he watches someone shooting at a young boy for fun and does nothing to stop it. He is unshaven and hardly says a word. Leone's style is operatic, with long-held shots that increase tension, then zooming into extreme closeups of faces or a weapon.

The music of Ennio Morricone adds powerfully to his effects. Morricone added unusual sounds to his score: whipcracks, gunshots, whistling. Leone was so impressed with his music that he would prolong a scene to allow it to finish. Morricone's theme for *The Good, the Bad and the Ugly* is famous and recognized even by people who have never seen the film.

Leone topped himself with *Once Upon a Time in the West* (1968) starring

Figure 4.5 Making the most of the Cinemascope wide-screen. *Once Upon a Time in the West* ©
Paramount Pictures. Screenshot captured by authors.

Charles Bronson, Jason Robards, and Henry Fonda. The first twenty minutes
of the film are almost without dialogue. Nothing seems to be happening except
we are watching some rough-looking men wait for a train. It is incredibly
suspenseful, all done with editing and close-ups of faces and the occasional
mosquito. Leone uses the wide screen to great effect, creating iconic images
that suggest the violence to come and honor just how big Western spaces are.

The villain is played by Fonda, a star of the Classic Era who always
played the good guy, the moral center such as Tom Joad in *The Grapes of Wrath*
(1940), *Young Abe Lincoln* (1939), and Wyatt Earp in *My Darling Clementine*
(1946). For him to be the blue-eyed villain, who we first see gunning down
a young child with a smile, was shocking and was meant to be. Fonda turns
out to be a terrific villain. This film aggregates and intensifies many of the
themes that define the Western, a culmination of fifty years of tradition. It is
one of the great Westerns.

Sergio Corbucci is another director of Spaghetti Westerns. The most
famous is *Django* (1966) starring Franco Nero as another lone gunslinger,
who we first see dragging a coffin (which, we will discover, does not contain
a body) and who goes into battle against a racist major and Mexican bandits
(a rather similar story idea to *Yojimbo* and *A Fistful of Dollars*). It was very
popular in Europe despite being banned in the UK (and unrated in the United
States) because of its extreme violence. There are a half-dozen remakes and
unofficial sequels by other Italian directors (most are not worth watching).
More recently, Quentin Tarantino made *Django Unchained* (2012), which
is not a remake but was inspired by the original (Nero has a cameo role,
opposite Jamie Foxx as Django).

Corbucci also made *The Great Silence* (*il grand silenzio*) (1968) starring Jean-Louis Trintignant as a gunfighter known as Silence, who is mute from having his throat cut as a boy, and Klaus Kinski as Loco, a bloodthirsty bounty hunter. It is a darkly grim story, snowbound and very violent with an unexpectedly sad and powerful ending. Many consider it a greater work than any of Leone's films.

Revisionist Westerns

Most of the American-made Westerns of the 1960s and 1970s were rethinking the Western, counteracting the traditional tropes and undercutting anything that would glorify the story of the Western frontier. These were the decades of Vietnam protests and voting rights battles in the South. It was a time when moral leaders were assassinated: John Kennedy, Robert Kennedy, Martin Luther King Jr., Malcolm X, and the civil rights workers James Chaney, Andrew Goodman, and Michael Schwerner. Westerns that glorified rough justice and killing Indians (now Native Americans) no longer sat well with young movie audiences.

A few Westerns were popular, though as a genre it had lost its luster. *Butch Cassidy and the Sundance Kid* (1969) with Paul Newman and Robert Redford was a lighthearted adventure about real historical outlaws. Its comic tone is undercut by their end in a hail of bullets. Sam Peckinpah's *The Wild Bunch* (1969) is about a group of aged outlaws looking for one last score in the West of 1913 that was no longer wild. They are no more the good guys than the posse of mercenaries who are chasing them or the revolutionaries they are trying to supply with weapons. The movie ends in a bloodbath, one of the most violent shoot-outs in movie history, marking not only the deaths of these men but, perhaps the creators thought, the death of the Western movie.

But Westerns don't die so easily. *Little Big Man* (1970), starring Dustin Hoffman and directed by Arthur Penn (who also did *Bonnie and Clyde* [1967], a revisionist gangster film with another brutal ending), introduces us to Jack Crab, 121 years old, who tells of his life in the West, captured and raised by Indians, marrying an Indian and witnessing Custer's Last Stand. It is the stuff of legend but brought down to earth, myths shattered as the Indians make it their story. *McCabe and Mrs. Miller* (1971), directed by Robert Altman and starring Warren Beatty and Julie Christie, takes a different tack, showing us the glum, shabby reality of life on the Western frontier. McCabe comes to a town in the Pacific Northwest to set up a whorehouse and tavern. Mrs. Miller, a whorehouse madam and opium addict, shows up later and the two go into business together. They make a success of it until a big mining company makes them an offer to buy their business. McCabe refuses, not realizing he is now a marked man. This is a melancholy piece, the cinematography emphasizing how cold and ugly life there can be. It is an elegy to the hopes of the frontier. Nevertheless, it is a beautiful and touching movie, and one worth seeing.

They keep making Westerns, and every once in a while one strikes a chord. In *Unforgiven* (1992), Clint Eastwood (who also directs) is an aging bounty hunter drawn back into violence. Some prostitutes in the town of Big Whiskey are unhappy with how the sheriff (Gene Hackman) handles things when one of them is cut by some cowboys. Hackman is just trying to keep things calm and quiet in the town, but that isn't okay with them. They put a bounty on the cowboys, which brings William Munny (Eastwood) out of retirement. He gets together with his old partner (Morgan Freeman), and a young gun too eager to prove himself in a killing (there is always a hot-headed youngster in these stories, needing to learn to cool down before he gets himself dead). Munny had hung up his guns when he got married. But now his wife is dead, and he is going to do one more job. He looks back at his life as a gunslinger and wants to atone for the killings he is responsible for: "It's a hell of a thing, killing a man. You take away all he's got, and all he's ever gonna have." This film won Academy Awards in 1992 for Best Picture, Supporting Actor (Hackman), Editing, and Director.

To bring things full circle, in 2013, the Japanese actor Ken Watanabe adapted *Unforgiven* as a samurai film. Here the aging samurai is called back to help collect the bounty on the men who cut and disfigured a prostitute. Same story, different world.

There are other ways to deconstruct the Western. Mel Brooks did it in *Blazing Saddles* (1974) with Cleavon Little as a Black sheriff, and Gene Wilder, as Jim, an ex-gunslinger, Madeline Kahn as Lili Von Shtupp (channeling Marlene Dietrich), and Harvey Korman as villain Hedley Lamar. This is a very funny comedy (with Richard Pryor as a co-writer), a satire not only on Western movies, but on race relations, and whatever else Mel had on his mind. There is the famous fireside scene, with all the cowboys eating beans, a flatulent chorus, and Brooks himself playing an Indian chief who speaks Yiddish. The N-word is used freely (something that would not pass muster today but is very funny here). Someone punches a horse in the nose. Brooks will do anything for a laugh.

Chapter 5
Film Noir

Key Films

Double Indemnity (1944)
Out of the Past (1947)
Touch of Evil (1958)
Chinatown (1974)

One glance at an image and you know you are in the world of film noir. What is it you see—what tells you? Just what is film noir?

First there is the look—the visual style. The noir look. Dark, strange low angles, single-source lighting leaving much of the screen in darkness, slashes of light. There will be sudden bursts of violence. Faces are hidden, and when revealed are unreadable, haunted, terrified, implacable, or resigned to their fate. Death is a moment away.

There's off-kilter camera placement—the world is out of joint it says, hard to fathom, scary, dangerous. Moral ambiguity is the rule—right and wrong are hard to know. The films may be black and white—but the stories are anything but. These films take place in the dark—not necessarily at night, but in the dark places of the world—the city alleyways, the darkened rooms. It's a world of shadows—what you don't see is often more important than what you do. Faces are hidden, then revealed, the camera very much telling us what to see and how to feel about it. **Dutch angles**, with the camera canted off the horizontal, leave us tense, unnerved—like the characters themselves.

That there can be such life, such energy in these stories of hopelessness, corruption, and human weakness, that these films can be so wonderfully effective after sixty years, is a testament to the craft of their creators. Often what we think of as noir style—the darkened image, the shadows, the crazy angles—were creative solutions to low budgets and not enough time. Those dark rooms are often dark because the studio couldn't afford to dress an entire set—or chose not to; so we only get to see what we need to see. No one in those days had any idea they were making film noir; they were just doing their jobs telling a story. But a particular kind of story.

Witty, Gritty, and Dark

There is much academic debate about whether film noir is actually a genre or just a style. Yet, why can't it be both? As a genre it has a common mood: disillusion, cynicism, and a sense that fate makes most decisions not worth making. There are standard elements that immediately tell you that you are in the world of noir: often there is a voice-over, the protagonist telling his story (it is always a "his"), sounding world-weary and defeated and announcing that "if only he had known where things were going." But usually he does know where it is going, and, feeling trapped and without agency, he goes there anyway.

In several of the best noir films, such as *Sunset Blvd.*, *DOA*, and *Double Indemnity*, the narrator is already dead or dying, and he is telling us how he got that way. He will tell us how he sees his situation, what he feels about it, and then how he could not pull himself away or figure out a way to fix it.

There is usually a woman who drives the protagonist to do something morally compromising, which he does because of lust or greed or what he thinks is love, each decision making things worse, either in a way unexpected or one we, the viewer, can see coming a mile away.

The look and setting of a noir film is defining: usually the big city, Los Angeles or New York, at night. There are flashing neon signs and lampposts not quite providing enough light. It's raining, or it just has rained, and the streets and dark alleys are wet (with reflections that make it seem like the city is a character, watching). The fog is often impenetrable. Even people together are separated by the dark, or the fog. That light piercing the fog illuminates nothing.

The action takes place in sleazy dark tenements or roominghouses, in nightclubs, in basements and lonely dark alleys. Odd camera angles and strong contrasts of light and dark with dramatic shadows are typical, but not necessary. What is necessary is a sense that the protagonist is fated to fail, and to lose everything. As Walter Neff says, in one of the best of the noir films, *Double Indemnity*, "I killed him for money and a woman; and I didn't get the money and I didn't get the woman." That's noir.

The films made in the 1940s were often B-movie crime stories, based on the pulp fiction that was popular in the 1930s. The magazine *Black Mask* featured tales of murder, corruption, and sex in the city. They had sharp, cynical dialogue with minimal description, portraying a stylized underworld. Many of the stories featured a private detective. There was Dashiell Hammett's Sam Spade played in the movie by Humphrey Bogart in *The Maltese Falcon*

(1941), and Raymond Chandler's iconic shamus, Philip Marlowe, also played by Bogart in *The Big Sleep* (1946) (opposite a definingly sultry Lauren Bacall), and by Dick Powell in *Murder My Sweet* (1944)—Powell, a popular crooner in Busby Berkley musicals of the 1930s, resuscitating his career as a tough guy. James Cain with *Double Indemnity* (1944) and *The Postman Always Rings Twice* (1946) and Cornell Woolrich with *The Phantom Lady* (1944) were the other pillars of the pulp style whose work helped define noir.

Many of these stories were made into crime films that were eventually called film noir. But when they were making them the writers, directors, and cinematographers had no awareness that they were creating a genre or inventing a new style. They were just telling a story as best they could.

The French film critic Marc Verbet wrote: "The Americans made [film noir] and then the French invented it." He has a point. These movies got their name from the French, well after they were made. The Nazi occupation of France enforced an embargo on films from Hollywood. Once the war ended, the Hollywood films made during the war filled the theaters in Paris. The first titles were *The Maltese Falcon, Laura* (1944), *Murder My Sweet*, and *Double Indemnity* and they made a big splash. The French had never seen anything quite like them. Enthusiasts noticed how different these films were from the ones they had seen before. An Italian-French writer, Nino Frank, called these films "noir" ("black" in French), noticing the downbeat fatalistic tone, the frequent violence, lack of sentiment, and how they often ended with the death of the hero. They seemed to be remarkably pessimistic, exploring the psychology of crime, as we follow a character making one bad decision after another driven by greed, or sex, or power, or a distorted idea of the right thing to do.

These are usually crime stories—but not always. But it is how they are told that makes a film "noir." The look of the film tells us things will go badly. The lead character may know what he wants—but he also is likely to fail in getting there. Fate is a character and Doom a close companion.

It's no coincidence that the great directors and cinematographers of film noir were often German or Austrian refugees, escaping to Hollywood from the early days of Nazi rule before the war: Fritz Lang, Billy Wilder, Robert Siodmak, John Alton. Their films convey a powerful sense of dread. Paranoia is in their bones.

They brought with them the German expressionist style from the 1920s and 1930s, with eccentric sets that reflected the twisted perceptions of characters, high contrast lighting, and key lights (smaller focused light sources) to make close-ups of eyes and faces pop, and use of these bright lights to create shadows enveloping the characters, cast by Venetian blinds, stair rails, and lamps inside and out. This dramatic emphasis on darkness and light is called chiaroscuro.

Chiaroscuro is a term used in the study of art, describing a style (most famously represented by the sixteenth-century Baroque Italian artist Caravaggio) of intense contrasts of light and dark, which adds drama and immediacy to the painted image. It does the same for these black-and-white films. Very often you will see a face in a half-light; one side dark and the other illuminated, a metaphor for goodness and evil, for how these characters, and by extension, all of us, contain both. In these films, the dark scenes, the shadows, and the eccentric camera angles as well as the stories being told, do something more. They all contribute to a feeling of anxiety and despair; of the world being out of control. And suggest that just one bad decision could lead any of us to moral decay. And yet these films are exciting, absorbing, and fun to watch. Much like horror films, as long as bad things are happening to someone who is not us (but who might be) we can enjoy watching.

There is much written about the "why" of noir. Why did this style happen when it did, tied as it is to the 1940s and early 1950s? It doesn't take much insight to see how those years were a time of awakening in America. With World War II, people were confronted with death and danger to an unprecedented degree; when their innocence about human nature and the world was challenged and often shattered by the nature of that war. The war years were a time of a new cynicism, a pessimism about, as radio's The Shadow "knows," "the evil in the hearts of men." Many were left numb by what they experienced; depressed and anxious, often hopeless, with a sense that they were not in control of their destinies.

These were times of social upheaval. When men returned home from the war, they discovered a world different from the one they had left. The traditional rules of the family no longer seemed to apply. Women were now in the workforce, doing jobs that had been only for men, and liking it. Many of the noir heroes are returning veterans, finding it hard to find a place for themselves again in society. Most are loners, and most cannot imagine a life of contentment in marriage or family. There is a sense of rootlessness; a disconnect from the middle-class world.

The noir films reflect that. The city becomes a world out of control, matching the corruption of the lead characters, their moral darkness. It is too often controlled by big shots who kill at will and do what they want with the little people, the people without money or power. There was an awareness that institutions were not to be trusted, that governments could lie; and that plans, an imagined future, could be undone in a moment, by bad luck or a bad choice—and often by events you could not comprehend.

In the 1940s, the works of Sigmund Freud became known in popular culture. Freudian symbolism becomes more and more explicit in many of the films of the time, not just the noirs. It underlies the concept that characters are subject to inner turmoil and psychological forces that they cannot understand or fully control and influences many noir stories—and the way they are told.

The negative view of women's sexuality seen in many of these films has been connected by some writers with the new independence of women during the war. Working in the higher-paid jobs of men who were off fighting, women seemed to threaten men's status. This coupled with an uneasiness about family, about the possibility of settling down, of trusting someone—all this figured into the noir sensibility.

In Robert Wise's *The Set-Up* (1949), a prizefight picture, you can sense the dread, the loneliness, the isolation of the character brilliantly played by Robert Ryan, a fighter who was supposed to take a dive but was not told by his manager until late in the bout. Feeling he was "one punch away" from being a champion, he fights his best fight and wins. The camaraderie of the fighters before they go out into battle, and the fight itself is both absorbing and suspenseful. But now the gangsters are after him—for doing the right thing. The silence in the alleyways matches the darkness, the shadows provide no comfort—the locked doors rattle—there is no place to hide.

If the Blues Were a Movie, It Would Be Film Noir

The noir films of the 1940s didn't only have a look and a mood. They also had stories and characters, variations on a narrow but rich set of themes.

Character types include the private eye (the "shamus"). Most of the stories in the pulp fiction magazines used Yiddish slang for underworld characters. Odd, since none of their authors were Jewish. The pulp names caught on with the people they were describing, and it became part of their language. The stories were filled with small-time crooks, gangsters, gamblers, over-the-hill prizefighters, showgirls, bargirls, and mistresses. Or we have the beat cop—a loner, burned-out, obsessed with the filth of the city. He's near the edge and about to go over. And we watch, fascinated. From the other side of the tracks, there are corrupt businessmen or politicians, or nightclub owners—the rich and the too-rich, convinced they can always buy their way out of trouble. We will find all of these types in the noir films of the 1940s.

Then there is the hood, the petty thief, the gonif. Trying to escape the bottom of the heap with a final score—usually a heist, elaborately planned. Film noir indulges our fascination with the planning of the crime, and then slaps us in the face as things go wrong. Trapped in their little worlds, these characters are doomed before they even get started. Can anyone be more defeated than Sterling Hayden at the end of the line in *The Killing,* directed by Stanley Kubrick?

There were examples of the noir style and attitude in earlier films, particularly *The Stranger on the Third Floor* (1940), with its story of a man wrongly accused, and its use of shadow, key lights, and Dutch angles. But it was hardly seen when it first came out, coming from a Poverty Row studio. The first film in this style that grabbed people's attention was *The Maltese Falcon* (1941) directed by John Huston.

It introduced the private eye, the shamus. He's what Raymond Chandler called a "knight in dirty armor," walking the mean streets of the city and usually getting roughed up for his trouble. He's got a code to guide his behavior—but more often than not he has no idea what he's got himself into. The archetype of the shamus is Sam Spade in *The Maltese Falcon.* This was the first film directed by John Huston and the film that made Humphrey Bogart an A-level star (after a ten-year career at Warner Bros. playing second banana to Jimmy Cagney and George Raft—usually dying halfway through the picture). Spade's quest for the priceless "black bird" statuette leads him to criminals, and to the supposedly respectable—which is never clear; no one can be believed; everyone is dangerous and lying. Authority is to be avoided or distrusted. This world is filled with hard-boiled patter and hard-boiled dames, with grand schemes, and petty thieves. Though the shamus is cynical about people's motives, he can be taken in by temptation—often in the form of the femme fatale—the woman who uses her sexuality to get what she wants—and often to get our hero dead.

The Maltese Falcon started it. Based on the novel by Dashiell Hammett, with sharp dialogue lifted directly from the page, and characters to match.

Elisha Cook Jr. is Wilmer, the gunsel, the Fat Man's gun-toting protector, but he is just a kid trying hard to act tough. His weak boyish face shows up in many of the best noirs—and he rarely stays alive for the finish. Spade sees right through him: "The cheaper the crook, the gaudier the patter."

When it comes to women, most noir heroes don't realize what they're dealing with until it's too late. And, as Robert Mitchum's Jeff Bailey in *Out of the Past* says, most are so enthralled that they "don't care." Mary Astor plays a beautiful dame who does very bad things. Here the lies keep coming—what exactly is her real name anyway? Spade sees through her lies, but he is tempted anyway: "We didn't exactly believe your story, Miss Wonderly. We believed your $200." She says, "I've been bad, worse than you can imagine." He replies: "That's good. If you were actually as innocent as you pretend to be, we'd never get anywhere."

The Maltese Falcon gets the tone and the attitude of noir—but the visual style would come later. It's a complicated story about the search for a priceless statue of a black bird, sharp dialogue, and larger-than-life characters (especially, Sidney Greenstreet, who we saw in *Casablanca* as the genteel-seeming Fat Man with a nasty edge, and Peter Lorre as Joel Cairo, with his gardenia-scented calling cards) make for great movie watching.

Look at *Murder, My Sweet* (1944) made a few years later, with Dick Powell playing the shamus, Philip Marlowe. It's based on Raymond Chandler's novel *Farewell, My Lovely.* That title sounded too much like it might be one of singer Dick Powell's old musicals—so it had to go. Directed stylishly by Edward Dmytryk, and written by Chandler and John Paxton, this one has it all: the sharp-talking shamus who we first see with his eyes bandaged telling all to suspicious cops, and he has three murders to explain. His wisecracking, self-deprecating voice-over guides us through the complicated plot, involving a stolen jade necklace, an elegant blackmailer who pretends to be a psychic, and a tough but oddly sensitive giant called Moose Malloy looking for his old girlfriend, Velma.

At one point, groggy from being beaten and drugged, Marlowe sums things up: "Okay Marlowe, I said to myself, 'you're a tough guy. You've been sapped twice, choked, beaten silly with a gun, shot in the arm [with drugs] until you're crazy as a couple of waltzing mice. Now let's see you do something really tough—like putting on your pants.'" He keeps on working because someone hired him, and that guy is dead. It's a matter of principle; he owes him. These tropes are close to the bones of *The Maltese Falcon* with its black bird. Oh, and there is the rich dame married to a doting rich guy thirty years her senior, who lies about who she knows and what she knows, pulls Marlowe close, tells him how much she needs him, and then gets him to agree to murder the psychic for her. Marlowe's got her measure, but at the finish, she is pointing her gun at him and about to pull the trigger. Claire Trevor plays this to the hilt, the template for the femme fatale. There is an expressionistic drug-induced nightmare and the dramatic chiaroscuro lighting that was missing from the *Maltese Falcon*: night, darkened rooms, smoky bars, fog, and shadows everywhere.

Raymond Chandler had been reluctant to agree to allow Dick Powell to play Marlowe; everyone knew him as a singer. But after seeing this movie he said that Powell was exactly how he pictured him. High praise. The movie was a big hit for the studio, RKO. A few years later, Chandler saw Bogart play Marlowe in *The Big Sleep* (1946), and he changed his mind; now Bogart was the image of his shamus.

Alfred Hitchcock, who never made a film that one could call noir, defined melodrama as "reality with all the boring parts taken out." The plots of some of these films were hard to follow, but they were never boring. More than that, they keep us guessing—the stories are often fractured—told through flashbacks, and sometimes with flashbacks within the flashbacks.

Another top-notch noir, *The Big Sleep*, also based on a Raymond Chandler novel, directed by Howard Hawks, with a screenplay by Leigh Brackett and, of all people, William Faulkner, and starring Bogart and Lauren Bacall, was famously so complicated that even the author finally didn't know who did what to whom. This was in part because Chandler had to twist his novel out of shape to accommodate the Hays Office, which among other things did not tolerate any suggestion of homosexuality on-screen. Hawks felt that if you told the story well enough, though, it didn't matter if it didn't make sense—and for this film at least he was right. It didn't hurt that the dialogue between Bogart and Bacall, who started an affair while filming, smoldered with innuendo.

Double Indemnity (1944)

The noir mood and style take center stage in Billy Wilder's delicious *Double Indemnity*—perhaps the best of all noir films. It is the perfect combination of a terrific plot, from a novella by James M. Cain, the hard-boiled dialogue of Raymond Chandler, and the wit of Billy Wilder. This strange partnership happened almost by chance. Wilder's regular writing partner, Charles Brackett, thought the Cain novel was low-class sleaze and he wanted no part of it. Wilder was convinced that audiences would love watching bad people do bad things. His producer suggested he work with Raymond Chandler. Chandler was an alcoholic who liked to work alone, and Wilder needed a partner he could bounce ideas off of. They were very different people and they despised each other. But they managed to come up with a brilliant screenplay. The films made from Chandler's novels had great dialogue but plots that no one could follow. Brilliant performances and direction made that less noticeable but having Cain's tightly constructed plot coupled with Chandler and Wilder's smart, sassy dialogue, and with Wilder's sharp direction and three terrific lead actors, and you had movie gold.

The gonif, the small-time fellow in over his head, thinking he's smart and willing to walk a cliff's edge for a dame, was epitomized here by Fred MacMurray playing Walter Neff (a perfect common-man name) an insurance salesman who has seen enough over the years to think he can pull off a murder and an insurance scam. But the thought doesn't occur to him until he meets Phyllis, the housewife who leads him down the garden path, played by Barbara Stanwyck. She is sexy and sultry, a nasty piece of work. The wonderful Edward G. Robinson is the moral compass—the insurance investigator who loves his job and has great instincts ("the little man in my stomach tells me"). Except, this time he didn't see it, the murderer was too close: Neff, his friend. Billy Wilder and Raymond Chandler give us suggestive situations and dialogue to match.

The movie opens with a car careening along dark city streets, going through a stoplight (metaphor alert: the light says stop but he just keeps going). The camera follows a man from behind as he enters his workplace, an insurance company, and heads to his office. We see he is bleeding; he has been shot. He starts talking into a dictaphone, addressing himself to Keyes, his friend and colleague. A confession: "I killed Dietrichson. Me, Walter Neff, age thirty-six, no visible scars, until a while ago, that is. . . . Yes, I killed him. I killed him for money and a woman—and I didn't get the money and I didn't get the woman. Pretty, isn't it?" So the story begins, with his voice-over walking us through it. He stops at the Deitrichson house to ask the man of the house to renew his life insurance and meets Phyllis, the man's wife. She is standing at the top of the stairs, wearing nothing but a towel. After she's dressed, he watches her legs as she walks down the stairs. He is smitten, and it shows. She invites him back when her husband will be home:

Neff: You'll be here, too?
Phyllis: I guess so, I usually am.
Neff: Same chair, same perfume, same anklet?
Phyllis: I wonder if I know what you mean?
Neff: I wonder if you wonder.

Figure 5.1 The shadows of the venetian blinds suggest dark doings, as Fred MacMurray and Barbara Stanwyck take each other's measure. *Double Indemnity* © Paramount Pictures. Screenshot captured by authors.

She wants him to take out an accident insurance policy on her husband, without him knowing. Neff at first walks away from this, seeing it as a setup to murder. But, she shows up at his apartment, and soon they are embracing and very much in this together. Later, Neff tells us: "Suddenly it came over me that everything could go wrong. It sounds crazy, Keyes, but it's true, so help me, I couldn't hear my own footsteps. It was the walk of a dead man." Even in the thrall of her and their plan, he sees death as how it ends.

Meanwhile, we are treated to the relationship between Neff and the claims inspector, Keyes. Keyes likes to try out his ideas on Walter, his friend, the one person in the office he thinks is smart enough to appreciate them. When he is on a roll, explaining how he sees through phony claims, Keyes is always taking out his cigar and Neff strikes the match and lights it. Their standard goodbye is a sarcastic "I love you." There seems to be great affection there, in a father-son way.

Once Dietrichson's murder happens, made to look like an accident, Neff watches Keyes closely as he becomes more suspicious that this death is not what it appears to be. Neff wants to pull out, not claim the insurance, but

Phyllis will have none of it. She repeats their mantra: "Straight down the line, Walter." That had started as a pledge that they would stick together, but now it comes out as a threat. She tells him, "I wanted him dead, but you figured out how to do it, and you did it." Soon, Phyllis is pointing her gun at Walter, ready to shoot:

Phyllis: We're both rotten.
Neff: Only you're a little more rotten.

So, the story comes full circle, and we are back in the office as Walter notices that Keyes has been standing there, listening to his dictated confession. You can see the sadness in Keyes's eyes, and all he can say is, "You're all washed up, Walter." A moment later he is kneeling next to his friend, who is dying, and for the first and last time, Keyes strikes the match to light Walter's cigarette.

Out of the Past (1947)

Some would argue that *Out of the Past* is the ultimate film noir. If it isn't, it sure is in the running for that title.

Robert Mitchum is another private eye in over his head. Atypically, this film opens in daylight, in the big sky country of mountains and lakes. Jeff Bailey runs a gas station in a small town there when he is seen by someone from his past and is summoned to meet with his old boss, Whit Sterling. Driving with his girlfriend, Ann, he tells her the story he had kept from her, which becomes an extended flashback. This structure is unusual; most flashbacks are summaries that bring a character and us in the audience up to date. But this one lasts half the movie.

Whit had hired Jeff to find Whit's girlfriend Kathie (Jane Greer), who shot him and ran off with $40,000. Jeff finds her all right. Following the trail to Acapulco, he falls for her, and it looks like she falls for him. Their time together is seriously sexy. We first get waves crashing on the shore, and then a spectacular rainstorm, drenching them. They take shelter in her house, laughing and drying off each other's hair with a towel. Then, Jeff flings the towel onto a lamp, which falls over, scattering light, the door slams open to torrential rain—then fade out. It's rapture, operatically over the top.

This was the 1940s, with Joseph Breen strictly enforcing the Hays Production Code. The code, instituted in 1934 by the Major Studios as a self-censorship mechanism to forestall government intervention, included a long list of morally objectionable actions that were forbidden: no swearing, no nudity, no sex in or out of marriage (married couples were not allowed to share a bed), no miscegenation, no homosexuality, nothing to challenge religious traditions or the institutions of another country (including Nazis, until well into the war years), and that the guilty must be punished. Studios were required to submit their scripts to the office for review and were not allowed to begin filming until the scripts were approved. All this proved a challenge to the filmmakers, who worked hard to suggest what they could not explicitly show.

Jeff and Kathie go off together, hoping to hide from Whit in San Francisco. Only Kathie's leading Jeff by the nose, and he doesn't see how devious and ruthless she is until she shoots and kills his partner, and runs, leaving Jeff to bury him and be suspected of the murder. Whit is played by a young Kirk Douglas, at a point in his career much like Bogart's before Sam Spade. Kathie, the vixen who leads both men astray, is played by a wonderfully scheming and seductive Jane Greer, who commits a dozen lies and three murders.

The flashback ends when Jeff reconnects with Whit, who wants him for

Figure 5.2 Robert Mitchum, Jane Greer. *Out of the Past* (1947). RKO Radio Pictures, Inc. / Photofest © RKO Radio Pictures, Inc.

another job. He isn't out for revenge, he tells him because, as Jeff discovers to his surprise, Kathie is back with him. And then, as though we are in a new movie, we are in the city, San Francisco, with Jeff caught in Whit's plot to frame him for the murder of a blackmailing accountant. Whit did want revenge after all. Now it is dark streets, nightclubs, neon signs, half-shadowed rooms, hallways, and faces—classic noir settings. It looks like Jeff is controlling the situation but looks can be deceiving when someone like Kathie is involved. It ends badly for both of them.

Every other line in this movie is memorable. At a casino, Kathie asks, "Is there a way to win?" Jeff replies, "There's a way to lose more slowly." Jeff, to Kathie: "You can never help anything can you? You're like a leaf that the wind blows from one gutter to another." About the gunsel, Joe: "[He] couldn't find a prayer in the Bible." Kathie: "I don't want to die." Jeff: "Neither do I, baby, but if I have to, I'm not going to die first." Kathie: "I don't know anything except how much I hated him [Whit]. I didn't take anything. I didn't, Jeff. Don't you believe me?" Jeff, kissing her: "Baby, I don't care." And, then, from his girlfriend Ann, talking about Kathie: "She can't be all bad. No one is." Jeff replies, "Well, she comes the closest."

Mitchum is the noir hero: seemingly strong, looking in control, but in over his head, in thrall to a woman, and resigned to his fate. This movie was directed by Jacques Tourneur, one of the best directors of the 1940s. His *Cat People* (1942) is one of the great horror films, all done with suggestion and shadows.

Mitchum had a wonderful career. Many of his best pictures are noir: besides *Out of the Past*, he was in *The Big Steal* (1949), costarring Jane Greer; *Blood on the Moon* (1948) (a noir-Western directed by Robert Wise; they weren't all crime stories!); *Cape Fear* (1962); the brilliant *Night of the Hunter* (directed by Charles Laughton), and a very good remake of *Farewell, My Lovely* (1975), where he played Philip Marlowe. Kirk Douglas also had an impressive career with films such as *Champion* (1949), *The Bad and the Beautiful* (1952), the antiwar story *Paths of Glory* (1957) directed by Stanley Kubrick, *Lust for Life* (1956) playing Vincent Van Gogh, *Spartacus* (1960), an epic of ancient Rome, which Douglas produced and starred in and that helped break the blacklist of Communist sympathizers by giving credit to the screenwriter, Dalton Trumbo, and *Lonely are the Brave* (1962), a modern-day Western. Douglas died in 2020, at age 104.

Touch of Evil (1958)

Noir reached a self-conscious culmination in Orson Welles's *Touch of Evil* some years later, in 1958. This is one of Welles's most effective movies, with a bravura suspenseful long opening tracking shot under the credits when we see a time bomb placed under a car that leads to the explosion minutes later which drives the plot. It's a twisty, nasty story of murder and police corruption in a town on the Mexican border. The camerawork and lighting are Welles at his most dynamic. He can be credited with the cinematography because he was as close to the complete auteur as the movies ever produced: writing, directing, editing, and controlling the camerawork in this movie as he did in every film he made after *Citizen Kane*.

Welles was a flawed genius, juggling more projects than he could manage. He left this picture after the filming was done but the editing was not complete. He planned to finish it when he returned. The studio was bothered by his unconventional editing and was confused by the plot. They assigned new editors and banned Welles from the editing room. Something similar happened with his first film after *Citizen Kane*, *The Magnificent Ambersons* (1942), a film many think is more a masterpiece than *Kane*. After Welles had disappeared to a new project, the studio cut an hour from the film and added a happy ending. The cut footage was destroyed. Even though it was not what Welles had filmed, nor what he intended, the release cut of *Ambersons* is still considered a masterpiece. With *Touch of Evil*, it happened again. Because they didn't understand the plot, in addition to their edits, they filmed two additional scenes, explaining what didn't need explaining. By the time Welles realized what was happening, writing them a fifty-eight-page memo detailing the changes he wanted, it was too late. We did not see a version of this film as Welles intended until the 1998 restoration project that corrected the edits using his notes.

Welles plays the obese, alcoholic, corrupt police captain, Hank Quinlan, and Charlton Heston, the Mexican cop who begins to investigate him. His playing a Mexican would not go over today, and it was ridiculed then. The studio had insisted the film needed a star and Heston did the best he could with the part. Janet Leigh is his wife, who becomes a pawn between them. And there is Marlene Dietrich, a fortune-teller and Quinlan's only friend. He asks her to read his future and she says: "You haven't got any . . . your future's all used up." That's noir.

More Noir Films Worth Watching

The Postman Always Rings Twice (1946). Based on a James M. Cain novel and starring a very effective John Garfield and Lana Turner. It doesn't have the signature camera effects of noir, but the story is as doom-laden as they come. Garfield is Frank, a drifter who stumbles on a job at a gas station/luncheonette and meets Cora, the wife of the owner. He is immediately smitten, and Cora seems to be too. In voice-over, Frank tells us right away that things are likely to go badly. Cora feels trapped with her older controlling husband (played by Cecil Kellaway initially as a sweet man but gradually showing his stubborn, angry side; a nice bit of acting), and soon they are planning his murder, so they can be together. The first attempt causes complications, but it doesn't stop them from trying again. Driving to a meeting, with Cora at the wheel, her husband beside her and Frank in the back, the camera closes in on Cora, we hear a struggle and then the sound of a bottle striking her husband's head. The violence is just out of the frame, with Cora, steely-eyed, in close-up, determined. They fake a car accident, but fate works against them and they are caught. You think the film is over but there is a final act, the trial, with each blaming the other, sworn enemies now, the lawyers as sleazy as the murderers. Frank is the sap, and Cora is coldhearted and ruthless. The mood and the plot are pure noir, but it has an MGM gloss that doesn't feel quite at home with the noir sensibility.

The Big Combo (1955). In this movie, Mr. Brown, the gangster head of the Combo, is played by Richard Conte. He is the charismatic center of the story. Cornel Wilde is the police detective trying to nail him with his crimes, who falls in love with the gangster's moll, played by Jean Wallace. She is no femme fatale but is a woman torn between darkness and light, in sexual thrall to Brown and helpless to leave him. The movie is out of balance because Wilde is stiff as an actor, and Conte quietly chews the scenery. The story also lacks the plot twists that give noir its energy. However, the cinematography is classic dark noir, with shadows and fog in abundance. John Alton, who manned the camera, wrote the first book by a studio cinematographer, with a title that says it all: *Painting with Light* (1949). He sure shows how with this movie.

Noirish

We've invented this term for films that don't cut it as noir, but have some elements of the style. These films are quite good, but they aren't noir.

Laura (1944). This is frequently filed under noir, but it doesn't come close.

It is a very good murder mystery, almost like an Agatha Christie, except that it doesn't take place in English country houses, but in Upper East Side New York apartments, and the detective is not some prissy Belgian, but a hard-nosed New York cop. Laura Hunt (Gene Tierney), a beautiful woman with a top job at an advertising firm who everyone seems to have loved and admired, is killed, shot in the face with a shotgun. No witnesses. Her portrait hangs on the wall in her apartment, and the lush haunting Laura theme plays repeatedly (it became a popular hit). The more the cop hears about her, and the more he stares at her portrait, the more he falls in love. "In love with a corpse," as Waldo says.

For the first half of the movie there is some very good acid dialogue, mostly from Waldo Lydecker (Clifton Webb), Laura's friend, a sort of effete Walter Winchell, a gossip columnist and radio personality who likes to write about a good murder. The cop is McPherson (Dana Andrews) terse, tough, who allows most of the suspects to tag along as he interrogates each of them; quite unprofessional, and quite unlikely. But it allows us to get to know them. There is a twist in the middle, which we won't spoil for you, but which you may well see coming. The whole thing feels artificial and unconvincing, but it fascinates, and the early dialogue is entertaining. Some examples: Waldo: "I don't use a pen. I write with a goose quill dipped in venom." Shelby (Laura's fiancé): "I can afford a blemish on my character, but not on my clothes." Waldo: "I'm not kind, I'm vicious. It's the secret of my charm." McPherson: "I suspect nobody and everybody." (Sounds very much like Hercule Poirot, doesn't it?)

There is no noir mood, no sense of fate or circumstance controlling one's life, and no heat in any of the relationships. It doesn't look like a noir film either. But because it's a crime movie from the 1940s, it gets pulled under the noir umbrella. Don't be fooled. But do watch it. It's good.

This Gun for Hire (1942). This one looks more like it might be a noir, with a trench coat-wearing hired gun named Raven (Alan Ladd, in his first star-making role), and Veronica Lake as Ellen, a woman who gets caught in the middle. After carrying out an assassination, Raven is paid in marked bills by Gates, his traitorous employer (this is happening during the war and Gates is suspected of selling deadly chemicals to the Nazis), setting him up to be caught for the murder. Entertainer Ellen works for Gates at his nightclub and is recruited to spy on him by the government. She and Raven meet accidentally on the train and he takes her hostage. But gradually they become friends, she sees his kindness to cats and children, and she offers to help him get to Gates. The movie looks like a noir, much of it taking place at night, all of it happening in the city or on a train. The plot, based on a Graham Greene novel, is complicated enough to stay interesting but there are no real surprises. Raven is a ruthless killer, but also a sad and lonely man. There is a lovely chemistry between Ladd and Lake that led to them making several other films together. But there is none of the world-weary, cynical fatalism that drives most noir films. And there is no femme fatale. Lake plays an openhearted woman with great sympathy for the killer. So, a solid crime movie, well-acted, with a good story. But we wouldn't call it noir.

The Naked City (1948). This one is also often filed under noir. It is a straightforward police procedural showing us step-by-step how they investigate a murder. Directed by Jules Dassin, it is very good and worth watching for several reasons. Filmed entirely on the streets of New York watching it is like looking into a time machine. You get a sense of the city back then. There is a voice narrating the story, commenting with mild sarcasm on the ordinary moments in the city as it awakens on a hot summer day. It's the omniscient narrator of a novel, not the noir thoughts of a central character in the movie. It has a documentary feel.

After broadly surveying the city, the narrator points to an apartment where a woman is being drugged and then killed. We don't see who it is, or who is doing it. That will become the case, says the narrator, talking about the murder and maybe trying a bit too hard to sound hard-boiled as we see a couple reading the newspaper during breakfast: "Yesterday she was just another pretty face. This morning she's the marmalade on everybody's toast." Barry Fitzgerald plays detective Dan Muldoon, with a broad Irish accent, compassionate with a sense of humor. He follows clues, interrogates suspects and gradually begins to understand who killed the girl and why. There is a terrifically suspenseful chase at the end, with the police after the one surviving killer. This has a bit of a noir feel, as the killer dodges his pursuers on the streets of the city and then onto the Brooklyn bridge and begins to climb the catwalks to escape. It takes real skill to film a chase, so you know where you are and where each character is from moment to moment. This movie nails it.

Chinatown and Neo-Noir

After decades of riots, conflict over civil rights, assassinations, political chicanery, and an unpopular war, there was something about the despair and disillusion of noir that spoke to filmmakers in the 1970s. *Chinatown* (1974) was directed by Roman Polanski, written by Robert Towne, and stars Jack Nicholson, Faye Dunaway, and John Huston (that's right, the director of the noir film *The Maltese Falcon*. He makes for a great villain!). It is often categorized as **neo-noir**, because of how self-aware it is about the 1940s mood and style they are re-creating.

Chinatown is set in 1937 Los Angeles, substituting the glare of eternal sunshine, and a big sky, for the dark shadows of the city. But when it gets to Chinatown those dark shadows are there too. It dials the beats and sensibility of noir up to eleven. There is a shamus who takes on a case he thinks is routine, only to uncover political corruption, a Mister Big pulling the strings of government; there is a woman in distress who is not what she seems. The shamus gets roughed up for his troubles, more than once, but, from a stubborn sense of principle he is even more determined to get to the bottom of things. He is Chandler's "knight in tarnished armor" standing on noble principle even as his best-laid plans lay an egg (he is never as smart as he thinks he is), confirming that the rich and corrupt hold all the cards. There is a final twist that ends in another death and a sense that everything, and nothing, has changed: the bad guy gets away with it, and the shamus is alone and defeated.

Jack Nicholson is Jake Gittes, a private eye who specializes in cheating spouses. Following Hollis Mulwray, the chief engineer for the LA Water Department, at the behest of a woman who claims to be his wife, he is soon

Figure 5.3 John Huston and Jack Nicholson square off, but Nicholson's nose bandage makes him look small. *Chinatown* © Paramount Pictures. Screenshot captured by authors.

investigating the illegal diverting of water from farmlands to Los Angeles. This is based on LA history, the fight for control of water and thus for control of this desert city. Mulwray winds up dead, his wife, Evelyn (Dunaway) turns out not to be who Gittes thought she was, and duplicity reigns. This is one of Nicholson's best performances. Dunaway is also terrific.

There are modern touches that tell you this movie could never have been done this way in the 1940s: the new permissiveness lets us see the sex that could only be hinted at then; the widescreen panoramas of the desert country outside Los Angeles are threatening the way the empty cornfields in Hitchcock's *North by Northwest* threatened Cary Grant; the soundtrack is alternately lushly romantic and percussively modern, depending on the moment, the sort of abrupt shifts they didn't do in classic Hollywood; there are subtle tracking shots to pull you into the action that didn't exist then. The dialogue snaps and the original screenplay keeps the surprises coming. The director Steven Soderbergh is not alone in calling it "a perfect movie."[1]

Almost as good is *L.A. Confidential* (1997) directed by Curtis Hanson, and starring Guy Pearce, Russell Crowe, Kevin Spacey, and Kim Basinger, based on a hard-boiled novel by James Ellroy, which takes place in the 1950s. The cops are violent and corrupt. One detective offers to testify against some officers, and one of them ends up dead in a mass shooting at a diner. Three detectives, each with his own baggage, and questionable morality, investigate. There are conspiracy, secrets, and blackmail. And a look at the underside of Hollywood glamour, with a prostitute ring based on hookers who look like famous movie stars. This was real. Who knew? This movie turns police procedure on its head; this is not the way you are supposed to do it, but the way it was done.

The look in both these films is noir; the complexity of the characters is at another level. But can noir be noir in color on a wide screen—can you have the mood, the claustrophobia, the paranoia, the double-dealing?

Well, in these films at least, but in few others, it works.

Noir is a more flexible form than you might suspect. You can have a sci-fi noir, like *Blade Runner* (1982) with Harrison Ford, which captures the noir feeling in a dystopian future Los Angeles. Danish director Nicolas Winding Refn's *Drive* (2011) is a noir action thriller, with style and energy. It stars Ryan Gosling as a movie stunt driver and garage mechanic, who moonlights driving the getaway car in heists. He has standards; he will drive but will not carry a gun or pull off the heist. To help out the husband of a woman (Carey Mulligan) he has fallen in love with, he offers to be the driver for a heist. It all goes wrong, and suddenly he is on the run, bloodied with a bag of Mafia money, and the woman and her son are in danger. *Blood Simple* (1984), the first film by the Coen brothers, starring Frances McDormand, Dan Hedaya, and M. Emmet Walsh is as dark as the darkest 1940s noirs. A bar owner in Texas suspects his wife of having an affair with one of his bartenders. He hires a private detective to provide proof and then tells him to kill the lovers. The detective has other ideas, and soon there are double-crosses, misunderstandings, and murder. The Coens are having fun with our expectations, and with the conventions of noir. And there are inside jokes, like the camera hopping over the head of a drunk as it tracks along the bar counter.

Many international works were inspired by noir. Jean-Luc Godard's À bout de souffle, English title: *Breathless* (1960), written by Godard, François Truffaut, and Claude Chabrol, stars Jean-Paul Belmondo as a young hood channeling Bogart, and Jean Seberg as the American student he tries to persuade to run away with him. *Alphaville* (1965) is another Godard film that nods to noir. Here, an American secret agent is sent to a city on another planet, looking for a missing scientist. It's a perplexing movie, a mixed bag, but worth seeing . . . once. Both of these films are in black and white. French director Jean-Pierre Melville's *Le samouraï* (1967), starring Alain Delon, is in color and works. Delon plays the cool silent hit man, Jef Costello. We watch him carefully plan a hit, including setting up an alibi. But he is seen and soon he is being chased by the police as well as the men who hired him. There is minimal dialogue, the pace is slow but suspenseful. A worthy tribute to noir.

Probably the best of the non-American noirs is *The Third Man* (1949), from England, written by Graham Greene, starring Orson Welles and Joseph Cotton and directed by Carol Reed. Holly Martin (Cotton) is a writer of popular Western novels, who comes to postwar Vienna when his old friend, Harry Lime (Welles) offers him a job. When he gets there, he discovers that Lime has died. The stories are inconsistent, and he tries to find out what happened. In one of the great "reveals," we see that Lime is still alive when a child's ball rolls against the foot of a man hiding in the shadows. The camera pans up, it is Lime. Holly is told that Harry is wanted by the military police for selling contaminated penicillin, which caused many children to die. Harry had faked his death to avoid capture. Tilted Dutch camera angles, dark shadows, dark secrets, and the iconic zither musical theme, put this very much in noir territory.

Harry is one of the most convincing psychopathic villains in film. He summons Holly to meet him in a cabin of the famous Wiener Riesenrad, a

Figure 5.4 The look of film noir: a dark street, a man in shadow, a ruined city, glaring light, shiny cobblestones. *The Third Man* © Selznick Releasing Organization. Screenshot captured by authors.

giant Ferris wheel. Paused at the top, Holly asks Harry if he has ever seen the victims of his adulterated antibiotic. Harry says, "Victims? Look down there. Tell me. Would you really feel any pity if one of those dots stopped moving forever? If I offered you twenty thousand pounds for every dot that stopped, would you really, old man, tell me to keep my money, or would you calculate how many dots you could afford to spare?" Holly fears that Harry might push him to his death and decides to help the police catch him. There is a brilliant final chase through the sewers. This is one of the most atmospheric films ever made and is also one of the most despairing.

There's a beauty in the darkness—it may portend danger and seem to threaten, but there is a beckoning sensuality too. As the cinematographer John Alton (*The Big Combo*) said in an interview: "The greatest things in the world happen in the dark—the good and bad, the murders and the marriages, the love scenes—all at night." Things change in the dark—and the films of the noir style glory in it.

These films noir are wonderful movies. They entertain, they tell terrifically intriguing stories with marvelously complicated characters. They stay with you. These are films that color your dreams in black and white.

Chapter 6
Comedy

Key Films

Bringing Up Baby (1938)
Airplane! (1980)
When Harry Met Sally (1989)

Comedy may seem like too broad a genre to fit into a single chapter. A disproportionate number of films released every year, dating back as long as you like in the history of film, could be categorized as comedies. According to a 2017 study, between 1998 and 2017, 51.6 percent of films produced in Hollywood were dramas (another broad category, of which more later), while 28.4 percent were comedies. The focus of other chapters was barely noted: Westerns and musicals were both less than 1 percent of the total output.[1] But this book is about how to get the most out of watching different genres and understanding them, and comedy is easier to wrap your head around. The short version is that it involves stories about situations that devolve through complications and are ultimately put right in the end, with bad guys punished and good guys living happily ever after. The affirmative ending, that all is cosmically and karmically right in the world presented by the film, is the key. And the films are usually presented in a quite straightforward way.

It should be noted that comedy as a film genre does not necessarily need to be funny. Comedies can be funny, of course, and many of the best ones are, but the term comes from the ancient Greek, *komos*, meaning "praise," and as early as the fourteenth century CE, it was defined as a "narrative with a happy ending" or "any composition intended for amusement."[2] Dante's *Inferno* doesn't leave you laughing in the aisles, but remains part of the genre—indeed, Dante's trilogy of epic poems is titled *The Divine Comedy* because they end happily for the protagonist. It is distinguished from tragedy, the other great genre of classical theater, from the Greek *tragikos*, which— with a nod to the fact that this is a bit comedic—literally means "about a goat," probably a reference to an early tragic play in which a performer took on the role of a satyr, a mythical creature who is a man from the waist up and a goat from the waist down (the term **satire** derives from the satyr, but we'll get there in a moment). In practice, tragedy refers to plays that highlight the *hamartia*, Greek for **tragic flaw** in the protagonist that brings about their downfall, leading to an ending that is disastrous to the protagonist. Their tragic outcome was meant as a morality lesson for the audience—their ending was sad rather than happy because of a tragic flaw in their personality. In ancient Greek tragedies, armies perished, cities fell, men accidentally slept with their mothers and killed their fathers, mothers killed their children—in general, bad stuff happens to flawed people.

In ancient Greek comedies, all manner of twists complicate the life of the protagonist, but all turn out well in the end. We know that all will turn out well because we know we are watching a comedy. As a result, we observe those complications with a wink—"Let's see how they get out of this pickle." Some ancient plays ended with the sense that the author hadn't come up with an elegant way to free their hero from the pickle. They chose, instead, what is called a deus ex machina (Latin for "God out of the machine") meaning that some god or goddess would appear at the last moment, just before hope is lost, and magically make everything right again—which usually involves a wedding.

Throughout the history of performance, writers, actors, and directors looked back to the ancient Greek playwrights (like Sophocles, Euripides, Aristophanes, and Aeschylus) and to ancient theoreticians (like Aristotle, whose book *On Poetics* was hugely influential) as the exemplars of dramatic performances. What Aristotle wrote about plays is still taught today. A play should consist of six elements.[3]

Plot: The events or incidents shown to the audience, consisting of problems that the characters must solve. Aristotle tells us that the plot should have a beginning, middle, and end. That might sound so obvious as not to warrant stating, but it wasn't self-evident in the third century BCE when he wrote it.

Characters: The agents of the plot, each of whom must have a motivation to be engaged in the plot.

Idea: The reason the playwright wrote the play in the first place—the "author's message."

Language: The dialogue, which Aristotle and the ancients felt should be "heightened," more poetic proclamation than realistic conversation.

Music: Sometimes translated as "rhythm," this is the pace of the plot and character development.

Spectacle: All that the audience sees happen before them (actors, costumes, lighting, sound, special effects).

Stage plays were the forebears of films, so the basic building blocks transferred over to the new cinematic medium. When it comes to film, the same elements hold, but with the addition of some technological aspects, like **shot**, which camera lens and angle a director uses, and **editing**, how quickly cuts are made. Most other elements remain.

Romantic Comedies

Romantic comedies, or "rom-coms," have traditionally been described as "boy meets girl, boy loses girl, boy finds girl and they live happily ever after."[4] This basic structure remains largely unaltered, though nowadays it may also be "boy meets boy" or "girl meets girl." Despite the countless films, plays, books, and more that adhere to this formula, it seems to always satisfy.

Most rom-coms start with our soon-to-be lovers in a **meet-cute**. This is a term for a charming, coincidental way in which a future couple meets for the first time. It is likely to be unusual and memorable. They often dislike each other at the start, though sometimes it is love at first sight. The implied understanding is that, even if they start at odds, the couple will fall in love by the end of the film.

Here are many iconic meet-cutes. In *Bringing up Baby* (1938), Katharine Hepburn interrupts Cary Grant's golf game and then takes over his ball by mistake. In *The Lady Eve* (1941), Barbara Stanwyck literally trips Henry Fonda so she can meet him; in *Love, Actually* (2003), Hugh Grant is the Prime Minister of England while Martine McCutcheon is a new member of his staff. Introducing herself, to her dismay she can't stop saying "fuck" to express her enthusiasm, and he is charmed. Gary Cooper, in *Bluebeard's Eighth Wife* (1938), is shopping for pajama bottoms when he meets Claudette Colbert, who only wants the tops. *Serendipity* (2001), starring John Cusack and Kate Beckinsale, channels this meet-cute when they both try to buy the same pair of cashmere gloves. He lets her buy them and she takes him out for a thank-you dessert, then the magic happens. In *Splash* (1984), as a child, Tom Hanks is somehow rescued from drowning by a young mermaid. As an adult, he almost drowns again and is rescued by the same mermaid, now grown up. She follows him to New York City, gaining legs when she reaches dry land.

But every rom-com must have an obstacle or complication to overcome before the final kiss. In *Splash*, the complication is that the girl is a fish (well, a mermaid, with a tail once she is back in the sea). Sometimes the complication is instant dislike when first meeting, which we will see in *When*

Harry Met Sally. But, more often, the obstacle is that one or both of the lovers are committed to another person, engaged, or even about to marry. It may be obvious to us that the other person is simply wrong, but it usually takes them a while to figure it out.

When Harry Met Sally (1989)

Sally (Meg Ryan) and Harry are carpooling. She will start grad school and he (Billy Crystal) a new job. Harry is dating Sally's friend, who suggested he and Sally share a ride. We immediately see that they annoy each other. Harry loves to snack, Sally only eats at mealtimes. Harry likes to take things as they come, Sally has a detailed driving schedule, including timed stops, for the trip.

At Katz's Deli in New York, they chat and Harry claims that no woman has ever faked an orgasm with him. Sally cannot believe it. In one of the most famous scenes in film history, Sally fakes an orgasm while sitting at the table in the deli, rather loudly for all to hear. One of the greatest comedic lines of all time is given to director Rob Reiner's mother, who is seated nearby. She summons a waiter, and orders, "I'll have what she's having."

The two go their separate ways and meet again every few years. Finding that they enjoy their conversations, they decide to be friends, even though they disagree about whether men and women can be "just friends" or if "the sex part gets in the way." These are no longer meet-cutes. They are just picking up from where they left off, and at first, they are both committed to other partners. But that changes a few years later when, at a New Year's Eve party, they share a midnight kiss and realize there is a mutual attraction. Still, they decide to stick to their deal to keep sex out of it.

By now even though they rarely see each other, they are constantly on the phone, commiserating about being single. One day, Sally calls Harry upset that her ex is getting married. He comes to her apartment to comfort her and they end up in bed. Sally is happy, but Harry feels awkward about it and regretful. Their friendship may be ruined. They part.

At the following New Year's Eve party, Sally is feeling lonely without Harry there. Harry wanders around New York and ends up at the party, where he professes his love to Sally. They kiss and get married—living happily ever after. So, many rom-coms have the same basic narrative arc, but it's the details that distinguish them. And it's a formula that never fails since all of us want to believe that, if we haven't yet, we will find true love, even if the situation doesn't look promising at the start.

Figure 6.1 After sex, Harry looks terrified, Sally is happy and satisfied. Billy Crystal, Meg Ryan. *When Harry Met Sally* © Castle Rock Entertainment. Screenshot captured by authors.

Farce/Slapstick

Groucho, Chico, and Harpo

The genre of comedy played most for laughs—laughs at all cost, regardless of realism, logic, or propriety—is the farce or slapstick comedy. In the best of these, anarchy reigns, and we have the Marx Brothers to thank for setting the standard.

Groucho, Chico, and Harpo Marx, with the occasional addition of brother Zeppo, were vaudeville performers who made the transition to movies as soon as sound came in. Groucho, with his famous stooped walk, his cigar, painted mustache, and sharp, smart comebacks, was the main attraction, but the other brothers had their fans. Chico, with an Italian accent (though the brothers were Jewish and very New York), was always looking for a card game, and sweet Harpo, with a silent mischievous innocence, and his "gookie," the uniquely funny look he would make, tongue sticking out and eyes popping. Anarchy ruled in their stage shows and Hollywood thought they needed to be tamed for the movies. Fortunately, it was hard to tame these guys and their rapid-fire, nonsensical comic set pieces with dialogue filled with puns and smart comebacks continued.

A Night at the Opera (1935) was their most successful film, a movie that took something highbrow and serious, like opera, and brought it plummeting down to earth. To fine tune their comic sketches for maximum laughter, they took them on the road before starting the movie, performing in local vaudeville theaters to live audiences.

Their films are filled with what are essentially stage routines. On a ship with an opera company headed for America, Groucho is given a small stateroom. His brothers are stowaways, hiding there. Groucho orders lunch to be delivered, adding dish after dish to feed the stowaways, with Harpo honking his horn every time he wants to add "two hard-boiled eggs." People keep knocking on his door and, one by one, Groucho invites them in, until they are piled on top of each other, hands and arms entwined. This is pure slapstick. The skit ends with the door to the stateroom being opened and everyone who managed to somehow fit inside tumbles out in a pile.

Later, Groucho goes over the opera contract line by line with Chico, with puns and one-liners galore. At one point he explains, "If any participants in this contract are not in their right mind, this contract is void. That's normal, it's a sanity clause." Chico laughs, "You can't fool me, there ain't no Sanity Claus." Producer Irving Thalberg insisted that there be songs and a romantic subplot to broaden the movie's appeal, and it made this their biggest hit. But manic craziness was their calling card, and today most people find those subplots a drag.

Figure 6.2 This "stateroom scene" was perfected in vaudeville theaters around the country before going into the movie. Somewhere in there are Groucho, Chico, and Harpo Marx. *A Night at the Opera* © MGM. Screenshot captured by authors.

In the earlier *Duck Soup* (1933), the boys were left to dominate the film from beginning to end, and the laughs kept coming. This one has sort of a plot. Groucho is Rufus T. Firefly, who has been made the head of the country of Freedonia by the rich widow Mrs. Teasdale (Margaret Dumont, his foil in most of their films). He declares war on neighboring Sylvania. His brothers are spies who keep shifting who they are spying for. There are musical numbers here, too, but they are intentionally overripe and silly, and a final war sequence becomes surreal, with non sequiturs and one-liners bubbling over each other.

One of their most famous stage routines shows up here. Groucho, in his night dress, suddenly sees himself in a doorway. Is he looking at a mirror? No, it's Harpo, wearing the same night dress, with the same painted mustache and glasses. Suspicious, Groucho moves. The mirror image moves. He tries again and again. Each time, it mirrors his movements. Until it doesn't. This is a clever pantomime, and very funny. Describing it is tough. You have to see it to find it funny. You can find this and the stateroom scene on YouTube. But better, watch these movies, complete. You will thank us.

Some of our favorite Groucho lines: to Mrs. Teasdale, "Married, I can see you right now in the kitchen, bending over a hot stove. But I can't see the stove." "Say, you cover a lot of ground yourself. You better beat it; I hear they are going to tear you down and put up a building where you are standing. You can leave in a taxi. If you can't get a taxi, you can leave in a huff. If that's too soon, you can leave in a minute and a huff," and to soldiers during the battle, "Remember you are fighting for this woman's honor, which is more than she ever did!"

Airplane! (1980)

A famous line in *The Naked Gun* (1988), a comedy very much inspired by these Marx Brothers movies, plays with the clichés of romantic comedy when a character says: "It's the same old story. Boy finds girl, boy loses girl, girl finds boy, boy forgets girl, boy remembers girl, girl dies in a tragic blimp accident over the Orange Bowl on New Year's Day." The funny part is the undoing of what we expect to happen. Surprise is the key. Jokes tend to set us up to expect one thing and pull the rug out from under us by presenting something else. That something else could be pithy and wise, or it could be random and silly. Farces tend to opt for the latter. The early film comedy star W. C. Fields provides an example of this with his famous line, "I like children . . . if they're properly cooked." The first three words set up the expectation of something more, well, expected. The last four lines, after the brief pause—just long enough for us audience members to calculate what we expect him to say next—invert our expectations in a surprising way. Because we know we are in the comedy genre, we're not worried that he's cooking children (save that for the horror chapter), so are prepared for mirth and a happy ending, which affects how we watch.

We confess that farces are our favorite type of film. To us they are the most escapist, and we watch movies because we want to enter an alternate reality for two hours and slake off whatever life presents us with preferably through the catharsis of laughter.

One of the other key terms used by Aristotle was *katharsis*, catharsis: "purification, cleansing, clarification." He wrote about it in terms of tragedy. We watch a tragic drama, *Titanic* (1997) for instance (it gives nothing away, we imagine, even if you've not seen it, to learn that the ship sinks and a protagonist doesn't make it), but do not feel lousy afterward. Tragedy, if too tragic, too realistic, without enough poetry, without the crumbs of positivity that come with the catastrophic ending, can be too much. It can pummel us with sadness or hopelessness.

Tragedy as a creative art form differs from the tragedy that surrounds us every day on the nightly news because there is some moral elevation or moving message, perhaps in the form of honorable self-sacrifice (as in the 1998 film *Armageddon*, in which one protagonist heroically volunteers to die to save planet Earth), that makes us glad we watched the film. While Aristotle thought of catharsis in tragic terms, we find it in comedy.

There is nothing that we find more purifying or cleansing than laughing. A film that makes you laugh pulls off one of the hardest tricks of all. You sit down to watch the film in one state of mind, maybe even in a bad mood, and a great comedy pulls you out of it. You feel good at the end and maybe you even laughed during it. An art form that provokes laughter creates an *ekstasis* (yet another Greek term, this time meaning "to stand outside oneself, a removal to elsewhere). An ecstasy literally means that the film pulled us out of ourselves, the way we were feeling before watching it, and changed us. This is as cathartic an experience as the moral elevation of watching a drama that might provoke tears or other strong, negatively associated emotions.

So what does this have to do with watermelons randomly dropping out of the sky or someone calling the Mayo Clinic and being patched through to a doctor whose bookshelves are lined with jars of mayonnaise?

One of our favorite films of all time is *Airplane!* (1980), surely one of the silliest farcical slapstick comedies ever made—and perhaps the funniest. Funny is a relative term, but this is a pretty universal choice: it was voted "the funniest comedy ever" in 2012 by *Empire* magazine and the BBC critics polled called it the seventh greatest comedy ever (*Some Like It Hot* was number one in that poll, and *Duck Soup*, number five).[5]

The story is also a satire, making fun of airline emergency dramas, particularly a 1957 movie called *Zero Hour!* (note that both have exclamation points in their titles) in which pilots on an airplane are poisoned by the fish option in the meal service, and a passenger is forced to land the plane.

The plot is largely irrelevant, as in most farces. It is merely a vehicle through which to tell jokes and insert absurd situations.

We're back to the history books to briefly understand the genre called **farce**. A farce is a comedic play that uses improbable, absurd situations and reactions to them to provide humor. Laughter is the goal, levity is preferred, and the humor is based on silliness. "Farce" is French for "stuffing" and originally referred to improvisations made by actors during religious dramas performed in the Middle Ages—the oldest farce by that name was written around 1266.[6] The "casing," the plot and character development, are largely irrelevant—we're watching it because of the "stuffing," the funny bits thrown in while the plot moves along.

Figure 6.3 Anything for a laugh. The masterpiece of non-sequitur humor. *Airplane* © Paramount Pictures. Screenshot captured by authors.

Airplane! is packed with absurdities and is an example of what might be called **non sequitur humor**. The surprise is what's funny, not specifically what happens. When, in the middle of a high-tension situation in the airport control tower, with staff frantically trying to help a passenger land an out-of-control airplane, a watermelon drops from nowhere and smashes on the floor—with no one reacting to it at all—what's funny is not the fact that a watermelon randomly fell from the sky, but the total lack of context. A non sequitur is a statement or idea that does not follow logically from whatever preceded it. *Airplane!* derives laughs from non sequiturs, as when the captain turns to a child and asks "Joey, have you ever been in a Turkish prison," as well as from jokes proper, as in:

"Surely you can't be serious!"
"I am serious. And don't call me Shirley."

When Noah was ten years old or so, he first saw *Airplane!* and there was one moment that made him laugh so hard that he kept rewinding the VHS (which shows how old he is). He could barely catch his breath for laughing so hard. He felt elevated, elated, euphoric, ecstatic. Each time he thinks back on that moment, he smiles. If that isn't catharsis, we don't know what is.

Satire, Parody, Spoof

Don't Look Up (2021)

The categories we mention are fluid. Satires can be worldly, romantic, or farcical. Mel Brooks is best known for his very silly farcical parodies, making fun of various film genres. We could have a parallel Mel Brooks comedy for many chapters in this book: *Young Frankenstein* (horror, 1974), *Blazing Saddles* (Western, 1974), *Space Balls* (sci-fi,1987). While the terms are often used interchangeably, spoof specifically means a film making fun of an entire genre by presenting itself in that genre, whereas a parody is a film that makes fun of a specific film. If we're getting technical, *Young Frankenstein* is a parody version of *Frankenstein* and *Space Balls* is a parody of *Star Wars* but *Blazing Saddles* is a spoof Western, since it mocks Westerns generally, not a single Western film.

In choosing an exemplary satire or spoof, the first one that came to mind was *Dr. Strangelove, or How I Learned to Stop Worrying and Love the Bomb*

(1968). If that's not one you've seen, watch it as soon as possible. This satire on film noir and the Cold War is a **black comedy**, a term meaning a comedy about dark subject matter, using humor to discuss serious things. It is ranked among the best films ever made and includes some iconic Hollywood moments, like a war enthusiast riding an atomic bomb as if it were a bucking bronco, as it falls to earth, about to launch a nuclear World War III.

There are also differences—and overlap—in satire versus parody. A parody is a film imitating the style of a particular genre or even a specific other film, whereas a satire uses humor to comment on or criticize some element of society or human behavior. *Dr Strangelove* is a parody of Cold War paranoia, *and* it's a satire about the Cold War.

But we might just as easily consider a contemporary satire, *Don't Look Up* (2021), written and directed by Adam McKay.

The story tells of an astronomy student who discovers a previously unknown comet—that is flying on a collision course with Earth. She and her professor leaked this news to the media, news that the US government felt was best to keep under wraps, and they became media sensations. The satire mocks social media and the news cycle, the reactions and hubris of government officials and Silicon Valley CEOs, while using the contemporary issues of the climate crisis and fake news. This also might be called a "black comedy" in that it uses humor to deal with serious matters.

Unlike most comedies, everyone dies at the end. And yet, there is a poetry to this and it feels "right." The movie ends with a positive feeling for the protagonists and a sense that justice has been meted out to the bad guys (the elite of Earth take off before the comet collides and fly through space, landing on a lush new planet that appears ideal for habitation—until they encounter animals there that eat them all). The message about humankind is bleak, but we feel okay about the handful of heroes of our story.

The ending reveals how *Don't Look Up* is an homage to its famous predecessor, *Dr Strangelove*. It is an homage because it mirrors some plot elements, but does not make fun of the previous film, as would be the case with a parody. *Dr. Strangelove* ends with a plan for the elite to survive a nuclear war by self-isolating, and the film concludes with global nuclear devastation set to the soundtrack of "We'll Meet Again" by Vera Lynn, while Bon Iver's "Second Nature" plays when the comet strikes Earth in *Don't Look Up* and as we see the debris that was once our planet in the moments shortly after.

Funny? Yes, but not ha-ha funny. Wise and pithy and using levity to hammer down heavy topics.

Screwball Comedies

Bringing Up Baby (1938)

Screwball comedies are a signature form that harkens back to farce plays, the most famous of which were penned by the French playwright, Georges Feydeau, in the 1880s to 1910s. They were characterized by romantic intrigues complicated with mistaken identity and the dialogue was fast-paced, intelligent, and more like fencing, with eccentric characters teasing each other. Women were usually the ones taking the lead—today that doesn't seem unusual, but in the patriarchal nineteenth century that was surprising and subversive.

Feydeau-style farces grew popular in the United States in the 1920s as stage plays, and the 1930s saw some of the earliest films in the style, for example, in *My Man Godfrey* (1936), starring William Powell and Carole Lombard. The woman in the lead was part of the new liberation of women post–World War I, the first time women were recognized as a valued part of the workforce. While this is decades before the sexual liberation of the late 1960s, female audiences appreciated seeing marriage as a partnership of equals, with women propelling the story, behaving with freedom, intelligence, and energy, and often "wearing the pants" in the relationship. There was also an escapist element since the popularity of this genre rose during the Depression—for the length of the film, you could forget your troubles and disappear into another world.

Cary Grant and Katharine Hepburn star in *Bringing Up Baby* (1938). It is noteworthy for having been cowritten by a woman (this was unusual at the time and unfortunately still is quite rare), Hagar Wilde.

Grant plays an awkward, shy paleontologist who falls in love with Hepburn's quirky, empowered heiress. Grant is nerdy, and Hepburn is worldly but scatterbrained. The distinctive twist is that Hepburn's character has a pet leopard named Baby, who has a taste for bones, including an important missing bone ("the intercostal clavicle") that will complete a skeleton of a brontosaurus that Grant is assembling.

The film introduces the protagonists with a meet-cute—they are playing golf, not with each other, when Hepburn accidentally plays Grant's ball.

A key is that the leading man and lady begin disliking each other— we, the audience, implicitly understand that they will eventually fall in love and be together in the end, and the pleasure is in seeing how that comes about. An important intangible element of a successful comedy is "chemistry" between the protagonists. We need to believe that they have an attraction to one another and feel it even when they are not speaking on-screen. On-screen couples who have had famously engaging chemistry include Grant and Hepburn, Tom Hanks and Meg Ryan, Fred Astaire and Ginger Rogers—there's a reason they are paired together in multiple films. Obstacles often make it seem impossible for them to get together, but our sense of the inevitability of their getting together is propelled by that invisible but palpable chemistry. When *Bringing Up Baby* opens, Grant is engaged to someone else. But the deal is implied and the chemicals bubble beneath the surface—they'll get there in the end.

There also must be complications. Otherwise, the film would be over in twenty minutes and there would be no tension. Tension is what drives us to watch. It needn't be tension in the will-they-escape-with-their-lives sense, but tension is inserted when the film poses a question (will they get together?) and intentionally delays the resolution.

Complications provide setbacks to the happily ever after, as mentioned in the rom-com section. There's Grant's fiancée, for starters. And his search for a missing intercostal clavicle, which Hepburn's dog manages to abscond with and bury in the backyard. And the big complication in this film, the one that makes it distinct from the cascade of romantic comedies on the

Figure 6.4 "I just went gay all of a sudden!" Today it's politically incorrect, but in 1938 it was likely an in-joke. *Bringing Up Baby* (1938). RKO Radio Pictures, Inc. / Photofest © RKO Radio Pictures, Inc.

virtual shelves of film libraries, is Baby. Hepburn's brother has sent her Baby from Brazil—a tame leopard who grows calm when she hears the song "I Can't Give You Anything but Love." It's the complication that is most vividly remembered, distinguishing this film from all other romantic comedies because it's "the one with the leopard."

Like all the best screwball comedies from this era, *Bringing Up Baby* has eccentric secondary characters, fast, funny dialogue, stars who really could deliver, and comically ridiculous situations. For instance, at one point Grant's clothes get drenched in the rain and Hepburn sends them to the cleaners to keep him from leaving. He is stuck wearing a frilly lady's bathrobe. When the imperious owner of the house comes to the door and demands to know why he is dressed like that, he leaps into the air and tells her, "I just went gay, all of a sudden!" This is arguably the first use of that term for homosexuals in Golden Age movies. Interesting historically, but mostly, because of the situation, it's just very funny.

Speaking of "fast," another Howard Hawks–directed comedy, *His Girl Friday* (1940), a remake (with a twist) of the early comic classic, *The Front Page* (1931), also stars Cary Grant, this time as the editor of a tabloid newspaper. His ex-wife and former ace reporter is Rosalind Russell. Grant is trying to stop her from marrying the wrong guy and entice her back to work to cover a sensational story about a convicted murderer who has escaped prison on the eve of his execution. The two are a great match. This film is famous for just how fast the dialogue goes. Urged to speed things up by Hawks, the two leads tear through the dialogue, trading barbs like a house on fire.

Some Like It Hot (1959)

This comedy combines elements of farce, slapstick, and rom-com into what many consider the greatest comedy ever made. Directed by Billy Wilder and written by him and his regular writing partner, I. A. L. Diamond, it stars Tony Curtis and Jack Lemmon as Joe and Jerry, two musicians who are forced to flee 1929 Chicago when they witness the Saint Valentine's Day Massacre. The mob is after them, so they disguise themselves as women, calling themselves Josephine and Daphne, and join an all-girls band on a train to Florida. Marilyn Monroe plays Sugar Kane, a ukulele-playing singer in the band. Watching the boys try to walk in high heels and manage their disguises is part of the fun, as well as situations such as Monroe asking to share a bunk on the train with Daphne, which turns into a party after Daphne finds some booze, with all the girls squeezing in. Curtis falls for Monroe and trades his female duds for a yachtsman's outfit. Sounding very much like Cary Grant at his most elegant, he introduces himself to her as a millionaire. Meanwhile, an actual millionaire falls for Daphne, and Jerry/Daphne likes it: "Why would a guy fall for a guy?" asks Joe. And Jerry answers right back, "Security!" Monroe is at her best, with terrific comic timing and a soulfulness that adds depth to the comedy. The boys are a great team, both at the top of their game. Sharp dialogue, unexpected complications, and one of the funniest last lines in movie history. This is the whole package.

Worldly

Manhattan (1979)

Manhattan is a favorite film, with *Airplane!* coming in a close second. Woody Allen's *Manhattan* is a romantic comedy with drama elements, but because it includes classic romantic comedy elements, and ends on a positive note (if not with the wedding bells that we might expect), it might be considered a worldly comedy. It has very funny parts (it's on Bravo's "100 Funniest Movies" list and the American Film Institute's "100 Years, 100 Laughs" list, too), but it's not played for laughs.[7] It's more philosophical and psychological, interested in character studies, why people behave the way they do. Most comedies are plot-driven, or the plot is simply a sleigh on which to tie jokes. For worldly comedies, characters are at the fore, as they discuss "big ideas."

Allen stars as a middle-aged comedy writer who is dating Tracy, a teenage girl—today this raises the hackles, and it did not go unnoticed as a taboo theme when the film came out, but that dynamic is not actually what the film is *about*. The film would have been equally effective if the girl had been twenty-one rather than starting the film as a seventeen-year-old, played by Mariel Hemingway.

The story is really about how Allen's character falls for the mistress of his best friend. Diane Keaton plays the mistress. They meet on a double date—not a meet-cute per se, but initially Allen doesn't like Keaton's character, considering her a snob. His opinion of her softens when they later meet-cute at a philanthropic event at the Museum of Modern Art. They chat all night, famously seated at sunrise against the backdrop of the Queensboro Bridge. They begin a relationship, despite Allen's feelings of guilt about taking up with his best friend's girlfriend—and having his own. He tries to do the right

Figure 6.5 Diane Keaton, Woody Allen. *Manhattan* (1979). United Artists / Photofest © United Artists.

thing and breaks up with Hemingway, encouraging her to go to London to study acting and to date other people closer to her own age.

But this is not the plot you'd expect. In *Bringing Up Baby* and *When Harry Met Sally* the story begins with the boy otherwise engaged and romantically unavailable—and disliking the girl he meets . . . before they eventually end up together. In *Manhattan*, Allen realizes that he does not love the girl he met, Diane Keaton, but loves the girl with whom he began the story, and who is now of age, Hemingway. In the famous penultimate scene, Allen lies on his couch and speaks into a tape recorder, listing what he feels makes "life worth living." He winds through a list of things he loves and comes to "Tracy's face." Inspired, he rushes to her, speeding through New York City—the other romance in this story, as the film is so beautifully shot in black-and-white that it can make you fall in love with Manhattan itself, which is otherwise not the most romantically photogenic of cities. He reaches her just before she heads off to the airport to fly to London. We feel good at the end of the film because we were cheering for this relationship all along, and it ends with an open-ended optimism that they might get back together for good, after all.

That open-ended optimism at the end, chasing the happy-ever-after from the start, is the mark of comedy, regardless of subgenre.

Chapter 7

Musicals

Key Films
Top Hat (1935)
Singin' in the Rain (1952)
Moulin Rouge (2001)

Are you someone who says, "I don't like musicals?" This seems to be the genre hardest for some people to appreciate, a special case, with many asking, "What's with people bursting into song or dance? It just isn't realistic; people don't do that."

It sometimes seems to be more difficult with musicals to suspend disbelief, something which many stories require, from meet-cute romantic comedies to action movies. How realistic are the superhuman heroes of the Marvel Universe who can fly or turn people into ice or become invisible? We seem to accept and enjoy them. Well, although people in real life don't usually burst into song and start dancing in the street, those actions are closer to what real people do than anything in a franchise fantasy. So how about giving musicals a chance?

A unique feature of musicals is that one can enjoy their best moments and not watch the whole movie. Each song or dance has a beginning and an end. You can get a taste of what the musical offers without committing yourself to the entire meal.

Why not watch a song or dance number (which rarely lasts more than five minutes) and let it work its magic on you? If a musical number described here intrigues you, search for it on YouTube and enjoy it for itself. Are you someone who just can't listen to music? Then enjoy watching the beautiful bodies in motion. If the rhythms of tap dance or the athleticism of the dancers don't amaze and delight you, then the graceful lines of the ballroom dances may.

Of course, in the best musicals much will be lost in not seeing how the song fits into the story. But, if you like what you see, you may find yourself wanting more, and the rest of the movie is yours for the asking.

If someone is having a bad day, nothing can cheer them up better than watching "Good Morning" from *Singin' in the Rain* or watching James Cagney whoop it up dancing "Give My Regards to Broadway" in *Yankee Doodle Dandy*. These musical moments immediately put people in a happy place. Give them a try!

Hollywood Finds Its Voice

On October 6, 1927, a movie opened that changed Hollywood forever. It was *The Jazz Singer*, starring Al Jolson and produced by Warner Bros. Though it was not the first sound movie, it was the first with synchronized singing and dialogue, and it was a sensation. Within a year, all the studios were making movies with sound, and the era of silent films was over.

In the movie, Jolson, a superstar in theater, with his jazz-inflected, heartfelt, blackface performances of minstrel songs, plays Jack Robin, the son of a cantor, torn between his father's wishes and his passion for popular song. The film includes several of Jolson's hits as well as *Kol Nidre*, the Jewish prayer of atonement. Though fictional, it parallels Jolson's life story.

After his first song in the picture, Jolson's first spoken words made history: "Wait a minute, wait a minute, you ain't heard nothin' yet!" Hearing him talk, the premiere audience went wild and were even more enthusiastic when a few minutes later Jolson, as Jack, speaks again, improvising a teasing dialogue with his mother. With five songs and less than two minutes of synchronized talking (all the other dialogue was on title cards), this became the biggest hit in Warner Bros. history, and the movie musical was born.

Most of these first efforts were borrowed from vaudeville revues. The singing was performed as though you were watching a live stage production, with crowds of ensemble dancers, which impressed more by their numbers than by any display of talent. The limitations of the sound technology in those early days made for primitive camera placements since performers had to speak and sing directly into microphones to be properly recorded. An MGM film, *The Broadway Melody of 1929*, a melodrama about rival sisters in a Broadway show, became the first sound film to win the Academy Award for Best Picture. It had a sequence in Technicolor and was the first all-talking Hollywood musical.

Love Me Tonight (1932), starring Maurice Chevalier and Jeanette McDonald, directed by Reuben Mamoulian and with songs by Rogers and Hart was an early musical hit. Influenced by European operetta, it is one of the first **integrated musicals**, where the musical numbers are not merely interludes but advance the story. Through song we are introduced to Maurice, a Paris tailor who is fitting an aristocrat for a new coat. Chatting with his client he happily sings "Isn't It Romantic?," and his client takes up the song, singing the words and humming as he leaves the shop, the song is passed on to a cab driver, then a composer who writes down the melody, then to soldiers, gypsies and then to a princess, played by McDonald. We have seen the world of the story, the social divides bridged by a melody, and have met the lovers-to-be. The rest is a witty pre-Code romantic comedy, filled with smart dialogue and sexual innuendo. Other operetta musicals followed (Chevalier and McDonald did four together) but once the Hayes Code tamed them (removing anything suggestive of grown-up sexual relationships), they were soon seen as old-fashioned.

The movies that set the template for backstage musicals in the early 1930s were *Gold Diggers of 1933* and *42nd Street* (1933), both from Warner Bros. First came *42nd Street*. We watch the grueling preparations for a Broadway show, with lots of backstage lore, the exhausting rehearsals, the bickering chorines, the irascible director, the financial backers looking to score with a chorus girl (a young Ginger Rogers plays one of those chorus girls, nicknamed "Any-Time Annie"). In a situation that became iconic, the star is injured on opening night and an unknown chorus girl must go on in her place. That unknown was Ruby Keeler. The director, an over-the-top Warner Baxter, grabs her by the shoulders, tells her how much depends on her success, the hours of work, the jobs at risk if the show fails, and ends with the famous line: "Sawyer, you are going out a youngster, but you've got to come back a star." There is a bittersweet ending. She is a sensation, and we see her celebrated as the director stands off in a corner, his hard work unrecognized.

The drama is absorbing and well done, but Keeler is not convincing as a potential star: she can't act, her singing is pedestrian, and she is an ungraceful dancer, stiffly watching her feet like someone just learning. It seems quite likely that she got her parts in the movies because she was married to Al Jolson. It certainly is not because of her looks or her personality. But, go figure, she became an audience darling and starred in several other popular musicals with Dick Powell. Powell, on the other hand, has an engaging manner and a sweet tenor voice and is charming when paired with her. Later, he would redefine himself by playing tough-guy detective Philip Marlowe.

The last twenty minutes of the movie are what make it a classic. They contain a sequence of numbers choreographed by Busby Berkeley. A former hoofer, Berkeley revolutionized the filming of production numbers, with enormous stages, hordes of scantily dressed chorus girls, odd props and sets (showgirls playing electric violins or at dozens of floating grand pianos, pretty girls splashing down water slides, and massive lines of men and girls tap-dancing with military precision), eccentric camera angles (both under and over the performers), often filmed from a great height (accomplished by cutting a hole in the roof of the sound stage), converting bodies into kaleidoscopic forms. His productions had an energy and scale that had never been seen before. Some of his shots are rather racy; he liked to swoop the camera between the legs of his chorus girls.

Gold Diggers of 1933 is another backstage story, with Ruby Keeler as the ingenue and Dick Powell as the young composer she loves. When the juvenile lead becomes ill, Powell agrees to go on in his place, putting his inheritance at risk since his family doesn't know he is involved with the show and would not approve. Of course, he too is a great success, and the Busby Berkeley numbers are too. But, boy, are they strange.

The opening number of this first *Gold Diggers* (there were two more to follow) is "We're in the Money" (meant ironically, since it was in the middle of the Depression) sung by Ginger Rogers, doing one verse in pig latin and fronting a parade of barely dressed chorines wearing oversize coins. The number "Petting in the Park" is more salacious than it sounds. We see Powell and Keeler and dozens of identically dressed couples, embracing in the park. A little boy in a raincoat, looking like a miniature dirty old man, is spying on the lovers. It begins to rain, the girls run for cover, hiking their skirts, and viewed from behind so we see their panties. Then they are in silhouette behind a screen, taking off their dresses and showering. The boy begins to pull up the screen, exposing an array of naked legs. When the girls come out, to the dismay of their beaus they wear bathing suits made of metal. The boy hands Powell a can opener which he proceeds to use on Keeler. We are not making this up.

In the final number, Joan Blondell, Keeler's roommate in the backstage story, sings: "Remember My Forgotten Man." "You put a rifle in his hand. You sent him far away. You shouted hip-hooray. But look at him today." Another woman picks up the song, and then another. We segue into soldiers marching to war, then the march continues but now they are wounded and bleeding, and then they are standing on bread lines. This is moving and in deadly earnest. This likely hit audiences of the day particularly hard, so soon after World War I. It works differently from the other numbers because of the bluesy sadness, sung simply and directly to camera, which continues over the images of soldiers and the down-and-out. Here, there is no dancing, no overhead shots meant to amaze—just documentary-like images of suffering and the Depression.

Gold Diggers of 1935's big production number was "Lullaby of Broadway." Another Berkeley extravaganza, it opens with a disembodied head, a woman (Wini Shaw) singing and a montage of a day in the city starting with the milkman making a delivery, a woman reluctantly getting up and getting dressed, people on the subway, then at work, then in the evening getting ready for a night on the town, with an extended sequence in a nightclub with dozens of dancers tapping in unison and looking rather too much like stormtroopers. It ends with a woman falling to her death. We kid you not.

These musicals were big hits and poured money into their studios. Grandiose and inventive as the musical productions are, there is something impersonal and cold about most of them. The bigger the ensemble, the more anonymous each performer is. Berkeley gives us mass and design, but we are watching from afar, meant to appreciate but not feel. The numbers are all part of an onstage show (impossibly extended in space, but still meant to be within a performance). There are no songs or dances expressing feelings between the characters in their offstage life.

But something very different and much better was about to happen, and their names were Fred Astaire and Ginger Rogers.

Astaire and Rogers Transform the Musical

They were secondary players in the RKO musical *Flying Down to Rio* (1933). Rogers, as a contract player, had been in several of the Warner Bros. musicals, but this was Astaire's first film. He was an established star on Broadway and in London's West End. He and his sister, Adele, had headlined shows written for them with songs by George and Ira Gershwin. But Adele had retired from show business to marry into British nobility, and Fred was on his own. He and Ginger have comic chemistry in their scenes together and have only one musical number here, but it defines the movie. The big production number, inspired by Busby Berkeley, with dozens of chorus girls strapped in formation to the wings of biplanes, pales in comparison with what happens next. Watching everyone dance "The Carioca," Fred and Ginger decide to give it a try. Pretending to be awkward (even bumping heads at one moment), they are having comic fun, and their joy is infectious. They would wind up doing nine pictures together and set a new standard for how to make a musical.

The first big innovation in creating the modern musical is that most of the songs and dances are *integrated* into the daily lives of their characters, moving the story and their relationship. They are not just something that happens on stage. In *The Gay Divorcee* (1934), the first musical with their names above the title, we see the first of many dances that show Fred in romantic pursuit and Ginger needing to be persuaded. The song is Cole Porter's "Night and Day." At a nightclub he asks her to dance. At first she keeps turning away from Fred, but when he takes her by the hand she twirls into his arms and begins to move with him, first romantically ballroom dancing, and soon tap-dancing side by side. A few more times she tries to leave, but she can't; Fred and the dance are too seductive. At the end she sits, quietly stunned, as Fred offers her a cigarette. This dance is not only pursuit and persuasion, it is barely concealed sex.

Top Hat (1935)

Top Hat, probably their most satisfying pairing, has a wonderful meet-cute. Fred is in the hotel room of his friend, played by comic sidekick Edward Everett Horton, tap-dancing his delight at being a bachelor, when the camera pans down to the room below where Ginger is trying to sleep. After complaining to the manager about the noise above, she goes up to confront the stranger directly and is reluctantly charmed by Fred's excuse that he has "St. Vitus dance" and can't stop himself. He is taken with her and seeing sand in an ashtray is inspired to help her go to sleep by doing a quiet sand dance, which puts all of them to sleep.

The songs are by Irving Berlin, with "Top Hat, White Tie, and Tails" and "Cheek to Cheek" considered American classics. The song and dance, "Isn't it a Lovely Day" finds them in a London park. It's a getting-to-know-you tap dance, a flirtation, with them alternating leading the steps, and increasingly enjoying each other's company. At the end of the dance, they sit, grinning and shaking hands. "Cheek to Cheek" is another overcome-her-reluctance number. Fred has been pursuing Ginger since they met, following her from London to Venice. Ginger thinks that Horton's wife is Fred's and is dismayed when she encourages Ginger to dance with him. Ginger is persuaded first by the enticements of the song and then by the impulse of the dance. She and Fred move onto an enormous art deco set, dancing alone, first ballroom style, and then gently tap dancing. The final moments, with Fred lifting her over his leg again and again and her final backward bend in his arms, ending

Figure 7.1 Fred Astaire, Ginger Rogers. *Top Hat* (1935). RKO Radio Pictures, Inc. / Photofest © RKO Radio Pictures, Inc.

in a quiet sigh, is a powerful evocation of sexual climax. Subtle, beautiful, powerful, and all in the dancing.

When you have two such talented performers, so well suited to each other, all you need to enjoy them is to make sure we in the audience can see them. The second innovation that sets their movies apart is that in Astaire's movies we always see the dancer's bodies in full and with long takes that let us appreciate their talent and technique. The only cuts are to give us a different view of the dance, but always with their full figures displayed. He accomplished this by insisting that a tracking dolly camera closely follow the dance to minimize how many cuts there would be, and make it seem that the dance was filmed without cuts at all. There are never eccentric angles or cutaways to waving arms or tapping feet, and only rare cuts to others watching; nothing is allowed to interfere with seeing the dance and the dancers, complete. This is central to the magic of his movies (including those he made with other partners). We will see that this purity is often violated in more modern musicals, which too often try to cover the inadequacy of the performers with complex editing.

Even with talents like Fred and Ginger, filming these dances is not easy. Fred was a hard taskmaster, a perfectionist, working with his choreographer, Hermes Pan, and with Ginger, for weeks of rehearsal and improvisation to get the steps right before they go before the camera and then, trying to get as much of each number in one take as possible. The goal of that hard work is

Figure 7.2 A dance partnership for the ages. Ginger Rogers, Fred Astaire. *Top Hat* © RKO Radio Pictures, Inc. Screenshot captured by authors.

for the audience to never see how hard it is, to make it all look effortless. More than any other dance team, time and again, they achieve that goal.

Every one of their films contains memorable musical moments. In *Swing Time* (1936), which, with songs by Jerome Kern many consider their best film, there is "Pick Yourself Up" a comic dance that starts with Fred pretending he doesn't know how to dance, and then turns into a tour de force of tapping and ballroom grace, with him and Ginger as his dance teacher. There is "Bojangles of Harlem," a solo tribute to the great Black tap dancer, which Fred performs in blackface to honor him, and "Never Gonna Dance," another example of dance, more than action or dialogue, showing the developing relationship between the characters, usually with Ginger discovering her love for Fred.

After nine films together the partnership ended. Rogers wanted a career separate from her association with Astaire. She had many successes and an Oscar just a few years later for her performance in the drama, *Kitty Foyle*. She and Astaire teamed up one final time in 1949 in *The Barkleys of Broadway*, an MGM picture and their only one together in color. It is a valedictory piece and has some wonderful moments. The tap number "Bouncin' the Blues" where they are in casual clothes rehearsing for a show is a favorite. Their joy in performing together is palpable—they are having such fun!

Astaire Changes Partners

Though none of Astaire's subsequent dance partners quite matched the chemistry he had with Ginger Rogers, he did make some wonderful musicals in the 1940s with some pretty terrific dancers. His tap duet to Cole Porter's classic "Begin the Beguine" with Eleanor Parker in *The Broadway Melody of 1940* is one of the greatest tap displays in movie history. They are technical equals and inspire each other. The film is a revue and is missable, but this dance is something to see.

Rita Hayworth was a remarkable beauty who was a trained dancer (born Margarita Carmen Cansino, she was trained by her grandfather, a famous classical Spanish dancer, and partnered with her father as the Dancing Cansinos). Astaire has admitted she was his favorite partner. Their two films together, *You'll Never Get Rich* (1941) and *You Were Never Lovelier* (1942) matched Fred's elegant reserve with her explosive sensuality and made for great dancing, both tap and ballroom. The films were big hits. In 1944 she danced with Gene Kelly in the Technicolor *Cover Girl*, making her the first woman to perform with both stars.

Astaire filmed two pictures with singer Bing Crosby. In *Holiday Inn* (1942), he danced with firecrackers on July Fourth. *Blue Skies* (1946) featured one of his most ingenious numbers, "Puttin on the Ritz," where in top hat, tails, white spats, and cane he first dances solo, using the cane as another source of tap, creating impossibly complex rhythms, then opens a curtain to reveal a lineup of doppelgänger Astaires, dancing behind him. He shocked his audiences when he announced that this number was his farewell dance and that he was retiring from pictures.

The retirement didn't last long. In 1948 when Gene Kelly was injured, Astaire stepped in to partner with Judy Garland in *Easter Parade*, with songs by Irving Berlin. In 1953, for MGM he starred in *The Band Wagon*, directed by Vincente Minnelli, with a screenplay by Betty Comden and Adolf Green.

Fred plays a musical comedy performer whose star is fading (mirroring Astaire's own story at the time). His friends (played by Comden and Green) write a new musical for him, but the director turns it into something pretentiously highbrow and hires a ballerina, Cyd Charisse, to costar. Initially hostile to each other, the two dancers doubt that their very different styles can be compatible. Once they recognize their mutual insecurity, they agree to try to make it work, and as they do, they fall in love.

Cyd Charisse is perhaps his sexiest partner, she simply exudes it with her long legs and sinuous moves, wearing a red sequined dress and dancing the femme fatale in the jazz-influenced "Girl Hunt Ballet." And then she is romance incarnate when "Dancing in the Dark" with Fred in Central Park, both dressed in white, the dance more ballet than ballroom. It is exquisite, quietly proving that they can indeed dance together.

This is one of the great musicals, every number a winner. Astaire has an opening number, "A Shine on Your Shoes," with one of his least storied dance partners, a real shoeshine man named Leroy Daniels who was discovered by the director shining shoes and dancing in New York City. Daniels inspired this number and is featured in it. He and Fred are so joyous here, with Fred made happy with the shine on his shoes and dancing his way through a penny arcade.

Musicals were very popular in the 1930s and 1940s with some fifty made each year, but then numbers started dropping and there were fewer than ten made a year from the 1960s to 1980s. With few exceptions, the films became more staid and less inventive, and audiences stayed away. One reason is that stars with the necessary skills were aging, and the new stars simply didn't have the skills. When sound first came in, the talent that raced to Hollywood came from vaudeville and theater. Many of them were triple threats—they could sing, dance, and act. For instance, James Cagney, who became famous in his roles as a ruthless gangster in Warner Bros. movies, had started as a hoofer. He was the best part of the Busby Berkeley musical *Footlight Parade* (1933), with his loose-limbed tap dancing. After tiring of his gangster roles, and wanting to do something patriotic at the start of World War II, he produced and starred in *Yankee Doodle Dandy* (1942), a biopic of the pre–World War I Broadway star George M. Cohan, who wrote and starred in his own plays, composed popular songs such as "Give My Regards to Broadway," and the military anthem "Over There," and, oh by the way, was a terrific tap dancer. Cagney channeled all of that into this film and he is wonderful. His ability to convey joy in the physical act of dancing, which is so central to the appeal of the best musicals, is perfectly exemplified by his tap dance down the stairs of the White House, after Cohan, meeting with President Roosevelt, is given the Congressional Medal of Honor for his support of the troops.

Judy Garland and Mickey Rooney: The "Backyard Musical"

One of the most popular musical series of the 1930s featured young Judy Garland (born Frances Gumm) and Mickey Rooney (Joseph Yule Jr.). Both were child stars who grew up in the studio system. And both were very talented. Rooney could sing and dance, play the drums, and act too. Even as a young girl Garland had a big voice, a swinging style, and a personality to match. She could dance and act with the best.

Garland started in films at age thirteen, too old to be considered a child, and too young to play adults. Unlike Shirley Temple, who from the age of five was the number one box office draw in the mid-1930s in films such as *Curly Top* (1935, singing "Animal Crackers in My Soup"), and *Bright Eyes* (1934, with her signature song "On the Good Ship Lollipop"), often playing the child as healer, fixing up estrangements in a family, or rifts between sweethearts. Temple danced on a staircase with Bill "Bojangles" Robinson in *The Little Colonel* (1935), the first interracial dance pair in Hollywood history. Garland's girl-next-door looks were not glamorous, but her energy and poise would excite any scene.

Mickey Rooney made his film debut at the age of six. At age fourteen he played Puck in a film adaptation of *A Midsummer Night's Dream* (1935). He played teenage Andy Hardy in a very popular small-town family comedy series in the late 1930s, and at age nineteen was nominated Best Actor for *Babes in Arms* (1939), the first musical he did with Garland. He was the number one box office draw in Hollywood for the years 1939–1941. He had a long career, with dramatic roles in *National Velvet* (1944) with a young Elizabeth Taylor, and William Saroyan's *The Human Comedy* (1943).

His films with Judy Garland were formulaic, invariably about the youngsters and their friends needing to put on a show to raise money to support some worthwhile cause. In *Babes in Arms*, they put on the show to stop Rooney's performing parents from going on the road with a show. It was based on a successful Broadway show with songs by Rodgers and Hart and energetic numbers choreographed by director Busby Berkeley. Most of the songs from the show were replaced (they did that a lot back then). Several of the new songs by Arthur Freed and Nacio Herb Brown, including "Good Morning" and "You Are My Lucky Star," were recycled ten years later for *Singin' in the Rain*. Other Rooney and Garland collaborations include *Strike Up the Band* (1940) with only the title song kept from the Broadway show and *Girl Crazy* (1943) the first film that allowed Garland to play a young woman old enough to be romanced, and this time including most of the music from the show, with songs by George and Ira Gershwin like "Fascinating Rhythm," "Embraceable You," and "I Got Rhythm." Dance was not featured in any of these films, just the small-town comedy, "Let's Put on a Show" production numbers, and the songs. But that was enough to guarantee their popularity.

Judy Garland in *The Wizard of Oz* (1939)

This musical fantasy is one of the most honored films in history. Nominated for six Academy Awards, including Best Picture, won for Best Original Song, and chosen as one of the first films selected by the Library of Congress for preservation because of its cultural significance. In 2022, *Variety* ranked it second on its "100 Greatest Movies of All Time" list. A perennial favorite, because of its repeated television broadcasts, it is rated the most-seen film in history.

With songs by "Yip" Harburg and Harold Arlen, including "Somewhere Over the Rainbow" and "We're Off to See the Wizard," remarkable sets and special effects (especially the marvelous transition from the sepia-colored world of Kansas to Oz, in glorious Technicolor), and comic support from Ray Bolger as the Scarecrow; Bert Lahr, brilliantly funny as the Cowardly Lion; Margaret Hamilton, incomparable as the Wicked Witch of the West; and Frank Morgan as Oz, the Great and Powerful, Judy Garland became a superstar with her sweet, spunky and beautifully sung portrayal of Dorothy.

Except for the eccentric dancing of Ray Bolger as the Scarecrow, this musical is all about the songs, the characters, and the production. There are extraordinary effects such as the tornado that delivers Dorothy to Oz,

Figure 7.3 Judy Garland as Dorothy, Ray Bolger as the Scarecrow, Burt Lahr as the Cowardly Lion, Jack Haley as the Tin Man. *The Wizard of Oz* © MGM. Screenshot captured by authors.

the good witch Glinda arriving by bubble, the Munchkins greeting Dorothy and introducing her to the Yellow Brick Road, flying monkeys, the Wicked Witch flying on her broom with smoke billowing behind her as she spells out "Surrender Dorothy" in the sky and then later doused in water and melting, and finally, the magic ruby slippers that take Dorothy home.

Beyond the fantasy, adventure, and humor, this is a story with a simple universal message: "There's no place like home." *The Wizard of Oz* was a hit when it was released in 1939, but because of how expensive the production was, it did not make a profit. After being shown on television as a special event in 1956, it not only made a profit but with annual showings, it became an enormously popular holiday tradition. Each year brought excitement about the coming broadcast, arranging the day and gathering the family so we could all watch it together.

Judy Garland Grows Up

Judy Garland's next film, *Meet Me in St Louis* (1944), is nearly as beloved as Oz. A very different experience, it tells the story of a loving family in 1903, as they excitedly await the opening of the St Louis World's Fair. This is one of the earliest films from the Arthur Freed Unit of MGM, which would turn out the best musical of that decade. In Technicolor, directed by Vincente Minnelli (he and Garland would soon marry, and she has never seemed more beautiful), and costarring six-year-old Margaret O'Brien (as young "Tootie," she won the Academy Award for Outstanding Child Actress). Garland is seventeen-year-old Esther, her first opportunity to play someone close to her real age, and has a crush on the boy next door. The story follows the family through four seasons of that year, rich in details of life in that "simpler" time. The title song is a "pass-along" and establishes how much this family enjoys each other. The joyous "Trolley Song" as Esther excitedly anticipates seeing the new boy she admires, is contrasted by the sadness of "Have Yourself a Merry Little Christmas" sung by Tootie and Esther as they contemplate having to leave St Louis because of their father's promotion to New York. Tootie has several memorable scenes: when on Halloween she is challenged by the other children to throw flour at a neighbor they all find scary; singing and strutting to "Under the Bamboo Tree" with her sister Esther, what passed for entertainment in those days before radio and television; and, in her upset at having to leave St. Louis, tearfully destroying the snowmen in their front yard. But it is Garland who shines.

As she does in all of the films she did then, including *For Me and My Gal* (1942), Gene Kelly's first movie, a story of vaudeville, and especially in *Easter Parade* (1948) with Fred Astaire, who came out of retirement to replace an injured Gene Kelly, and even in *Summer Stock* (1950), a backstage musical with perhaps the number that best captures her special talents, despite the terrible personal emotional roller coaster she was on.

Garland had been addicted to pills given to her as a child by the studio to keep her weight down and help her sleep. The pills caused mood swings, problems with balance, unexplained illnesses, and weight changes, which ruined relationships, upended her personal life, and cost the studio money in lost time. She had become unreliable, and MGM had threatened to fire her several times (they took no responsibility for causing her addiction). With *Summer Stock*, Gene Kelly was extending his hand to help save her career. Kelly created one of his most memorable tap dances on the song "You, Wonderful, You" where he played with a creaking floor and an open newspaper, and also did a rousing tap dance solo on "Dig Deep." Garland continued to miss work, causing the film to go six months over schedule. Despite that, she managed some wonderful performances here, a tap dance duet with Kelly in the barn dance number, and her solo, "Get Happy," which was filmed after several months' break. By that time, she had lost weight and gotten some rest. She looks terrific in a peaked fedora hat and a shirt-length tuxedo that displays her legs to advantage; her singing has never been better.

Nevertheless, she was fired as soon as *Summer Stock* finished filming. Her career looked over. But, boy what a comeback! In 1954, she starred for Warner Bros. in a Cinemascope remake of *A Star Is Born*, directed by George Cukor and with a screenplay by Moss Hart. It was based on a 1937 dramatic film that starred Frederick March and Janet Gaynor. A story about a fading movie star, Norman Main, played here wonderfully by James Mason, who discovers a young singer, Esther Blodgett, encourages her career, falls in love with and marries her, and watches her career soar as he gets lost in drink and self-pity. They first meet when Norman drunkenly interrupts her performance, and she rescues him from embarrassment by pretending it is part of the act. Afterward, Norman wants to apologize and goes looking for her, finally finding her in a small after-hours bar. We watch as her emotional singing of "The Man That Got Away" entrances him. He had no idea she was that good. Garland's performances in this movie are uniquely powerful—with her signature clarion singing voice underscored by a tremulousness and fragility that is finally heartbreaking. With such a strong story, perfectly cast, and the magic that Garland brings, this is one of the great musicals.

This story has been remade twice since then. In 1976, starring Barbra Streisand and Kris Kristofferson, and in 2018, with Lady Gaga and Bradley Cooper (who also directed). It can be very interesting to compare these remakes, as well as the original film from 1937, and, if you are really a completist, the first iteration of this story from 1932, the pre-Code "What Price Hollywood" also directed by George Cukor. Each has something to recommend it. Which do you prefer?

Singin' in the Rain (1952) and Gene Kelly

Singing in the Rain is the top musical of all time according to the American Film Institute, and the AFI ranks it number five in its "greatest American movies of all time" list. We couldn't agree more with both rankings. It has the remarkable choreography and dancing of Gene Kelly, a very different dancer from Fred Astaire but in his way just as creative. Kelly got his start on Broadway, initially as a choreographer, but the role that made him a star was dancing the lead in *Pal Joey* (1940). After that Hollywood came calling.

Kelly thought of dance as every bit as masculine an activity as a sport. He hated that it was considered "sissy" for men to dance. His persona in films was the everyman, often blue-collar, who simply best expressed himself in dancing. Kelly's dancing is athletic. He rarely wears formal clothes, preferring an outfit of jeans and a T-shirt with white socks and loafers. As we saw in *Summer Stock*, he loved to find common objects to dance with, there with a newspaper and a creaking floorboard, in another picture, with a mop, and in another, *Anchors Aweigh* (1945) with an animated cartoon of Jerry the Mouse. With support from Stanley Donen, Kelly also pioneered filming dances outside of the soundstage. *On the Town* (1949) had several scenes filmed on the streets of New York.

Kelly was a remarkable tap dancer, but he had great respect for ballet and modern dance and included them whenever he could. He was very good at mixing the dance types, with taps interspersed with balletic leaps and modern dance stretches that distinguished his dances from those of Astaire. *American in Paris* (1951), which costars the ballet dancer Leslie Caron, ends with a seventeen-minute ballet number. This was unheard of. But then *Singin' in the Rain*, one year later, includes an extended ballet and modern dance production, "Broadway Rhythm" where he is partnered with Cyd Charisse dressed in green, vamping him with the sexiest legs in movies.

Singin' in the Rain has a clever screenplay written by Comden and Green (who also did *The Bandwagon* for Astaire a few years later) inspired by the difficult transition movies had abandoning silent movies to sound. It is very much aware of the illusions of Hollywood. Kelly plays Don Lockwood, a swashbuckling movie star in silent movies. At the premiere of his latest silent film, he is interviewed on the red carpet and tells of his formal training in the dramatic arts, "We went to the best conservatories," and repeats "My motto was . . . dignity . . . always dignity," but as he tells his tale we see the truth. He and his friend Cosmo (Donald O'Connor) got their training in burlesque and vaudeville, doing comic dance numbers, and his start in the movies was as a stuntman, getting blown up regularly.

When the audience clamors for talkies and they try to add sound to the new film they are making, they are undone by the limitations of the technology at the time, and by his leading lady, Lina Lamont, who can't talk and can't act, in a very comic performance by Jean Hagen. When they show their new sound version to a preview audience they get laughed out of the theater. It looks like a disaster until Cosmo gets the idea of turning the film into a musical and having Don's new girlfriend, Kathy (a young Debbie Reynolds) dub Lamont's voice. Their delight in this idea becomes the song "Good Morning" with Kelly, O'Connor, and Debbie Reynolds expressing their happiness at finding a solution. They are just having fun, tap dancing together, up and down the

Figure 7.4 Gene Kelly dancing for joy. *Singin' in the Rain* © MGM. Screenshot captured by authors.

stairs, clowning with their raincoats, one of the most exhilarating numbers ever filmed. This is later matched by the "Moses Supposes" number with Kelly and O'Connor tapping up a storm, making fun of the elocution lessons imposed on actors trying to make the transition to talking pictures. O'Connor and Kelly are some of the best tap dancers in Hollywood history.

The movie was directed by Stanley Donen, who was also credited as co-choreographer (he started as dance assistant to Kelly, much like Hermes Pan with Astaire). There are so many wonderful, iconic songs and dances. Most memorably, the title number, when Kelly, discovering his love for Kathy and, heading home after their date, ignores the rain and dances joyously with his umbrella, and then discarding it, revels in water, tap splashing in puddles. A picture of new love's happiness, unbound by so-called proper behavior. It is one of the great dance numbers: one man, dancing alone, in clover.

"Make 'Em Laugh," a copy of Cole Porter's "Be a Clown" number from *The Pirate* (1948), which Kelly had danced with the Nicholas Brothers (probably the best tap dance duo act in history), is a solo number here, sung and danced by O'Connor, exhausting himself and us with pratfalls and gags showing the artifice of moviemaking: he does a backflip on what looks like an open hallway but is a solid wall with a life-size photo of one, but then tops it by trying the same thing on another wall, and going through it, when it turns out to be paper.

A bit of irony. A comic element in the story is that Kathy dubs the speaking and singing for Lina, and when Don reveals that to the audience, he declares she is the real star of the movie. It turns out that the two ballads sung by Debbie Reynolds, "Would You" and "You Are My Lucky Star" were dubbed by Betty Noyes. Reynolds only sings for herself in the "Good Morning" number. Noyes was one of several "ghost singers" who, uncredited, dubbed the singing for her and the likes of Deborah Kerr in *The King and I* (1956) and Audrey Hepburn in *My Fair Lady* (1964). Both of these actresses were dubbed by Marni Nixon, considered the "queen" of dubbers.

Musicals Go Out of Favor

By the late 1950s tastes had changed. The songs of the Golden Age of Musicals were part of the American Songbook, songs people knew by heart and sang in the shower, by composers like Cole Porter, Irving Berlin, and the Gershwins. But now rock and roll was popular and the Songbook seemed old-fashioned, from another time. In addition, to combat the increasing popularity of television, movies were now emphasizing widescreen color systems like Cinemascope and VistaVision, giving people a reason to leave their living rooms. The wide screens posed a creative problem for the filmmakers: how to fill those bigger spaces? The solution for musicals was to return to production numbers crowded with dancers, compromising the intimacy of watching one or two dancers develop a relationship through dance. As a result, there was a bombastic heaviness to many of the musicals of the late 1950s and on. And the habit of enjoying musicals was being lost.

The only musicals that made an impact were ones transferred from established Broadway shows, like *South Pacific* (1958) or *Oklahoma* (1955), meant to be family entertainment, usually losing whatever edge the original productions might have had. They were special events, heavily promoted, but no longer part of everyday viewing. *Gigi* (1958), starring Leslie Caron and Maurice Chevalier, was one of the few musicals not from a prior show that had some success.

Every genre needs reinvention from time to time, to bring a new energy and relevance. A new way to tell the story, with a different kind of hero, perhaps, or with musicals, to highlight the popular music and dance of the day. To bring something new to the table, with new stars performing at the top of their game.

The two musicals written by Richard Adler and Jerry Ross did that by going back to basics. *Pajama Game* (1957), with Doris Day and John Raitt, and *Damn Yankees* (1958) with Gwen Verdon, Tab Hunter, and Ray Walston, were both directed by George Abbot and did something smart. They brought the entire original cast of each show into the movie, with the addition of one "bankable star" for each—Doris Day and Tab Hunter. And they kept the original choreographer too—Bob Fosse.

Bob Fosse Kick-Starts the Reinvention of the Musical

Fosse had a small career as a dancer early on and choreographed his one number in *Kiss Me Kate* (1953), but now he was making a name for himself as a choreographer on Broadway. His dances were distinctively modern, very sexy, with signature moves (if you've heard of "jazz hands," that's Fosse). This was new. "Whatever Lola Wants," the seduction number he created for Gwen Verdon in *Damn Yankees*, was defining, though she had to tone down her sexuality for the movie. Carol Haney danced "Steam Heat" in *Pajama Game* wearing a man's black suit with a bowler hat (a prop Fosse relied on to hide his bald head but which became standard in many of his dances) with the angular moves with turned-in knees, rolling shoulders, swaying hips, gloves, and white socks, that became Fosse trademarks. Fosse himself danced "Who's Got the Pain (When They Do the Mambo)?" with Verdon in *Damn Yankees*, one of his last appearances as he shifted to film directing and choreography. Both of these numbers are filmed full-figure, with very few cuts, only slightly changing the angles of view. Though the dances are new they are filmed with classical restraint. You are watching what might as well be a live performance, without any camera tricks to hide behind.

Another thing that is different here is a willingness to choose talent over looks. Verdon and Haney were not conventionally pretty, but they had created their roles and were seriously talented dancers. Too often, the suits in Hollywood would choose a pretty face or an actor with a fan base over the performer who defined a role, and something was lost in translation. But every once in a while they made a smarter choice.

When they chose well, it made quite a difference. *Saturday Night Fever* (1977) and *Grease* (1978), both starred John Travolta, a TV actor who had both talent and looks. He was a trained dancer but had only done small roles in movies before being chosen for *Fever*. This movie features disco dancing, a new fad of the time, and added the drama of performance contests and the moves of Travolta: cocky, graceful, electric. He followed up this success with *Grease* and, as they say, "A star is born!"

A quite successful transfer from the New York stage was Frank Oz's film *Little Shop of Horrors* (1982). The songs were new, pastiches of 1950s rock and roll, clever and catchy, and Oz kept Ellen Greene from the original stage production in the role of Audrey, the love interest. Greene was not traditionally pretty and not well known in film, but she had great presence, and her performance of "Suddenly Seymour" stopped the show on stage and is a standout in the movie. Frank Oz surrounded her with smart comic performers such as Rick Moranis, Steve Martin, Bill Murray, and with Levi Stubbs (of the Motown singing group the Temptations) as the voice of the giant plant, Audrey II. Oz's fluid camerawork immersed us in the fanciful story of a plant from outer space that requires blood to survive and intends to take over the world. It was a hit and has developed a cult following.

There was no doubt that when a movie was made of the stage musical *Funny Girl* in 1968, Barbra Streisand would star in it. The original New York production had won every Tony award for a musical in 1964. Streisand was a phenomenon, playing Fanny Brice on Broadway and also in the West End production in London. Though she had no experience in films, *Funny Girl* really couldn't exist without her. The suits wanted Shirley MacLaine for the role. Ray Stark, the producer, refused. It was Streisand or no one. Even though a novice in films, she was no shrinking violet, demanding extensive retakes of her prerecorded singing, and was a perfectionist on set, frequently arguing with the director, William Wyler, who was experienced enough to stand up to her. The movie was a big hit and Streisand won the Oscar for Best Actress.

The first movie Fosse directed was *Sweet Charity* (1969). By that time, he was an established director and choreographer of musicals on Broadway, usually starring his wife, Gwen Verdon. She had created the role on Broadway, and he wanted her to star in the movie, but he was overruled and Shirley MacLaine was cast instead. MacLaine was an experienced dancer and she worked very hard on the part, but she wasn't the dancer that Verdon was, and the film suffered for it.

Fosse's next film was *Cabaret* (1972), based on a stage musical by Kander and Ebb, directed by Harold Prince. Here we are telling a different story and in a different way, set in Berlin in the 1930s as the Nazis are gaining power in Germany. Fosse made it his own, creating the dances and directing, giving Liza Minnelli, the daughter of Judy Garland, her first chance to sing on-screen (her touching performance as Sally Bowles, and her singing and dancing of the title song, won her the Oscar for Best Actress) and keeping Joel Grey (from the original Broadway production) as the sinister Emcee at the Kit Kat Klub where Sally works.

Unlike the show, where many songs advanced the plot, all of the songs in the film are sung on stage, reflecting the ominous political changes

Figure 7.5 Liza Minnelli as Sally Bowles. *Cabaret* © Allied Artists Pictures. Screenshot captured by authors.

occurring at the time. There is one powerful exception. At a beer garden we see a young blond boy sing what sounds like a celebration of nature and the young ("Tomorrow Belongs to Me") but when the camera pulls back from his angelic face we see he is wearing a Hitler Youth uniform and the song becomes a martial anthem, with the adults and Hitler youths rising to sing it together. The shift is chilling. This was a musical everyone wanted to see. It won every award it was nominated for except Best Picture.

One of the most successful original musicals from this period (not based on a previous show) was *Mary Poppins* (1964), giving Julie Andrews a chance to demonstrate what a wonderful job she would have done in the film *My Fair Lady* (1964). She had starred in the Broadway show but since she was an unknown in movies the studio insisted on giving her part to Audrey Hepburn, who was very good, but couldn't sing. All of Hepburn's numbers in *My Fair Lady* were dubbed.

West Side Story (1961) was another big hit at the time, with the opening Jerome Robbins dance number filmed on the streets of New York, capturing the original show's energy, and the excitingly danced "America" led by a magnetic Rita Moreno. But, then much of it is lost in the wan performances of the leads (all the singing was dubbed). The 2021 version directed by Steven Spielberg emphasizes its Latin roots by putting dialogue in Spanish (but not offering subtitles) and shows respect for the original. Many numbers are cleverly staged. "I Feel Pretty," sung by Rachel Zegler as Maria is particularly well done, but the "America" number, danced by Ariana DeBose with the company, is hampered by hectic editing, with too many close-ups and shots from on high to appreciate the dancing. It's a shame, because in many ways this is a decent remake.

The producers of *The Music Man* (1962) were smart enough to keep the lead from the original cast, Robert Preston, master of the con-man patter song "You've Got Trouble in River City" and match him with Shirley Jones as Marion, the librarian. It's happy old-fashioned entertainment.

Umbrellas of Cherbourg (1964) is a French musical directed by Jacques Demy with music by Michel Legrand and starring Catherine Deneuve. It is one of those films you either love or hate. All the dialogue is sung, the colors are pastel, and the palette changes as the story becomes more serious. It is a story of romance and longing, as the lovers are separated by war. Deneuve is at her loveliest. It seems a fantasy, not just that everyone sings, but that everyone is good-looking and that even the sleaziest of settings seem beautiful too. A fantasy about people you care about and that ends sadly. An original film.

The 1960s featured a couple of films starring The Beatles. Their first, *A Hard Day's Night* (1964), is a performance film. It's an opportunity to see and hear the group in rehearsal and performance, capering through London and having fun. Directed by Richard Lester, it invented a new form, anticipating the music videos of MTV. The editing and cinematography share their restless energy and creativity.

Musicals That Just Don't Work

There are other more recent movies worth seeking out for their originality and creative revitalization of the form, and they are listed in the "Movie Playlist" at the end of this book. But there are lots to avoid, making the mistake, too often, of presenting the dancing badly or of casting performers who can neither sing nor dance. A prime example is *Paint Your Wagon* (1969), starring, believe it or not, Lee Marvin and Clint Eastwood. Neither actor can sing nor dance. What were they thinking? It was a minor musical on the stage, but it was an embarrassment with this cast.

The film *Chicago* (2002), directed by Rob Marshall, is another missed opportunity. An example of what can happen when the movie creative team wants to make a show its own, and putting its stamp on it, removes much of what made it great. The original Broadway show *Chicago* (1975) was directed by Bob Fosse and starred Gwen Verdon and Chita Rivera, both of whom were too old by the time the movie was made to play their parts. In a story of 1930s Chicago, Roxie Hart and Velma Kelly are in jail for murdering their lovers. With the help of their high-priced lawyer, Billy Flynn, the public's interest in their salacious stories turns them into celebrities; a career in showbiz beckons, if they don't hang first. The show was too darkly cynical for its time and was a modest hit. But times change. The 1996 revival starring Anne Reinking and Bebe Neuwirth was a sensation and now holds the record for the longest-running musical in history. The songs and original Fosse dances are terrific. As of this writing, it is still running on Broadway.

In the movie, the only trained dancer with a major role is Catherine Zeta-Jones (playing Vera). The other leads, Renée Zellweger and Richard Gere, can neither sing nor dance. The choreography has energy but is a pale imitation of Fosse's style and substitutes razzle-dazzle editing and posturing for actual dancing.

There is an odd end credit declaring that all three of these leads did their own dancing. Perhaps they did, but the flashy editing sure does all it can to hide the result. It's all pizzazz and no art. Nevertheless, the movie was a hit. Zeta-Jones won the Academy Award for Best Supporting Actress, and the film won for Best Film Editing and Best Picture. Watch it and decide for yourself. Or even better, go see the live show on Broadway.

Similar issues compromise the more recent *La La Land* (2016). Directed by Damien Chazelle, it starts wonderfully with "Another Day of Sun," an exuberant dance number in a traffic jam in Los Angeles. With cars going nowhere, the camera swoops and darts among the dancers as they leave their cars to party on the freeway. This recalls the best of old-time musicals, with a modern shot of adrenaline. But then the tone changes to glum and it stays pretty glum throughout. Emma Stone is a very good actress. Her most effective number is the audition sequence, which is an acting tour de force. Ryan Gosling seems to be without energy. Their dancing together is leaden, without grace or beauty or passion. Stone seems about to break into dance when she is with her girlfriends doing "Someone in the Crowd" but all she can manage is to wave her pretty blue dress around. Why would you choose as your lead in a musical an actor who can't sing and can't dance? This movie was highly praised as a new way forward for the musical. But, as a lover of musicals with songs and dances that stay with you, and performers with technique and talent who know how to sell them, it just seems sad.

But Things Are Looking Up

However, a new trend that seems to be revitalizing the musical is the biopic of popular performers such as *Walk the Line* (2005) about country singer Johnny Cash, *Rocketman* (2017) about Elton John, *Bohemian Rhapsody* (2018) about Freddie Mercury and the British band Queen, *Jersey Boys* (2014) about Frankie Valli and The Four Seasons, and *Elvis* (2022) about, well, Elvis. All these films brought talented newcomers to the screen and have generated a lot of buzz.

The **jukebox musical** tells an original story using old songs, not written for that film. This concept goes back a long way: *Singin' in the Rain* used the songs of Arthur Freed and Nacio Brown, *Easter Parade* and *White Christmas* (1954) used the songs of Irving Berlin, and *An American in Paris* (1951) used the songs of Gershwin.

Some jukebox musicals are based on the songs of groups like Abba, *Mamma Mia* (2008) (with a sequel in 2018), or singer-songwriters like Prince, *Purple Rain* (1984). The Beatles songbook inspired several films: *Yellow Submarine* (1968), a psychedelic animation based on the *Sgt. Pepper's Lonely*

Hearts Club Band album; *Yesterday* (2019), a clever film imagining a world where no one knows the songs of The Beatles except one young man who pretends to invent them and becomes a celebrity; and *Across the Universe* (2007), directed by Julie Taymor, which mixes live action with animation and psychedelic colorings, and somehow mingles 1960s youth culture, the Vietnam War, civil rights protests, and a love story with more than thirty Beatles tunes.

Instead of featuring one composer, the music can be more varied, chosen from different periods and musical styles. *Happy Feet* (2006), an animation about a tap-dancing penguin, covers "Heartbreak Hotel" and "Somebody to Love." *Pitch Perfect* (2012), a surprise hit with Anna Kendrick and Rebel Wilson, is a comedy about an a cappella group college competition. Sort of *Rocky* with singing, you know exactly how it will come out. But it is funny, and the performances of current hits are excitingly sung and choreographed. *Pennies from Heaven* (1981), starring Steve Martin and Bernadette Peters and written by Dennis Potter, is an interesting experiment. It tells a story of the Depression, with the leads lip-synching to classic recordings from that time. The stars are charming and give it their all, but the story is quite a downer. *The Blues Brothers* (1980), with John Belushi and Dan Ackroyd, is a slapstick comedy complete with car crashes, that distinguishes itself with rhythm and blues legends such as Aretha Franklin, Ray Charles, and Chuck Berry singing their classics. *School of Rock* (2003) stars Jack Black as a substitute teacher at a private high school who turns his class into a rock band and enters them into a "Battle of the Bands." It features songs from Led Zeppelin, Blondie, Jimi Hendrix, and Pink Floyd.

Moulin Rouge! (2001) may be the ultimate jukebox musical. Directed by Baz Luhrmann (who also did *Elvis*) and sung very well by Nicole Kidman and Ewan McGregor, it is a fever dream, a fantasy of nineteenth-century Paris with a mash-up of pop love songs, from "Diamonds Are a Girl's Best Friend" to "Material Girl," from Elton John's "My Song" to The Beatles' "Simple Love Song," "Lady Marmalade," and "Roxanne" from The Police. You haven't lived until you see Jim Broadbent sing Madonna's "Like a Virgin." It is hyperactive, wildly colorful, loud, ridiculous, romantic, and quite entertaining. Every other word seems to be "love." It breaks every rule about how to film dance, with cuts, close-ups, and new camera angles on almost every beat. Busby Berkeley on speed. You will either love it for its excess and sentiment or hate it for the same reasons. But it grabs you and has the energy to burn.

Chapter 8

Suspense and the Heist Film

Key Films

The Wages of Fear (1953)
The Birds (1963)
The Italian Job (2003)

It is 1936. Terrorists in London are planning to set off a bomb in the Piccadilly tube station. The young boy Stevie lives with his sister and her husband. The husband, who runs a movie house, is secretly a member of the terrorist group. He asks Stevie to deliver some film canisters to another cinema across town and to bring a package to the cloakroom at the Piccadilly tube station by 1:30.

We know there is a time bomb in the package. Stevie has no idea. As he pauses at a flea market, the camera pulls in close to the package and superimposed over it we see a handwritten note, "Don't forget the birds will sing at 1:45," then it zooms in on the time, "1:45." The soundtrack music ticks like a clock.

There is a large crowd waiting to watch a parade. When Stevie tries to cross the street in front of the parade, a policeman sends him back to the curb. Stevie glances at a clock on the street. It is 1 p.m. The parade starts and he is having a great time watching. An image superimposed over the parade shows a clockwork, ticking, then the clockface. It is 1:20.

After the parade passes, the crowd disperses. Stevie can barely get through, but he manages to board a bus. The conductor challenges him, notes that he is carrying two film cans: "You can't ride the bus, film is flammable," but Stevie persuades him to let him ride. He sits down next to a lady with a small dog. A glance at a clock on the street: it is 1:35. He is running late.

Then, there is a close-up of the package on the seat next to him. Stevie plays with the dog. The music becomes more intense. The bus stops to let pedestrians cross. Stevie checks that his packages are safely next to him on the seat. We see backed-up traffic—it is a busy time in the city. Stevie is worried about how late he is. He keeps on turning to look at the clocks on the street. Meanwhile the music resumes its tick-tock cadence, but faster.

Another close-up of the package. Then another clock. It is now 1:44. Back to the package.

The boy pets the little puppy. The light changes, the music ticks, and Stevie rests his arm on the packages, to keep them close. Another clock, another look at the package. It is now 1:45. The music moves faster and faster.

The light changes, the bus begins to move, we see, close-up, the clock ticks to 1:46. A quick cut to the package. Then a big explosion destroys the bus. The boy, the puppy, and everyone on the bus are killed.

This is the iconic moment in *Sabotage* (1936). Early Hitchcock, it defines what he does best. Stevie's otherwise ordinary journey across London has us on the edge of our seat, as we are reminded again and again of the bomb, set to go off at 1:45. There is a moment of relief when at 1:45, nothing happens. But then, at 1:46 it explodes. This is a surprise. Until this film, movie tradition did not allow you to kill off an innocent child, much less a puppy. And we were prepared for 1:45, not a minute later. That is Hitchcock playing with us, setting up a moment of relief, before undoing it.

Suspense happens when we know the danger, and the protagonist does not. Or if he or she does, the suspense is about how that danger will be resolved. Very different from surprise or shock: when something sudden happens out of the blue, with no warning. In this case, Hitchcock manages both in one five-minute sequence.

We all know what suspense feels like, that sitting-on-the-edge-of-your-seat sensation, watching some action that may go very wrong at any moment. It creates an intensity of feeling and identification with the protagonist that many people seek out in movies and others try to avoid as too anxiety-provoking. It is essential to action-adventure movies, thrillers, horror, and heist films.

There will be plenty of suspense in the action thrillers we discuss in the next chapter. Here, we will focus on slow-burn suspense, the tension of waiting for something to happen or of the slowly revealed threat.

How does it work? What do these films do to make us so invested in what will happen next?

Alfred Hitchcock, known as "The Master of Suspense," has often answered the question this way: "Two people are sitting at a table chatting about baseball, women, the state of the world. It is simple and boring. But, if the camera shifts to look under the table and we see a bomb there, and there is a close-up of a ticking timer . . . the bomb is set to go off . . . then that conversation takes on a very different tone. We listen but are aware of something that they are not . . . they are in danger. We are in suspense until something happens: either the bomb goes off killing them, or someone notices it and reacts to defuse the danger."[1]

That kind of suspense is the slow burn. It is what Hitchcock did in *Sabotage*. A situation is set, something dangerous that the protagonist doesn't know but that we do, and we anxiously watch to see what happens. It increases our investment in the situation and our emotional connection to the character. What will it take for him to find out about the danger, and what will he do? How will the danger play out?

The film has created apprehension and anxiety in the audience and increased alertness to details and the action. There needs to be a payoff. Something active and dramatic must happen to resolve the suspense . . . or increase it.

The Birds (1963)

Alfred Hitchcock's film *The Birds* is another brilliant example of slow-burn suspense. Tippi Hedren is Melanie. She has met Mitch awkwardly in a pet shop in San Francisco and, taking a shine to him, she is bringing him a pair of lovebirds as an apology. She is on a boat heading to the town dock in Bodega Bay north of the city, where he is visiting his mother and young sister. Suddenly, a seagull swoops down on her head, drawing blood. This is not suspense; this is a shock or surprise when danger happens suddenly and without warning (the horror monster pouncing from a closet). This odd attack sets up the story.

Birds are behaving strangely. More strange things happen. Sparrows swoop into the house down a chimney; a man is found dead with his eyes pecked out by birds. Melanie and Mitch are increasingly concerned and decide to take his sister out of school.

Melanie goes to pick her up. When she arrives at the schoolyard, she sits down to wait. We hear children singing in the school. The camera shows us one bird, a black crow, flying past behind her and landing on the jungle gym in the playground. Melanie doesn't notice. In a medium shot, she lights a cigarette. Then the camera shows us three crows sitting on the jungle gym. Close-up again of her smoking, oblivious to what is happening behind her. We, in the audience, are aware that something is brewing, that there is a figurative "bomb" under the table, but the main character has no idea. Unlike the bomb, we don't yet know the nature of the danger, or how bad

Figure 8.1 Birds quietly, ominously, gather at the school jungle gym. *The Birds* © Universal Pictures. Screenshot captured by the authors.

it will be, but that unknown only increases the suspense. Next, we get to see that twice as many birds are sitting there. Then there is another close-up of her impatiently waiting and smoking and we have another glance at the playground—more birds have gathered. She still has no idea. Hitchcock stretches this out, the birds gathering behind her, silent and unseen.

Now, we have a longer close-up, she is more impatient, still waiting. She finally notices a crow flying high in the air and turns, following its path. For

Figure 8.2 And then the attack. Tippi Hedren. *The Birds* © Universal Pictures. Screenshot captured by the authors.

the first time she sees the jungle gym and it is teeming with crows. She rises slowly in alarm and begins to walk toward the school, watching the sitting birds. She warns the teacher, who instructs all the children to leave quietly and run when she tells them. We see the birds again, barely stirring, and then suddenly they swarm and begin to chase the children, who are now running screaming as they are attacked.

This is quiet, gathering suspense. Then, a payoff: the attack, which amps up the intensity because now we are seeing violence, which had only been threatened before.

One of the most famous suspense scenes in movie history is from Orson Welles's *Touch of Evil* (1958). It opens with a close-up of a man placing a bomb underneath a car in a Mexican border town. In a tour de force three-minute-long crane shot we watch the car drive through town. As it turns left the camera begins to follow a man and woman walking, our protagonists, Mike Vargas, a Mexican police detective (Charlton Heston), and Susan, his new American wife (Janet Leigh). The car stops at the border crossing, and is given the okay to go, even as the woman in the car complains, "I'm hearing a ticking noise in my head." The camera finds the walking couple again, they stop to kiss, and are startled by the noise of an explosion. Now comes the first cut of the movie: we see the car on fire, destroyed.

Here we are given some information right away: there is a bomb under a car. We have no idea why the bomb was placed, or who the people are in the car. That lack of information can create suspense too, encouraging us to imagine the reasons. Meanwhile we are no longer passively watching. We become active participants in the story, thinking "When will they discover the bomb, will they be able to stop it from exploding, why don't they do something!"

A different sort of situation has the hero doing something dangerous that may go wrong at any moment, like Mel Gibson as Riggs disarming a bomb in *Lethal Weapon 3* (1992), a situation which is both suspenseful and funny, or Tom Cruise climbing the outside of a skyscraper in *Mission Impossible: Ghost Protocol* (2011). We watch as a dangerous situation gets worse when the unexpected happens, cranking up the suspense. In *Ghost Protocol*, a climbing glove device stops working; in *Lethal Weapon*, Riggs isn't sure whether to cut the red wire or the blue. This is played for laughs, but it is also nerve-racking. We and the hero are equally aware of the risks, we are all in suspense, until the danger is neutralized, or the job is done.

Steven Spielberg is another master at creating suspense, in such popular films as *Jaws* (1975), *Jurassic Park* (1993), and *Raiders of the Lost Ark* (1981). Often his suspense is quietly suggested, waiting for something intense to happen. In *Jaws*, Quint (Robert Shaw), the experienced sailor, is in search of the great white shark that has been attacking swimmers off a resort island. He is in a boat with the police chief of the town and a marine scientist. Quint sees his heavy-duty deep-sea fishing line lightly tugged in the water. A close-up shows him carefully watching as the line tightens. There is a cut to the police chief, unaware, practicing knot tying. Cutaways like this lengthen the moment, adding to our suspense: is this the shark? What will happen next? Why doesn't the chief notice anything?

The lack of certainty about what is happening and what is about to happen adds to the suspense. We see Quint quietly put on his shoulder belts, and then lift the heavy fishing rod from its mount and position it for action. Then, in a close-up of his hands, he slowly clips himself to the reel and positions his feet, readying for a fight with a big fish. These details tell us that Quint knows what he is up against, even if we in the audience (and the police chief playing with knots) don't. Then, there is another shot of the fishing line, with bubbles in the water. Something is coming to the surface. Not a word was spoken. Nothing very dramatic has happened yet, but we are again on the edge of our seats, anticipating the battle to come.

There are so many other ways for a film to generate suspense. A shot where something is happening in the background behind the protagonist (with increased depth of field), something he doesn't see but we can, that may be a threat, or may just be something we don't quite understand because we haven't been given enough information. Long traveling shots, following the hero closely, increase a sense of danger: what might be happening just behind him, or around the corner? Increasingly intense music, or repetitive sounds like the tick-tocking of the soundtrack in *Sabotage* can create suspense, letting us know that danger is lurking. A sudden silence or attention to the diegetic sounds of where the hero is (street sounds, footsteps, someone talking indistinctly, a radio suddenly being turned off) can increase our sense of dread. Watching your character trying to decide what to do next, especially if we have some information he does not yet know. Sometimes the director will play with us, showing the character something that we are not privy to: she looks at a photo or reads a note and reacts in shock, but at that moment the film does not let us see it. Again, we are in suspense, waiting for the reveal that will allow us to breathe again.

The Wages of Fear (1953)

This is one of the most suspenseful films ever made. Directed by Henri-Georges Clouzot, who is sometimes called the "French Hitchcock." Clouzot also directed *Les diaboliques* (1955), a murder tale with a shocking moment that Hitchcock so admired, and envied, that it inspired him to try to top it with *Psycho* (also because he had bid on the novel it was based on and was upset at losing it to Clouzot, who then made such an effectively terrifying film).

The Wages of Fear stars Yves Montand and Charles Vanel. Montand was then famous as a singer. This was his first film. He later starred in the conspiracy thriller *Z* (1969), the heist film *Le cercle rouge* (1970), and *Jean de Florette* (1986) based on a famous novel by Marcel Pagnol. Vanel was an old hand and had a long career, appearing in more than two hundred films, including *Les diaboliques* and Hitchcock's *To Catch a Thief* (1955). *The Wages of Fear* won Best Picture at Cannes and in Berlin and was a big hit internationally, in a time when foreign language films were rarely a success outside their home country.

A remote South American village is a dead-end for many workers of an American-owned oil field. There are no more jobs, the roads go nowhere, and none of the workers has enough money to fly out. When there is an out-of-control fire at one of the rigs, the only way to stop it is to explode it with

Figure 8.3 Yves Montand. *Wages of Fear* © Distributors Corporation of America (DCA). Screenshot captured by the authors.

nitroglycerin (liquid dynamite). Four desperate men are offered big money to drive two trucks to bring jerrycans of nitroglycerin three hundred miles to the site. However, the road through the jungle is rough, nitroglycerin is highly unstable, and the slightest vibration could cause it to explode. It is a suicide mission.

The two trucks are kept thirty minutes apart so if one explodes the other can go on. The journey is nerve-racking, the heat is overwhelming, and rivalries among the drivers fester. The trucks never go faster than six miles an hour (a walking pace) and for minutes at a time, there is no dialogue as they deal with one hazard after another. There is a stretch of very rough road called "the washboard," a rotting bridge that threatens to collapse, a boulder blocking their way. This is slow-burning suspense that never lets go; and then there is an explosion. There is much more to tell but we are avoiding spoilers. If you want to see what happens and how suspense is done by a master, watch this movie.

The Heist Film

For a healthy dose of suspense without the hectic action and violence of most thrillers, nothing beats a heist film. These films about planning a robbery or a scam have a form and pace that defines and distinguishes them. The intensity comes from watching the plan unfold but not knowing exactly what comes next, and whether it will work, with the possibility of something unexpected undoing it, of the predictable (because it always seems to happen in these films) wild-card member of the gang making a mistake or changing his mind, or deciding he is being double-crossed, or planning a double-cross himself.

In these films, something of value will be stolen, often from a villain who got it by devious means in the first place, so there is the pleasure of guilt-free schadenfreude (joy at another person's failure) in watching the bad guy be duped or undone. For the bad guy, the stakes are money and reputation. For the protagonists pulling off the heist, the stakes are often personal, for revenge or to right a perceived wrong, or because they are on the skids and need money quickly.

Or it might be simply for the challenge of pulling off the deed, which can make the film more of a comic caper. *Gambit* (1966), with Michael Caine and Shirley MacLaine, is a caper film worth seeking out. Caine is Harry Dean, planning a con and a heist. He needs a woman who looks like the deceased wife of Shahbandar (Herbert Lom), a recluse and "the richest man in the world." MacLaine is Nicole, the woman whom he meets in a Hong Kong dance hall.

Nicole is dressed to remind him of his wife and, as they hoped, Shahbandar invites the couple for dinner. Harry takes the opportunity to scope out the apartment and the prize, a valuable ancient Chinese bust. He steals it and gets away with the loot. So, where's the suspense? For the first thirty minutes of the movie, Nicole does not say a word. We discover that what we are watching is Harry explaining this perfect heist to his colleague before he has even approached Nicole. Once he does, the movie gets into gear, because nothing he has predicted happens the way he expects: Nicole has a mind of her own, and the "mark" is not the recluse he appears to be; he is smart, modern, and immediately suspicious. There is real suspense as one thing after another goes wrong, and a satisfyingly funny plot twist at the end. There is a rom-com angle, too. This is lighthearted thievery at its best.

Every heist film starts with something to be stolen (jewels, money, gold bullion) and a plan to steal it. Often the security system seems impregnable and the theft impossible. Which challenge makes it seem even more desirable.

We are introduced to the mastermind who has the plan: to avenge a double-cross, *The Italian Job* (2003), or to steal a treasured work of art because he can, *The Thomas Crown Affair* (1999), or a few million from a bank he works at, *The Thomas Crown Affair* (1968), or a London bank of a million pounds cash delivery, *The League of Gentlemen* (1960), or a hoard of cash from three Las Vegas casinos, *Ocean's Eleven* (1960 and 2001), or the jewels from a jewelry store safe, *The Asphalt Jungle* (1950) and *Rififi* (1956).

The mastermind then gathers a gang, each member has a special skill and a reason to want or need to commit the crime. In *The League of Gentlemen*, ex-army men with a grudge are having a hard time adjusting to peacetime. In *Topkapi*, with a plan to steal a jeweled dagger from the Istanbul Palace museum, the gang includes a sexy con woman, a driver, a mechanical expert, a strongman, and an acrobat. These experts are the equivalent of the gadgets James Bond gets from Q in every Bond film, tools that conveniently provide exactly the function he later needs in his latest adventure. The experts will offer a distraction, the muscle, the driving skills, the sophisticated knowledge to disable the computer system or confound an alarm, and the ability to open or blow up a safe.

There will be at least one scene in which the mastermind walks the team through the details of the plan, which we in the audience may or may not see all of. If not, what we don't know of the plan will likely add to the suspense when they confront what seems to be an insurmountable problem. Or if we do know all the details that sets us up for an intense reaction when something unpredictable happens: the entry code was changed at the last minute, a guard stops to flirt with a woman colleague, putting his rounds off-schedule, the safe explosion is too strong and sets off alarms (or is too weak and doesn't open the safe).

We then watch them prepare. Perhaps they need special equipment, which they organize to steal or "borrow" from an unsuspecting source.

The high point of each of these films is the heist itself. In *Rififi*, a 1956 French film with a gritty underbelly, there is a sequence that sets the standard for every heist film that came after. For thirty minutes, with no dialogue, we watch every step as the crew breaks into the jewelry store safe from the apartment above. All we hear are the sounds in the room or from the street outside. It feels like it's in real time and it is very suspenseful.

Topkapi mimics it but ups the ante with the theft of a jeweled dagger from the Istanbul Palace Museum. The floor of the museum is sensitive to pressure so that, after hours, once the alarm is set, any contact would set it off. We watch the gang secretly climb to the roof of the museum, open a window, and lower the acrobat on a rope, inch by inch, toward the case holding the dagger. Controlling the rope is difficult and several times he almost touches the floor.

This dangling idea is both clever and memorable and has been copied frequently. In the first *Mission Impossible* (1996), Tom Cruise is slowly lowered into a computer room so he can download the codes they need for their theft. He too cannot touch the floor without setting off an alarm. There is a moment when the strong man holding the rope almost lets go when a rat comes too close and another when the sweat from Cruise's brow threatens to drop, and he catches it at the last moment (unlikely, but it works to up the suspense). In *Ocean's Eleven*, the floor of the safe is also touch-sensitive. The solution there is less interesting: the acrobat is delivered to the safe inside a box. When he climbs out, he jumps to a high shelf and helps open the safe from the inside, never touching the floor.

Very often one of the gang gets injured, the explosion goes wrong, or one of them gets shot by the police. The cliché is that the gang member most likely to die during this caper is the most sympathetic: he has a family or a sick mother, or he's old and this was to be his "last job." Most of these films end with the gang turning on each other, or getting caught, often because of one slipup. In *Rififi*, the safecracker César pockets one of the jewels for his girlfriend. That is enough for things to go wrong. With *The Asphalt Jungle*, from the beginning you know things will go badly, and they do. Not only do two members of the group get shot (one by a policeman who interrupts the robbery, the other, after the heist, by one of the gang trying to take all the money), but the mastermind gets caught too, when, on the run, he lingers too long watching a nubile teenage girl dance to a jukebox in a diner. It is the fatalism of film noir.

Capers

When these films are capers, as opposed to heists, there is usually little sense of danger. *Ocean's Eleven*, the remake from 2001 with George Clooney, Brad Pitt, and a gaggle of other big-name stars, was a big hit when it came out and remains popular. But the film is a bit of a con itself, pretending to be a heist film but getting by on cool charm, a flashy Las Vegas setting, and a clever director (Steven Soderbergh). It points to the standard beats of a heist film but then cheats on every one of them.

Gathering the gang, each member has a special skill (and each in a different city, channeling the global travel chops of a Bond film), Clooney is Danny Ocean, just out of prison and ready for a score (with the added not-so-hidden agenda of wooing back his ex-wife, played by Julia Roberts). He describes the plan: robbing three casinos in one night by getting into the hyper-secure safe they all use for their cash. Danny makes it clear that this is impossible to pull off—with an underground safe, high-tech security, passcodes, guards with Uzis, and the cash too bulky to carry away. For each impossibility, he simply says we will deal with it, nodding to one of the experts, and the gang accepts that.

When it comes time to see the actual heist, every obstacle is easily overcome but we never see how, or if we do see something that might explain it, it is either too conveniently easy to be interesting or too ludicrously over the top to be believed (yes, heist films, especially those presented as capers like this is one, require some suspension of disbelief, but this film stretches it). For instance, the explosives guy, played by Don Cheadle (with the least convincing cockney accent since Dick Van Dyke in *Mary Poppins*), reports a problem with cutting off electric power long enough to get by the laser-light barriers to the safe. His solution? Steal a mini nuclear reactor (which they manage ridiculously easily) and blow out all the power in Las Vegas with its magnetic pulse. Really?

At no time is there even a trace of suspense. The bad guy casino owner acts exactly as predicted and never confounds their plan. Even when something goes wrong, it is immediately fixed, and nothing serious or unexpected ever happens. With no real sense of risk, and the details of the heist all smoke and mirrors, there is no narrative tension, nothing at stake.

And yet, the movie is entertaining. We are in the company of charismatic, charming leads, with some veteran actors like Elliot Gould and Carl Reiner getting late-career opportunities to steal scenes, some funny bits of dialogue, and the Las Vegas setting. Somehow it works. But it is no heist film.

The Italian Job (2003)

This is a heist film that gets it right. A remake with Mark Wahlberg, Charlize Theron, Edward Norton, and Donald Sutherland of the 1969 movie of the same name (which starred Michael Caine and Noel Coward), it significantly altered the original, which has not aged well (it comes across now as slow, and not as clever or funny as it seemed fifty years ago). The best thing about the Caine version is the cliffhanger at the end, which is one of a kind, and still really works.

The only thing the 2003 *Italian Job* has in common with its namesake is a trio of small cars (Fiats in 1969, Mini Coopers here), controlling traffic by hacking a computer, and the prize: a pile of gold bullion. Otherwise, this is a very different film, and much better than the original.

It begins in Venice, Italy, in the middle of a caper. John, played by Donald Sutherland, calls his daughter Stella to tell her he has just sent her a present: "It sparkles."

She is immediately worried, "Do you have a receipt?"

When she hears he is in Venice, she asks if Charlie is there. John is a career thief. "I promise I'm done after this," he tells her. He is having fun, putting young Charlie, his protégé, in charge of things. In just a few lines we see his devotion to his daughter and to Charlie. These are people we like.

We meet members of the heist gang, bantering with each other. Then, we are in a grand villa on the Grand Canal. The computer expert guides careful placement of two painted squares on the floors of two rooms, one above the other. In the top room, we see gangsters watching TV and polishing their guns. There is a safe in the room. Suddenly, there is an explosion, and the safe drops through the holes, two floors into the boathouse basement below.

The team drives a speedboat out into the canal. The gangsters immediately go after them. Suddenly, we are watching a terrifically staged speedboat chase through the canals of Venice. But then we cut away and see other team members underwater in that basement, wearing scuba gear. John is carefully opening the safe. The speeding boat was a diversion, the safe was never on the boat; it had dropped directly into the water. We cut back and forth between the racing boats and the slow opening of the safe. The different paces balance each other. The safe is full of gold bars, worth millions. The race is exciting, and the underwater sequence is suspenseful. Will they load the bullion before the police arrive?

Then we see the gang driving a van across the border into Austria and pausing in the mountains to celebrate. John credits Charlie with their success. The team tells each other how they imagine spending their winnings, and we get to know them. Left Ear, the explosives expert wants to buy a house in Spain and fill it with rare books; Handsome Rob, the driver, plans to buy an Aston Martin to impress girls; Napster, the computer nerd, wants a top-of-the-line speaker loud enough to "blow women's clothes off"; and Steve doesn't want to play this game and says he hasn't decided.

John takes Charlie aside to tell him how he regrets not being a better father to Stella. He has spent too much time traveling the world stealing and too much time in prison. He cautions Charlie, who he treats like a son, not to do the same, "Find someone you want to spend your life with and make it happen. I love you, kid. You did really great."

This heart-to-heart conversation, a pause after the excitement of the opening, convinced this viewer that John was not long for this world. This is a frequent trope of thrillers: the old-timer, ready to retire or make a change in his life, is likely the one who gets killed. Whether it is a surprise because you don't expect it, or something you suspect will happen, it can be gratifying if it is done well. And it is done very well here.

Steve, played with just the right degree of sneer by Edward Norton, has his plans. Suddenly the gang is surrounded on a bridge, guns fire, John is indeed killed, the gold is removed from the van, and Rob tries to drive away but the van goes off the bridge into the water. Steve viciously fires into the water to be sure they are all dead and drives off. But only John is dead, with Charlie tearfully mourning his friend.

It's a year later, and we meet John's beautiful daughter Stella breaking into a safe. She is played smartly by Charlize Theron. We are shown each step until the safe opens. It turns out she does this legitimately, opening safes for the law. For her, most of them are easy. She loves to drive fast and she drives a Mini Cooper.

Charlie approaches her to join him and his gang to take revenge on Steve, and get back the gold. They have located him living in Los Angeles. She is reluctant, but Stella agrees to help to avenge her father's death.

As in most heist films, they each have a specialty, which we saw in the Venice job. Handsome Rob is the driver and mechanic, his moment of glory was setting the record for the longest freeway chase; Left Ear, the explosives guy, has been blowing things up since tenth grade; the computer genius Lyle is called Napster because he claims his college roommate stole his idea for the groundbreaking and lawbreaking music sharing site of the late 1990s. Stella is the safecracker.

Then the film goes into high gear, the reason we love heist films. Charlie outlines the plan, how they will steal the gold, and, most importantly, how they will get away. Timing is everything. We see them timing the drive from Steve's house to the train station. We see Napster checking out his security system, Left Ear reporting about the wire fence, an armed guard at the gate, and two guard dogs, telling them how he would deal with each. The traffic looks like it might defeat Rob, but Napster offers to try to hack the computers that control the traffic lights. We watch step-by-step as they interrupt Steve's cable signal and then organize for Stella to pretend to be the repair person, so she can get a picture of the location of the safe in his house.

Napster gets the dimensions of the house. How will they get all that heavy gold out of the house quickly enough? He measures the width of the hallway, and Stella has an idea. A Mini Cooper could fit. They test it, with her driving with weights in the car on a mock-up of the route inside the house. They will need three Minis. They find Wrench, a skilled mechanic, to remove extra weight from the cars and soup them up to outrun anyone chasing them, even though loaded with the weight of the gold bars.

Then there is a montage of each expert working on his part of the scheme. Napster is trying to get computer control of the traffic system and then testing it by changing lights from red to green, and causing a few minor crashes. Left Ear trying out explosives to blow the gate. Wrench working on the car suspensions and engines. Then there is a sequence of the three Mini Coopers driving fast, testing the new engines on the famous dry Los Angeles River Culvert, the scene of many movie chases (including *Grease*, *Chinatown*, and *Terminator 2*).

No more spoilers. Things don't go according to plan and Steve finds out

Figure 8.4 When a remake is better than the original. *The Italian Job* © Paramount Pictures. Screenshot captured by the authors.

they are alive and after his gold. When they discover he is running to Mexico with his gold, Charlie realizes they can grab the safe in transit. They have to come up with a new plan, but their preparations give them the tools to figure it out. They will use the "Italian Job" as a template. You will need to see what happens. But we will again get to see the detailed steps of the plan, which is smart and exciting, with a couple of final twists that are completely satisfying. This is best of breed, and one very entertaining movie.

Heists are hybrids: they are suspense films dotted with action. In a later chapter, we'll look at movies with action at the fore, sometimes with all other aspects thrown to the wind.

Chapter 9
Horror

Key Films

Cat People (1942)
Halloween (1978)
The Babadook (2014)

In Michael Powell's masterful *Peeping Tom* (1960), a gothic horror psychological thriller, the pathetic Mark Lewis is obsessed with the study of fear. He is a serial killer who forces his victims to watch their own deaths. "Do you know what is the most frightening thing in the world?" he asks. "It's fear." This may not be a universal truth, but it is certainly true that, like Mark, we in the audience viewing a horror film, in the comfort of the dark and the company of other watchers, enjoy seeing the fear of those about to be killed. And we like sharing our fright: seeing a horror film with others in a darkened auditorium is much more exciting, and finally satisfying, than watching it alone in our living rooms.

There have been many theories, and psychological studies, that try to define "horror" and explain our fascination with it. Their observations are often interesting but none of them is entirely convincing, neither for the general public nor psychiatrists, who spend their days considering the machinations of the human mind. We all indeed share some basic primitive fears that are likely hard-wired through evolution: fear of the dark, of what can't be seen, fear of creatures with sharp teeth, or crawly things like snakes, rats, or spiders, of thunder and lightning and, especially, the fear of death.

In his essay *"das Unheimliche"* (The Uncanny), Sigmund Freud suggested that horror comes from the **uncanny**. This describes situations that touch our nightmares, things that seem ordinary, but aren't quite, the familiar altered just enough to be scary. Freud said these sensations occur "either when infantile complexes which have been repressed are once more revived by some impression, or when primitive beliefs which have been surmounted seem once more to be confirmed." Think of *Frankenstein* (1931), with the Monster made up of body parts, looking human, but not quite; or *The Invasion of the Body Snatchers* (with two excellent versions from 1956 and

1978), in which alien pods placed next to a sleeping person replace them with emotionless look-alikes. In a more recent trend, there are zombies, who seem human, even ordinary, except that they walk with a strange lumbering gait (or are, in some films, unnervingly fast) arms outstretched, with dead eyes. Just different enough to be "uncanny." Of course, they want to kill and eat human flesh, so zombies cross the line from uncanny to the demonic. Ghosts are also uncanny, human-like but without a body.

A doll, a child, a snowman—all with murderous intent are uncanny. In *The Babadook*, the monster becomes the mother (or the mother is the monster; either way it's terrifying). The boy's mother uncannily becomes an extension of the Babadook, someone the child becomes afraid of even as he turns to her for safety. In Wes Craven's *A Nightmare on Elm Street* (1984), Freddy Krueger uncannily escapes from nightmares and kills with his claw-like knives. The Babadook has an elongated body and similar knifelike fingers; he is quite scary, but not as scary as when he becomes the mother.

This hiding of identity adds to the sense of the uncanny. Many of the monsters in slasher films (in which a killer stalks a series of victims, usually killing them with a sharp weapon) wear masks—ordinary or grotesque, these masks hide the creature behind them and are all the more frightening because of that. Michael Myers in John Carpenter's *Halloween* (1978) is a famous example, and there are many more: Leatherface in *The Texas Chainsaw Massacre* (1974), Jason in *Friday the 13th* (1980), and Ghostface in *Scream* (1996).

The monsters in horror films can change with the anxieties of the era in which they are made. In the 1950s, with the Cold War and the threat of mutual annihilation by the hydrogen bomb, monsters were the result of nuclear accidents (for instance, giant ants in *Them!* (1954), one of the best horror films from that era, or *The Creature from the Black Lagoon* (1954), one of the worst), or they reflected the terrors of the "organization man," as people became concerned about the dangers of conformity (*Invasion of the Body Snatchers*). *Body Snatchers* also played on the uncanny—are these really the people in my life? They seem not quite right. In the 1970s, when baby boomers' children were entering adolescence and beginning to challenge their parents, slasher films put teenagers in their place, making them the victims. And in the 2000s, with Ebola and other viral pandemic fears, zombies stumbled ravenously into our movie palaces.

When we are children, we are prone to nightmares. Our worlds are less clearly delineated between the real and fantasy. Children learn through play and pretending, and play encourages fantasy and imagination, which children learn to separate from the real world they are just beginning to understand. Even as adults, it is sometimes hard to be sure that something we dreamed so vividly didn't happen. This is part of ordinary development, but it's not well understood neurologically. Some children even have night terrors—a form of nightmare that doesn't want to "turn off" when you wake up. Again, these are not well understood and they usually fade as we become adults. But the sense of the fantastic that is part of most dreams, and of many nightmares, stays with us—and it can be tapped by the better horror films. This is why we suspend disbelief when confronted with the impossible in these films: the creatures that fly, that jump out of dark corners, that change shape before our eyes.

One of the most terrifying images is from the original Bela Lugosi film *Dracula* (1931). *Dracula* is a black-and-white classic, very old-fashioned and rather corny now, but it defined Dracula for generations. When Bela Lugosi first walks down the massive castle stairs, enveloped in a black cape, and declares in that wonderful middle European accent, "I am Count Dracula," you know you are in for it. The spookiest moment was a later glance out the castle window: we see the Count crawling down the outside face of the castle—headfirst. Talk about uncanny!

Many movie moments can invoke that disturbing feeling: the young girl Regan in *The Exorcist* (1973), possessed by the devil, contorting herself backward to crawl headfirst, spiderlike, down the stairs, and later slowly turning her head around, 360 degrees; the ghost girl in *Ringu* (*Ring*, Japan, 1998) her face hidden by her hair; the moment Hugo, the ventriloquist dummy in *Dead of Night* (British, 1945) begins to talk on his own, and the final scene when Maxwell Frere, the ventriloquist, transforms into Hugo; and several moments in *Repulsion* (1965), when the rooms in Carol's apartment begin to change shape, becoming larger, the bathroom becoming a jungle dripping with vines, and, in the hallway, hands reaching out from the walls to grope her.

In horror films, we can relive these nightmares, knowing now that they are not real. Not just that they are fantastic and could never happen, but that they are not happening to *us*. We can experience a fright vicariously: it's happening to someone else, and that someone is not real. To the extent that we identify with a character, we may fear for them, and experience the fear as our own. The better the film and the more we identify with a character, the more intense our fear. But then the film ends, the monster is vanquished, and we are relieved. The lead character may live or die, but we are okay. Meanwhile, we have had an adrenaline rush, an excitement of the sort that is lacking in our ordinary life.

The better horror films give moments of pleasure throughout—not just when they are over. Some of those pleasures are social. In the slasher films that followed *Halloween* and the first *A Nightmare on Elm Street*, there is an almost Victorian morality at work. The teenagers who have sex are guaranteed to be victims—they are getting what they "deserve" for behaving badly. Mathias Clasen (a literature scholar at Aarhus University) notes that in zombie monster films (and TV shows like *The Walking Dead* [2010]), "the zombies drastically reduce the moral complexity of life. They are unequivocally bad, they need to be killed . . . there is no moral shade of gray." These films appeal to people who have little tolerance for ambiguity—it's clear in these films who the bad guy is, and who deserves to die.

Brain studies show that when we are watching a horror film, the amygdala, the part of the brain that responds to fear and danger, is *not* the most stimulated. Instead, the thalamus and the prefrontal cortex go into overdrive—these are the parts of the brain associated with attention and problem-solving. What we actually may be doing when we watch these films is rehearsing how we might respond in such a dangerous situation—and comparing our response to what happens in the film. Would we go into that dark room without a weapon to protect ourselves—and without putting on the light? Imagined practice for dangers that we are reassuringly unlikely to find in our everyday lives.

Unlikely, that is, but for the one danger we all face—the existential reality of death. Horror films allow us to contemplate this with a sense of distance and control. We see fantastic versions of our fears acted on by others, and we can play with our responses and calibrate our reactions. We can see how others respond (one reason it is more fun to see these films in a group), recognize that our fears are shared, and are not alone. And we can enjoy the frisson of suspense and surprise, the delight in being alive in the moment, that the best of these films provide.

Horror Movie Beginnings

The Cabinet of Dr. Caligari (1920), which we discussed in the chapter on silent movies, was the fever dream of a psychotic, imagining that his doctor was a serial killer. The stylized, odd-angled sets, meant to look artificial, conveyed that this was a cock-eyed worldview. They also made the film feel uncanny and frightening. The German film *Nosferatu* (1922) has the same sensibility, this time telling the story of a vampire, with a plot borrowed from the nineteenth-century novel, *Dracula*. The image of the monster in the recent horror movie *The Babadook* is directly borrowed from this film.

The Phantom of the Opera (1925), starring Lon Chaney, created an uproar when it first premiered. Chaney was famous as "The Man with a Thousand Faces" and the makeup he devised for the Phantom caused women to faint and people to scream in fright when his mask was removed. This is both a horror film and a love story and it holds up well. The Phantom lures the woman he loves, Christine, into his darkly gothic home beneath the opera house, down a labyrinth of stairs leading to an underground lake. There is a scene at a costume ball in Technicolor (a new technology at the time) with the Phantom looking terrifying, dressed as the Red Death.

When sound came in, Universal, which was a minor studio, made a success with *Frankenstein* (1931), directed by James Whale and based on the gothic novel by Mary Shelley. It is the story of a scientist intent on creating life using body parts from the dead. A crashing thunder and lightning storm, a laboratory in an ancient tower crackling with electric sparks (which became the template for evil genius lairs to come), the Monster being raised on a platform to the open roof so that lightning could activate him, and Colin Clive as Henry Frankenstein hysterically crying out, "It's alive," as his creation begins to move, asks the question: is this genius or madness? The Monster, with makeup designed by Jack Pierce, was played by Boris Karloff, which started Karloff's long career in horror films.

Karloff's appearance in the movie is quite different from how the Monster is described in the book, but the look became famous: bolts in his neck, a broad forehead, stitches on his face, a lumbering gait. He is both terrible and terribly sympathetic; an innocent in this world, too easily becoming violent if angered or scared. An iconic scene has the Monster wordlessly meeting a little girl by a pond. She is not frightened by his appearance and asks him to play a game, tossing flower petals into the pond. He likes this game, but when he runs out of petals, not understanding, he tosses the girl into the pond and she drowns. Soon the whole village is after him, a torch-carrying mob, trapping him and Henry in an old mill and setting it on fire. Henry is rescued, as the building collapses over the Monster. The movie was a big hit and inspired the even better sequel, *Bride of Frankenstein*, also directed by Whale, in a rare example of the sequel outdoing the original.

Bride of Frankenstein (1935)

We first see Mary Shelley (Elsa Lancaster) explaining to her husband, Percy Bysshe Shelley, and their friend, Lord Byron, that the story she wrote had a moral message: warning against any man who tries to play God. Then the scene shifts.

Picking up right where the first movie ended, we discover that the Monster survived the fire. Henry Frankenstein visits the laboratory of his old teacher, Dr. Pretorius (Ernest Thesiger), and sees the miniature people he has created, who he keeps in bottles. Pretorius offers to make an artificial brain if Henry agrees to make a new body and create a mate for the Monster. Henry refuses.

Figure 9.1 The lady says no. Elsa Lanchester, Boris Karloff. *Bride of Frankenstein* © Universal Pictures. Screenshot captured by the authors.

That night the Monster hears a violin playing "Ave Maria," and encounters a blind hermit in the woods, who invites him into his cottage and teaches him the words "friend" and "good." When hunters come upon the cottage, they recognize the Monster and try to kill him. He chases them away, taking the hermit with them, and he accidentally sets the cottage on fire. Later, the Monster spies Pretorius removing bodies from a grave. Pretorius greets him and tells him that he is making him a mate.

The Monster tells Henry that he wants him to help create the mate, a "friend," and Henry reluctantly agrees, growing excited as the Bride nears completion. She, too, is raised to the roof to be activated by lightning. When the Monster comes down the stairs to the laboratory and sees her (Elsa Lancaster again, with her iconic lightning-struck hairdo) he reaches out and asks, "Friend?" She screams at the sight of him. He goes berserk, destroying the laboratory equipment and threatening them all. He looks at Henry and his wife Elizabeth and says, "You live. Go!" He insists that Pretorius and the Bride stay. "We belong dead." The Bride hisses at him and the Monster, tearful, pulls a lever that destroys the laboratory and the tower.

Thus, we have the Monster as an inarticulate brute who is touchingly sympathetic, trying to find his place in the world, and looking for a "friend." This was the mold for several Universal horror monsters, from the silent *Phantom of the Opera* to *The Hunchback of Notre Dame* (1923), also starring Lon Chaney, and *The Wolfman* (1941), played by Lon Chaney Jr.

Other monsters from that studio are not so sympathetic: *Dracula* (1931), starring Bela Legosi, is reptilian in his cold aristocratic manner and pure evil; *The Invisible Man* (1933), played by Claude Rains, who would later play Captain Renault in *Casablanca*, is a nasty piece of work, diabolically enjoying the power invisibility gives him. These films hold up remarkably well, considering how long ago they were made. The sets, the cinematography, the writing, and the performances may show their age, but they were state of the art in the 1930s, bringing a sense of humanity to even the most extreme characters.

Val Lewton and the Power of Suggestion: *Cat People* (1942)

Then there are the films produced by Val Lewton for RKO Pictures, another minor studio at the time. He was head of the horror film department but with the severe limitations of low budgets, contract actors (mostly unknowns), a seventy-five-minute limit, and no control over the film titles. His first horror film was *Cat People*, directed by Jacques Tourneur. It is the story of Irena (Simone Simon, a French actress whose accent conveys a sense of otherness), a woman from the Balkans who is convinced by a village legend that she is cursed: if she ever experiences an intense emotion, she will turn into a panther and attack. The story moves into the modern world—no ancient castles or horse-drawn carriages, but a city zoo, an office, and a brownstone apartment.

Supposedly, the filmmakers tried to create a panther costume with the money available, and every costume looked phony and ridiculous. So

Lewton and his director came up with an idea, an insight that has influenced every horror film since. Why not keep the monster hidden, in the shadows, suggested by glimpses barely seen, allowing the audience's imagination full rein? It unnerves you by suggestion. Since then, withholding the full view of the monster has become a horror staple. In this film, the monster is never fully seen, while in most others our view of it is withheld long into the film, to raise tension, before an ultimate reveal.

There are images of cats everywhere in this movie. When Irena enters a pet shop, the birds become agitated. When she accidentally kills the canary that her new boyfriend, Oliver, bought her, she is upset. She becomes someone we care about who does not want to do anyone harm. Later, she is afraid to be intimate with her new husband and shows her frustration by quietly clawing the couch.

She imagines that Oliver's work colleague Alice is after her husband. We see Irena follow Alice as she is walking home from work on a dark street, along a stone wall, through a tunnel. Alice hears footsteps behind her but can't see anyone. It feels like she is being followed. The footsteps stop and then begin again, and she begins to walk faster and then almost run. A wind comes up, tree branches shake, she looks behind her and sees nothing. Suddenly a bus pulls up, the opening door making a loud cat-like hiss.

The Lewton bus became the film industry term for a sudden shocking sound or action that turns out to be benign, an innocent **jump scare**. Jump scares also became a horror trope. Tension builds, we sense danger, and then—*bang*—something suddenly happens to make us jump in our seats. It has been used countless times since, but this is its origin.

Figure 9.2 The Lewton touch: claw-marks on the sofa reveal all. Simone Simon. *Cat People* © RKO Radio Pictures Inc. Screenshot captured by authors.

Alice goes to the gym for a swim in the pool. She is alone. The reflections of the water on the wall, what seems to be the shadow of a panther on the stairs and the growl of a big cat, cause Alice to scream, her scream echoing until Irena turns on the lights and asks her, "What is the matter, Alice?" These two scenes became iconic, all mood and suggestion. But there will be violence and a climax, as the psychiatrist that Irena has been seeing to help her overcome her fear of changing into a panther, comes to her house to seduce her, telling her he is not afraid of her. This turns out to be the wrong thing to say. As he tries to kiss her, suddenly we hear a cat growling, the psychiatrist backs away: there is a panther in the room, and we see in the shadow that he is mauled and killed. Though the studio was bothered by how little actual violence there was in this film, audiences were enthusiastic. The movie did so well that it saved RKO from bankruptcy.

Lewton's subsequent films, with lurid titles that he never chose, like *I Walked with a Zombie* (1943), *Leopard Man* (1943), and *The Curse of the Cat People* (1944), all contain the subtle use of shadow, sound, suggestion, and ambiguity that we experienced in *Cat People*. They are very much worth seeking out and represent important cinematic firsts.

The Conventions of Modern Horror

Mark in *Peeping Tom* may state that the most frightening thing to experience is "fear itself," but many would agree with H. P. Lovecraft (an author of horror fiction with a cult following) that the oldest, most elemental kind of fear is fear of the unknown. Horror films play on both of these ideas, and more: the supernatural, the devil, the apocalyptic, the monsters of myth such as vampires, werewolves, and ghosts, and monsters from our nightmares, blood, the grotesque, and clowns.

There are standard elements to every modern horror film that define them, with many variations.

The Setting

It might start with an old house or a hotel with a terrible history as in *Halloween* (1978) or *The Shining* (1980), or an isolated shack in the woods in *Evil Dead* (2013), or an empty highway with a group of teens on vacation in *Friday the 13th* (1980), or a family heading toward their new home (*The Shining*) or a woman hoping to start a new life with stolen money in *Psycho*

(1960). But it also might begin in a tranquil small town (*Halloween*), or a comfortable middle-class suburb (*Nightmare on Elm Street, Scream*). The more ordinary the venue, the more shocking it is when something uncanny or evil happens. The characters go someplace they shouldn't (the Bates Motel in *Psycho*), or knock on a door of a house that looks deserted, calling out, "Anyone there, is anyone at home," and discovering the terrifying response, as in *The Texas Chainsaw Massacre* (1974).

In the Shirley Jackson novel *The Haunting of Hill House* (one of the scariest books ever written), the basis for the movie *The Haunting* (1963), she describes the house as "not sane. It is an undiscovered country waiting to be explored." The house is a gothic mansion, filmed from low angles to make it seem to be hovering, ready to strike. Inside, as the heroine (Julie Harris) begins to unravel mentally, the camera tilts back and forth, a distorting mirror reflects her increasing panic, and she becomes tangled in a window curtain as though evil spirits in the house are attacking her.

There is a tradition of such haunted houses. Castle Dracula in Bela Lugosi's *Dracula* has the same ominous sense of threat, both as it is approached for the first time, and once inside the coldly cavernous rooms. When Lugosi as Dracula first descends those steps to meet his guest, his old-world greeting has the undertone of threat. This film shows its age. It is slow, and the dialogue and some of the acting are very old-fashioned. It no longer scares, but it sure works in creating a sense of dread and of the uncanny. It also established the trope of the venue for horror as one oozing foreboding darkness before anything nasty happens.

On the other hand, sometimes, the evil is not apparent at first. In *The Shining* (1980), directed by Stanley Kubrick and starring Jack Nicholson and Shelly Duvall, the family driving to the Overlook Hotel are impressed with how grand it is. It is only as their young son Danny goes riding his tricycle in the hallways, followed by a Steadicam camera placed at child level (a new device at the time this movie was made that made smooth extended tracking shots possible) that we begin to sense that there is evil in this place. Once Danny stops and sees twin girls calling out to him to "come and play with us," and then sees an image of them dead and bloodied on the floor, both he and the audience are terrified. This is one of many very scary images in this film (one of the most famous is when an elevator door opens and a cascade of blood thunders its way out of it), all confirming that this hotel is indeed haunted, that there is something evil here. There are no jump scares in this movie, just increasingly frightening occurrences until the monster is revealed to be Jack Nicholson, murderously possessed by the spirits of this hotel.

Sometimes there is a warning that something dangerous lurks. In *Friday the 13th*, the camp handyman first startles the young counselors when they arrive, and then warns them not to stay there, saying "This place is cursed." This is a false jump scare, a "Lewton bus"—we jump with surprise, but it turns out to be nothing dangerous. Of course, they don't listen (otherwise, we would have a very short film).

Camera Placement and Lighting

Tilted camera angles, mirrors, and distorted lenses increase our sense of dread, that something is "off" about this place. The house or building itself might seem to embody some sort of evil, in *The Haunting*, *The Conjuring* (2013), *The Shining*, or, as in Roman Polanski's *Repulsion* (1965), it seems to come alive as threatening hands reach out of the walls to grope Carol, the young woman who lives there. This film is a special case. The distortions of Carol's apartment are experiences of her acute psychosis. There are no evil or supernatural causes, it is all happening in her mind, which can be even more frightening. This became a trope—we learn to mistrust the protagonist, who in some cases may turn out to be the monster we think is threatening her.

So often, in a horror film, the protagonists are in the dark and so is the audience. Literally. The shadows become places of the unknown. Characters frequently fail to turn on the lights at night. The camera often takes the POV of the character as she (it is usually a young woman) investigates something mysterious happening in the house. The camera stays close behind her, we see what she sees, but now we are not able to see what might be sneaking up behind her, setting us up for the jump scare.

Jump Scare

Suddenly a hand reaches out from behind; it's her boyfriend wondering where she went—a false jump scare. Or someone suddenly steps out of a doorway: it's her roommate, up to get a glass of water. These are "Lewton bus" moments. The young woman is startled and scared, and so are we. But then we and she are relieved when we realize there is no danger. We get a chance to breathe, and our anxiety lessens. This is a common trope of horror films, and it is a setup. For the next time there is such a jump scare, it will be for real. This time the person coming out of the dark will be the monster, an antagonist brandishing a kitchen knife or, in *Nightmare on Elm Street*, Freddy Krueger's knife-gloved hand.

There are several examples of jump scares in *An American Werewolf in London* (1981). Our hero, Jack, and his friend are on the moor in England, and they hear what sounds like a wolf chasing them. They run for their lives when suddenly Jack drops to the ground. His friend turns and sees that he has just tripped and says, "You really scared me, you shithead." So, a moment of almost comic relief. Another "Lewton bus" moment. Then, he reaches to help Jack up, and suddenly a wolf attacks him. The friend is dead.

Jack has been bitten by the werewolf and is in the hospital. We see his father answer the door at his home, and when he opens it, monstrous creatures with military helmets fire a machine gun, killing him. Jack cries out and one of the monsters cuts his throat. Jack wakes up suddenly.

It was a nightmare. We feel relief. There is a nurse at his side, who reassures him and gets up to retrieve some medication to help him sleep. She opens a curtain, and another monster stabs her in the heart, blood splattering everywhere. Jack wakes up again; another nightmare. This is a double false jump scare: the filmmakers are playing with us.

One of the most famous jump scares occurs at the end of the film *Carrie* (1976), directed by Brian De Palma. This is one of the best films ever made from a Stephen King novel (and that's saying something, as the prolific King has had dozens of his novels and stories made into films). A must-see film for any lover of horror, it avoids most of the standard conventions.

Carrie (Sissy Spacek, nominated for an Academy Award as Best Actress for this role) is a teenager who lives with her religious fanatic mother, so sheltered she doesn't even know about a girl's period when she has her first in-the-school shower. When she tells her mother (Piper Laurie), she is told that menstruation is sinful and is locked in a closet to pray. Carrie is teased and made fun of at school by some of the students (one, Billy, is played by John Travolta, in his first significant movie role—horror movies often provide early opportunities for actors who will have major careers). Billy's girlfriend, Chris, hates her. What Carrie begins to learn is that she is a telekinetic. She can move objects with her mind, especially when she is upset. An ashtray shakes and falls when the principal of the school keeps getting her name wrong; the mirror in her bathroom bends and breaks with her anger at her mother.

Her mother, discovering this hidden power, calls Carrie a witch. At the prom, Billy, Chris, and their friends pretend to elect her prom queen, and as she stands on the stage to receive her crown, thinking that she is beginning to be accepted, Chris pulls a cord to pour pig's blood over Carrie's head, drenching her. Upset and angered, imagining that everyone is mocking her, Carrie telekinetically slams shut all the doors of the gym, and turns the fire hose on the trapped students. One of the teachers is killed by a falling basketball backboard, others are electrocuted, which sets the gym on fire. Carrie walks out, sealing the doors behind her. Billy and Chris try to run her over. She makes their car turn over and explode. At home, her mother tries to stab her and Carrie causes knives to fly through the air, pinning and crucifying her. The house begins to self-destruct. Carrie dies and the house burns down around her.

At the end of the film, her one friend Sue (Amy Irving) brings flowers to the site of Carrie's house, the image slightly soft, the mood melancholy and sweet. She reaches down to place the flowers and Carrie's bloodied arm reaches up from the ground and grabs her. She screams, the music becomes antic, and we see that Sue is having a nightmare and she can't stop screaming.

When you saw that in the theater, you screamed, too. And even though you are reading this, when you see the movie, it will still get you. Even if you know it's coming. This was particularly unexpected because, though there was much violence and destruction in the movie, there were no jump scares. Until this one.

Soundscape

The sounds of a horror film add much to the sense of dread and suspense. The excellent horror film *The Ring* (2002) has creaking noises, ominous silences, heavy breathing seeming to come from nowhere, or animal sounds, screeches, and screams. Sometimes the sounds are ordinary and **diegetic** (meaning they are sounds fixed to the world of the movie), such as piano scales being practiced in another apartment in *Repulsion*, or a radio or television broadcast; in *Halloween* the children are watching *The Thing* (1951) and *Forbidden Planet* (1956), two classic horror movies. In their ordinariness or repetitiveness, these sounds become ominous. If they stop, the sudden silence increases the sense of dread. Has something bad happened? Is there someone or something there?

Non-diegetic sounds, like a musical soundtrack, can make a big difference, too. *Halloween*'s soundtrack was composed by the writer and director John Carpenter, and it adds powerfully to the effect of the film. It is spooky, with simple repeated notes, much like the music of Philip Glass. The repetitions become ominous and suspenseful.

When Alfred Hitchcock was filming *Psycho*, he told the composer Bernard Herrmann that he wanted no music for the famous shower scene where Marion is killed. Hermann composed a score for that scene anyway and played it for Hitchcock, who immediately agreed it was better than the silence he had planned. The shrieking violins when Mother comes to stab Marion really make that scene work and have become iconic, the musical "stabs" dramatically increase the immediacy of the violence on the screen.

The Monster

Monsters in a horror film come in many guises. In *Frankenstein*, he is a creature made by the crazed scientist Dr. Frankenstein, whose assistant Igor has accidentally given him a criminal brain. Once made alive, the Monster is innocent, understanding little and killing only accidentally or when he is provoked. The real "monster" is the doctor, intent on challenging God by creating life from death.

Other monsters come from another world, like the space creature in *Alien* (1979), or the Cave Crawlers from *The Descent* (2005), a film which feels like a thriller for its first half, as a group of women divers explores deeper and deeper into the cave, but then becomes a horror film when they discover creatures living there. Monsters may come from a supernatural beyond such as Freddy Krueger from *Nightmare on Elm Street*, who, though he is the monster in your nightmares, can reach out into the real world and kill you, or they are possessed by the devil as in the young girl Regan in *The Exorcist* (1973).

Often these creatures can only become active if they are invited. Regan and her mother play with a Ouija board and accidentally release the evil. In many vampire movies, the creature is often invited into her room by a young woman charmed and ready to be seduced by the vampire in his human form, before he transforms, sucks her blood, and turns her into a vampire.

In the classic silent film *Nosferatu* (1922), starring Max Schreck and directed in an expressionistic style by F. W. Murnau, Count Orlok, very much like Count Dracula, has a castle in the Carpathian Mountains. He is intrigued by a photo of Ellen, the wife of Hutter, who is selling him a house near his own. As Orlok travels by ship to his new home (sleeping by day in a coffin), a deluge of rats and the plague follow him from town to town. Ellen senses the coming of evil and learns that a woman "pure of heart" can defeat the vampire if she sacrifices herself. She invites Orlok into her room and allows him to bite her neck. As the sun rises, Orlok vanishes in a puff of smoke.

Of the many films based on *Dracula*, Bram Stoker's 1897 novel which was the primary source for most early vampire movies, Francis Ford Coppola's film *Bram Stoker's Dracula* (1992) is one of the best, with a powerful performance by Gary Oldman as the Count.

Horror with a Difference

Let the Right One In (2008), a Swedish film, is an original vampire tale. Eli, a young vampire girl, moves next door to twelve-year-old Oskar in a Stockholm suburb. She tells him that they can't be friends, but they begin to communicate by Morse code, knocking on the wall between their apartments, and a friendship develops. Oskar is being bullied at school and Eli urges him to fight back. He spends his evenings planning revenge and wishing he could murder the bullies. Meanwhile, Eli's father goes in search of blood for her and kills a passerby. There are other killings and, when her father is caught trying to drink the blood of a boy at school, he disfigures himself so as not to be identified and protect his daughter. In the hospital, he offers Eli his blood to drink. When she drains him, he falls out of a window. There are other dramatic moments, without the gimmicks of jump scares or spooky effects, though there is a lot of use of eerie sounds, like heartbeats and loud breathing to increase tension and unease.

A schoolgirl, Virginia, is attacked by Eli but gets away. She finds she is suddenly very sensitive to light. When she visits a friend, cats attack her viciously. Meanwhile, Oskar realizes that Eli is a vampire and confronts her. She tells him that she is not a girl, that she is two hundred years old. She persuades him to accept that she kills only so she can survive. Virginia, in the hospital, asks an orderly to open the curtain. When the light streams in, she bursts into flames. At the end, we see Oskar on a train, with Eli in a box next to him. They are communicating by morse code.

This is not a generic vampire movie. It is more of a story of lonely children finding each other in a world that has no place for them. It is beautifully filmed with many quiet moments, all quite uncharacteristic of the horror genre, which makes it special.

Another horror film that avoids the clichés of franchise films is *Don't Look Now* (1973), based on a short story by Daphne Du Maurier and starring Julie Christie and Donald Sutherland. Directed by Nicholas Roeg, it is a very sad and intense story of a couple, John and Laura, whose daughter accidentally drowns in the pond behind their house. There is a scene of their lovemaking that is remarkably sensuous and edited to play with time (we see it interspersed with moments of them getting dressed)—a feature that this film pioneered.

They go to Venice for his work. The city becomes a sinister character, its churches, alleyways, and dark canals both claustrophobic and ethereal. There, they encounter two elderly sisters, one of whom claims to be a psychic and tells them she has seen their daughter wandering among the canals. Laura is intrigued and John is skeptical, but he begins to see glimpses of a small figure in a red coat like their daughter's. He begins searching for her. This film is atmospheric, with a suspenseful and finally shocking ending. A class act among horror films. It incorporates flash-forwards, abrupt cuts that show a moment that will happen later in the film, before returning to the chronological moment in the plot. We're used to flashbacks, scenes that show something that happened in the past before the action of the film's plot began. But flash-forwards were new and intentionally disorienting. They would become staples of films of all genres, but they began here.

Another original is the made-on-the-cheap movie *Night of the Living Dead* (1968) which revolutionized the zombie film. Directed by George A. Romero, it is filmed in black and white, like a documentary. We meet Barbra and Johnny, a brother and sister visiting their father's grave. A man approaches them, kills Johnny, and attacks Barbra. She runs to a nearby farmhouse, where she finds a woman's body, half-eaten. Soon there is a gathering of "ghouls," the name used in the film for zombies. These are the undead, made alive by some radiation accident. They kill and eat their victims, who then become undead and add to their numbers.

Meanwhile, several people are hiding in the house, trying to keep the ghouls at bay. A particularly scary moment happens when Karen, a young girl who was bitten and badly injured, dies in the basement, and then becomes undead, kills her mother, and eats the body of her father. Barbra is dragged away by her undead brother, leaving only one person alive: Ben, the lone Black in the group. The next morning, a vigilante gang, shooting any ghoul they find, sees Ben in the window and, mistaking him for a ghoul, shoots him. This was a not-very-subtle commentary on the society of the time. The critic Pauline Kael called this "one of the most gruesomely terrifying movies ever made" and she is not wrong.

This, and Romero's other *Dead* films, particularly *Dawn of the Dead*

(1978), established the zombie film as a horror subgenre. What Bram Stoker's *Dracula* novel did for vampires, Romero did for zombies, establishing the "rules" for how they behave and how they are killed. *The Walking Dead* television series (2010–2022), which takes place in an apocalyptic future when the undead are walking the earth, owes its whole concept to Romero's films. Directed by Danny Boyle, *28 Days Later* (2002) is an excellent film that couples zombies with the story of a devastating virus that turns its victims into rageful monsters before killing them, leaving cities oddly peaceful in their emptiness. Though it is a terrifying concept and there are frightening images, this movie comes across as more of a thriller, a genre with crossover elements to horror.

Get Out (2017), written and directed by Jordan Peele, is another horror movie with a sociopolitical message, this time about the many guises of racism. The film opens on a dark suburban street. In a long Steadicam sequence before the credits, Andre (LaKeith Stanfield), a Black man, is walking and talking on the phone, "I'm lost in a creepy-assed suburb. I feel like a sore thumb out here." He glances uneasily as he turns the corner. A white car drives past, the camera angle shifts to watching him from the front, and we see the car stop and make a U-turn behind him. The car comes alongside him and pauses. He abruptly turns around, walking the other way. As he begins to cross the street, we see that the car has stopped, its brake lights are on, and the driver's door is open. Suddenly, out of the shadow, someone in a helmet jumps on Andre and wrestles him to the ground. He goes limp and is dragged toward the car. Then the camera shifts to a wide shot. Andre is dumped into the trunk of the car, the car drives away, and the credits start. We will see Andre again much later, in very different circumstances. This abduction sets up the story and its racial subtext.

Chris (Daniel Kaluuya), a Black photographer, is nervous about meeting the parents of his white girlfriend, Rose (Allison Williams). She tries to reassure him that her parents are liberal and very accepting. They do seem welcoming. Her father is a neurosurgeon, her mother a psychotherapist. They introduce him to their friends, who are both complimentary and condescending toward him. There is humor here and social commentary on liberal patronizing hypocrisy. The Black servants seem oddly distant and hostile, the all-white party guests ask too many questions about "what it's like to be Black," and Rose's mother is overly insistent on helping Chris stop smoking by using hypnosis. There are sinister doings here, and Chris is in real danger, his desire to "fit in" and ingratiate himself is making it hard for him to see where this all leads. There are standard horror tropes, with violence, jump scares, and musical stings to up the tension. When Chris tries to leave, Rose and her parents lock him in. They have plans for him, involving body parts, and something called "the sunken place." This film was nominated at the 2017 Oscars for Best Picture, Best Director, and Best Supporting Actor (Kaluuya), and won Best Original Screenplay, the first time for a Black person. Rare accolades for any film, but especially for a horror movie.

Children's toys and imagery can be scary too. There are monstrous children such as Damian in *The Omen* (1976), clowns found in *It* (1999), and dolls, playing into our childhood fears that they might become alive when we are not looking. Chucky in *Child's Play* (1988), the android doll in *M3gan* (2022), as well as Annabelle in *The Conjuring* are all possessed and evil, encouraging their child "playmates" to murder, or do it themselves.

These are all elements of horror films. And when a film is a hit, it can often, zombie-like, proliferate into sequels. Enough sequels, and you have a franchise on your (bloody) hands.

Franchise Horror: *Halloween* and *Nightmare on Elm Street*

Franchise horror movies began with *Halloween* and included *Nightmare on Elm Street*, *Friday the 13th*, *Saw* (2004), *The Texas Chainsaw Massacre*, and many more—their popularity generated sequel after sequel. It was *Halloween* that got the ball (or perhaps I should write "heads") rolling. It found great success by combining titillation and a sort of Victorian morality. The monster's prey in the first *Halloween* but also in these other franchise movies were invariably half-naked or half-dressed teenage girls, and the occasional young man, who are sexually obsessed and sexually active.

Halloween opens with a first-person view of a simple clapboard house, the camera acting as the eyes of an unseen character peering in the windows and watching a young couple sexually teasing each other and then going up the stairs to a bedroom. The music is ominous and suspenseful. The camera looks up at the second-floor window as lights go out, then finds an open door in the back and enters the kitchen. We see a hand reach into a drawer to find a big chef's knife and then the still-unseen person climbs the stairs. The hand reaches out again and picks up a Halloween mask from the floor. Putting it on, now the view is narrowed, through the eyeholes of the mask.

Entering the room we see the girl at her dressing table, naked except for her panties. The camera glances at the mussed sheets on the bed and looks at her. She turns, surprised, and cries out "Michael," as the POV character begins to stab her over and over. She falls, bloodied and dead. We may know his name, but we still have not seen him. The masked camera goes down the stairs and out the front door, where an older couple is just arriving home. Then the camera angle changes, and, the mask is removed, we see Michael Myers, an innocent-looking six-year-old boy in a Halloween costume, standing there quietly, holding a bloody knife. His parents stare at him. The camera draws back.

This is bravura filmmaking.

Then it is fifteen years later. Michael escapes from the mental hospital he has been incarcerated in for all this time. His psychiatrist goes after him, describing him to the sheriff: "[he had] a blank emotionless face and the blackest eyes . . . the devil's eyes. What was living behind that boy's eyes was purely and simply evil." Michael stalks two sexually active teenage girls in the neighborhood, then strangles and kills them with his knife. He wears a blank white mask that hides his face.

The girls' friend, Laurie (played by Jamie Lee Curtis), notices a car following them and glimpses Michael watching from a distance. She doesn't know what to make of it, but it registers. Unlike her friends, who are oblivious until the moment they are attacked, Laurie notices things. She is smart, resourceful, a problem-solver, and a virgin. She will be the **final girl**, the one who defeats the monster and survives—another trope established here, the one survivor being the moral one.

The Final Girl

Carol Clover's *Men, Women, and Chainsaws: Gender in the Modern Horror Film* (1992) explores and names this phenomenon. The final girl in horror movies, especially the bloodier slasher films, is often androgynous, a serious person, and a virgin, wary of sex. She is watchful, while her friends are carefree and unobservant. Unlike them, she takes action to protect herself. She confronts the killer and is the character with whom we most identify.

There is no suggestion that Michael has any supernatural powers: he is just an evil killer. Though, at one particularly spooky moment, he does seem to have unnatural strength. As he is strangling one girl's boyfriend, he lifts him with one hand until his feet are off the floor. This is uncanny. As is the ending, when even though he has been shot several times and falls two stories to the ground, his body disappears (making way for the sequels).

Figure 9.3 Michael Myers threatens the Final Girl. Jamie Lee Curtis, Tony Moran. *Halloween* © Compass International Pictures. Screenshot captured by authors.

We will see moments like this in other franchise films when something happens that doesn't make sense with the logic of the story. These moments are there to keep the villain alive for the next installment.

Another iconic final girl is Nancy (Heather Lagenkamp) in Wes Craven's *Nightmare on Elm Street*. Her friend Tina has had nightmares of a man with a grotesquely burned face and a gloved hand with knives on each finger chasing her through a boiler room. She is terrified and her mother notices four slashes on her nightgown. Nancy and her boyfriend, Glen (Johnny Depp in his first role), tell her they also had a nightmare about a man with a disfigured face. Tina's mother will be away, so Nancy offers a sleepover at her place so Tina can feel safe. Her boyfriend, Rod, interrupts the plan, so he can sleep with Tina. Later that night, Rod is awakened by Tina thrashing about on the bed, then being pulled up to the ceiling by an unseen attacker, slashed and bleeding until she drops to the bed, dead. Rod is arrested for her murder.

Nancy falls asleep in class the next day and dreams of the same man chasing her to the boiler room. In the dream, she burns her arm on a pipe, which awakens her. There are burn marks on her arm. Nancy is the final girl, who is beginning to figure out what is happening and what she can do to prevent it.

She first tries to avoid going to sleep, knowing that to sleep is to die at the hands of this killer. But you can only avoid sleep for so long. In the bath, she begins to drowse and is pulled underwater and almost drowns. When she allows herself to sleep, she has Glen stay to watch over her. In her dream, she sees the man walk through the bars of the jail cell and begin to strangle Rod, who dies hanging, as though he had committed suicide. Her alarm clock wakes her up. She is being both clever and smart by allowing herself to sleep, trying to learn more about this supernatural threat and to discover how to defeat him, and protect herself and her friends.

Nancy's mother tells her that, years ago, there was a man named Freddy Krueger, a murderer who killed twenty children but got off on a technicality. Parents in the neighborhood chased him and burned him alive. Freddy is a spirit demon now, out for revenge. At a sleep clinic, Nancy, while dreaming, grabs Freddy's hat and holds onto it, dragging it into the real world. His name is written inside.

Glen, who lives across the street, has promised to stay up to help Nancy keep awake, too. But he falls asleep, and Freddy kills him. There is a terrifying image when they discover that Glen is dead: a deluge of blood cascading upward to the ceiling from a hole in the bed that Glen was dragged into.

Nancy sets up booby traps throughout her house, *Home Alone* (1990)–style: wires set low across a doorway, a sledgehammer poised to drop, things for Freddy to trip over. Freddy chases Nancy through the house and the traps work to slow him down. Logic isn't always present: this approach contradicts the rules of the story since we have seen that Freddy is a spirit who can walk through the bars of a cell unaffected, so these traps shouldn't faze him—but they do. You don't register this inconsistency while watching the movie because it is so well done. But when you think about it, you realize it's a cheat. Nancy throws gasoline on him, sets him on fire, and locks him in the basement, but not before he kills her mother, with the two of them vanishing into her bed. When Nancy's back is turned, Krueger rises from the bed. She realizes that he feeds off her fear, so she keeps her back to him even as he approaches ready to pounce and he suddenly vanishes. Freddy is gone.

Like Michael Myers disappearing at the end of *Halloween*, we then get an ending that contradicts much of what we have seen. Nancy is leaving the house on a beautiful spring day. Her mother is alive and sends her off to be with her friends, who are also all alive and in a car, oddly colored like the orange stripes on Freddy's sweater. Once Nancy is in the car, they are suddenly locked in and it begins to drive away, with no one in the driver's seat. They are screaming, trapped. Nancy's mother is grabbed from behind and pulled through the window of the front door. A jump scare that works but this whole scene makes no sense. Is it another nightmare, is Freddy still out there? It turns out that Wes Craven, the writer/director, was forced to add it to set things up for a sequel.

The sequels in these franchises are most often poor imitations of the original. They are usually not written or directed by the original team, and since so many of the characters are killed off in the original, the casts are usually different, too, with the monster, the final girl, and maybe the setting (the summer camp in *Friday the 13th*, for instance) as the only connecting element. With rare exceptions, these sequels are best avoided. The word "schlock" comes to mind. They are not the passion projects of the originals but are just there to make money.

The Babadook (2014)

The Babadook is a film that avoids the conventions of a typical horror movie. It is a quietly unnerving film, a psychological horror story about Amelia (Essie Davis), the mother of Samuel, a six-year-old boy, whose husband died in a car accident while taking her to the hospital to give birth. She is still grieving and is increasingly overwhelmed by taking care of her son, who is prone to nightmares. He finds a pop-up book in their house called *The Babadook*, which is about a very tall scary-looking creature in a top hat with lance-like fingers. The text is threatening and Amelia tears the book into pieces and throws it away. Samuel is a difficult child, always demanding attention and constantly worried that this creature will come and kill them, so he constructs all sorts of weapons for protection. Neither mother nor son can sleep.

This film captures how hard it is to be a single mother and how overwhelming grief can be and, as we watch the mother unravel, we are not sure whether we are witnessing psychosis or the supernatural. This is typical of psychological horror. Amelia finds the book sitting on her doorstep and, when she opens it, it has been repaired and the pop-ups now show her killing their dog and Samuel. She is terrified and burns the book. Then she begins to hear sounds and see things that suggest that the Babadook is in the house. Trying to get some sleep, she sees him on the ceiling above her, and as she screams, something gets into her mouth.

Watching television late at night, she sees scary images from old movies transform into the Babadook. Soon she is terrorizing Samuel, telling him she wishes he had died instead of her husband and threatening to kill him. He runs from her, crying, "You're not my mom," and he is right: she seems possessed and evil, with a threatening scream to wake the dead. At one point she chases him with a kitchen knife and later quietly puts her hand around his neck to strangle him, telling him it's time for him to join his father.

Samuel uses his weapons to knock her out and, when she awakens, they are in the basement and she is tied to the floor. After struggling and emitting more unearthly screams, she vomits a bloody substance and seems to return to herself. But then things change. Samuel is dragged up the stairs by something unseen and repeatedly slammed against the wall. Amelia stands up to the Babadook, who she now sees hovering in the dark of her room. "This is my house, this is my child, you are nothing!" she screams, and the creature goes limp and runs to the basement. We never actually see it clearly, which makes it even more scary.

This is another horror trope. The fearsome thing feeds off of fear. To stand up to it, to not be afraid, will disarm or destroy it. We see that happen here (and also in *Nightmare on Elm Street*, and Stephen King's *It*). "We have nothing to fear but fear itself," said Franklin Delano Roosevelt, and in horror films, he is often right.

Later, we see Samuel's mother calm, with Samuel loving and relaxed, able to enjoy his birthday. They are gathering worms, which Amelia takes into the basement, to pacify and feed the Babadook, which is timidly living there. Some monsters can't be killed (like the death of a husband), but you can live with them if you can put them in the basement. Though this is literally what happens here, it is a powerful metaphor for the therapeutic approach to trauma and loss in traditional psychotherapy.

Metaphor or not, the last thirty minutes of this movie are hair-raising. This is one flat-out scary movie.

Figure 9.4 The ferocity of motherly love. Essie Davis. *The Babadook* © IFC Films. Screenshot captured by authors.

Chapter 10
Action

Key Films

The Bourne Identity (2002)
Nobody (2021)
Run Lola Run (1998)

It's useful to distinguish between action and suspense because there is almost inevitably an overlap in any given film. Suspense films will have action sequences and action films will be suspenseful. The nature of the question that drives you to watch is the real distinguishing factor. You can have suspense films with almost no action at all (see much of Alfred Hitchcock's oeuvre as an example), and an action film with almost no suspense (as in any of the *John Wick* films).

Action, mystery, thriller, suspense, police procedurals—all these films are about toying with tension. We are constantly asking questions about what is happening, why, and who is behind it. This can be moment to moment ("Is anyone hiding in the closet and about to jump out?") or run the length of a film such as who is Keyser Söze in *The Usual Suspects* (1995)? What is the nature of the modus operandi of the villain? Who is the bad guy? And in any given scene, what is going to happen or what is happening? Our confusion and trying to solve the puzzle alongside the protagonist is part of the fun. In action films, however, the question is not so much about what is happening, or who did it, but rather how the protagonist is going to deal with the crisis or issue at hand.

Let it be said that there is a lot of fluidity between suspense and action and the many other genres that include attributes of them. As noted in a previous chapter, tension can come from the plot or it can come from what we in the audience are allowed to see, for instance, we are aware of a danger before the protagonist is aware of it. But the core question, what versus how, is the distinction between our categorizations of suspense versus action.

To contextualize this, consider two very popular, long-form television series. *Bodyguard* (2018), a BBC production, has a huge amount of dynamic action, but much of it is driven by the protagonist trying to answer what's happening or who is behind it. This is especially the case in the gripping opening scene, which takes place on a train. It involves the protagonist recognizing that there is a potential terrorist situation and trying to figure out who the terrorist is, what their plot may be, and how to defuse it. Then he encounters someone who appears to be a victim of the terrorists, a woman strapped with an explosive device—or is she the terrorist herself?

By contrast, there is a very similar series in terms of style, and even format, called *The Night Agent* (2023). In its opening scene, the protagonist is also on a train, in this case, a subway. He sees a man wearing a hood leave a briefcase under a seat on the subway before exiting the car. The protagonist immediately suspects it's a bomb. He opens the bag and sees that it is. With that sorted, the reason we are engaged and want to watch is the imminent danger. We are curious to see how the protagonist will save the day.

He does so by pulling the emergency brake, which causes the train to skid to a halt. He yells for everyone to get off the train, grabs a child who is frozen with panic, and leaps off, just as the bomb explodes behind him.

After minimizing the damage of this terrorist explosion, the protagonist sits on the bumper of an ambulance, when he sees the suspicious-looking figure from the subway right there in the crowd gathered in front of him. Again, there is no question as to which person is the bad guy. They're spotted right away. The protagonist gives chase. The question is not who the bad guy is, but how the protagonist will apprehend him.

Though *The Night Agent* is enjoyable, *The Bodyguard* is far more gripping and effective. What is missing in *The Night Agent* is suspense. It is all about action, with relatively little in terms of us trying to guess who the bad guy is or what is happening. There are a few twists, but they are relatively flat. Action, with no (or almost no) twists or plot-driven surprises at all, can be a delight, but then it becomes either a chase film or a film that we'll categorize as "joyous violence."

Chase Films

Some of the most memorable moments in action films are chases: on foot, in cars, down mountains. Chases add an urgency to action. Chase scenes can provide extended set pieces or the climax of films, as they feel bigger, more elaborate than other, less mobile action sequences. The difficulty in directing action films is that the action must get progressively grander, involving more people, a higher body count, more pace or danger as the film continues, otherwise it can feel like a letdown rather than a crescendo to the climax.

Car chases owe much to *Bullitt* (1968), which features a scene described as the best car chase of all time. Star Steve McQueen did his own stunt driving in a scene that runs eleven minutes long. That is an epic amount of time to hold viewer interest, and yet it still retains its appeal, even today, in an era of ever-shorter, punchier scenes with lots of chopped-salad edits. As *Carbuzz* magazine described it, "*Bullitt* essentially did for movie car chases what *Star Wars* did for science fiction films."[1] The stunts were real, with no use of traditional rear-screen projections and no speeding up of scenes in postproduction to make them feel faster.

But the chase in *Bullitt* is just 11 of the 113 minutes of the film. That's a lot for a single scene. A famously gripping car chase in *The Bourne Ultimatum* (2007) is quite long for contemporary films and is only three minutes. Speed isn't everything. *The French Connection* (1971) sought to better *Bullitt* with a "slow chase," slow because the car is chasing a train on elevated tracks. But this is exciting all the same because the car is weaving through the middle of city traffic, veering to just avoid collisions.

But what of films that are, almost entirely, a single, very long chase sequence? This is action at its purest—nothing but action, sandwiched by some light plot points that provide a rationale for all that driving or running.

From the driving side, *Speed* (1994) consists of a "car chase" with no one giving chase. The plot follows a bus that is rigged with an explosive that will detonate if the bus drives at less than fifty mph. It's not about the vehicle being chased, but it's about maintaining speed in the face of obstacles.

A running example is *Run Lola Run!* (1998), a German film that manages to be artful, winning numerous awards, while providing pure action throughout. It is not a chase in the sense of someone following the protagonist, but of the protagonist racing against time.

The plot is set in motion when the gangster boyfriend of Lola, the protagonist, loses a bag containing 100,000 deutsche marks. If he cannot replace the money in twenty minutes, his boss will kill him. So off Lola runs—and she runs for the rest of the film, literally and almost without pause. (This must have been a great way for the star actress, Franka Potente, to keep in shape). What gives the film its artistic twist is an ingenious trick in which, when Lola runs past someone, we see brief flash-forwards of what will happen to them in the future. This also happens with Lola, who can replay certain moments and, when they go wrong, live them again and alter her fate.

Figure 10.1 Franka Potente. *Run, Lola, Run* (1998). Sony Pictures Classics / Photofest © Sony Pictures Classics.

After receiving her boyfriend's call about his predicament, Lola rushes down the stairs of her apartment building and passes a man with his dog on her way to the bank, where she plans to ask her bank manager father for help. There she finds her father having a conversation with his mistress, who reveals her pregnancy. An argument ensues between Lola and her father as he discloses that he is leaving her mother and that Lola is not his biological child.

Because the argument delays her, Lola arrives too late to stop her boyfriend from robbing a supermarket with a gun. She decides to help him. They manage to steal 100,000 deutsche marks before the police surround them, shooting Lola, who is killed. That could be the end of a short film, but then the sequence of events restarts, with Lola back at home, just hearing of her boyfriend's troubles.

This time, when Lola sprints out of her home, she trips over the man walking a dog and arrives late at her father's bank. Instead of being confronted by her father about his mistress, she becomes enraged after overhearing her father's conversation. She takes a security guard's gun, holds her father hostage, and robs the bank of 100,000 deutsche marks. Lola meets her boyfriend on time, but he is fatally hit by an ambulance.

The events restart once again, and Lola arrives at the bank earlier than the previous two times. She then wanders and ends up at a casino, where she wins 129,600 deutsche marks by betting on the number twenty twice in a row at roulette. Her boyfriend spots the money bag and manages to steal it back. Lola arrives just in time to witness him handing off the bag to his boss. This is the happy ending—the problem that initiated all that action is solved, and in this iteration of the story, the couple is wealthy, too.

This is not a film only about action, there are philosophical ideas at play with the redoing of key moments of one's life, and the chaos theory concept of how a single, seemingly unimportant event (like tripping over a man walking his dog) can lead to a chain reaction of life-changing import. But the action motors forward throughout the film. It is why we watch. One long sprint.

Joyous Violence

How often have you skipped ahead to watch, or rewatch, the fight scenes in action films? They are usually the highlights. In *Star Wars Episode II: Attack of the Clones* (2002) there's a scene in which Yoda fights—something he never did in the original *Star Wars* films, despite being a renowned Jedi master. When the moment approached, everyone in the theater leaned forward in anticipation. Was the two minutes and forty seconds of Yoda's lightsaber duel with Count Dooku worth the ticket price? It was certainly the best, and the only memorable scene from the film.

Since fight scenes are the highlights of action films, why not make a film that is almost entirely fight scenes? The pleasure of watching is in the joyous violence. This is violence that is fun to watch without guilt or repercussions. The effects of violence on characters—on their bodies, in terms of focusing on pain or recuperation, or on emotion—is minimal. And this provides an easier, more enjoyable, wild ride through fun fight scenes and chase sequences.

We viewers can (rightfully so, as compassionate humans) be "burdened" by the repercussions of violence. Directors can help relieve this burden of compassion by making the violence more cartoonish. This can be done by making the bad guys relatively anonymous, never introducing them with a name and backstory, or making them masked and interchangeable (like stormtroopers in *Star Wars*) or, even better, robots, for whom we need not feel sympathy.

What inhibits our joy in watching violence, the sort that is a specialty of kung fu movies, is the choice by the filmmaker to focus on the repercussions of violence and to lend humanity to its victims. If we know that a stormtrooper has a wife and seven kids at home, and a mortgage to pay, and no life insurance, we'll be significantly less gleeful when he's blasted by a photon torpedo.

Filmmakers can, and often do, choose to build stories about the outcomes of violence. These are films that can be full of action. War films about brotherhood and self-sacrifice, like *Saving Private Ryan* (1998) or *Zulu* (1964), for example, use moments of violence and war to tell a story about people, with plot developing character. These are heavier, and more emotional, which is a good thing, but is in its own category, "action drama."

By contrast, joyous violent action films seek to provide fun without the weight—they are bubble moments, floating as entertainment unmoored to real-life consequences.

Action dramas are more character-driven, focusing on the emotional repercussions of violence, and they can be much more gory, highlighting the physical consequences. The violence can be "cartoonish," even if we see blood and death, if the focus does not linger on the suffering of those injured, and if we have not humanized the victims. This is the opposite of joyous violence.

An example of a joyous action violent film is *Nobody* (2021), starring Bob Odenkirk as a former special operative killer for US government agencies who is trying to live the quiet life of a suburban family man before an incident

Figure 10.2 Bob Odenkirk. *Nobody* © Universal Pictures. Screenshot captured by authors.

brings out his dormant boogie and he returns to his fighting days. A burglary results in the thieves stealing his daughter's favorite stuffed animal, which proves to be the straw that breaks the camel's back and leads him back into violence.

From beginning to end, this film is a pure pleasure. We are never really concerned about the well-being of the protagonist or his family. It's just about seeing Odenkirk's character in action. There is some character development, although not in the traditional sense, nor does the film open with a bang, which is also unusual for action movies.

Viewers of action movies, or indeed readers of action novels, are immediately drawn in when there is violence and someone's life is in danger. It is an easy way to engage us right off the bat. And so a lot of films and books begin with an action sequence, preferably with mortal danger involved. Once we are hooked and this happens within the first minute or so of a film, or the first page of any book, we mentally "opt in" and decide that this is something we are going to enjoy. We've been tricked into doing this, and we will give the film the benefit of the doubt and sit through quieter moments, such as exposition, character development, or backstory because we already know that we are in good hands in terms of being entertained by the action sequences.

There are relatively few action films that start slowly. *Nobody* is a film that is surprising because it begins with a slow burn. We start in the first third of the film trying to figure out who the protagonist is and why we are watching him living a perfectly pleasant but repetitive and not very exciting suburban existence. It is only at the end of act one when he decides not to foil a burglary at his own home when he could do so, that he clicks back into his old self and prepares to kick ass.

Some aspects of act one give clues as to what will come. For example, we see him jogging each day, which seems like a reasonable pastime for a suburban commuter father, but he also does a very elaborate series of pull-ups every day after his run at the overhang of a local bus stop. This gives us a bit of pause because this seems a level more elaborate than most casual fitness. Only in act two of the film do we see him deciding to set off and resume his life of violence, which he dearly missed, and which then escalates into two very elaborate fight scenes, as he dismantles the operation of the Russian mafia.

This slow start is an exception to the rule of beginning with a bang, and it works here. But it is risky in this era of film-surfing, as is possible with streaming services, where you can dip in, try a film for the first five minutes or so to decide whether you want to stick with it because, if you don't, you can just go on to one of the thousands of other films available on demand, at your fingertips. It would be interesting to know the statistics on how long streaming viewers gave *Nobody* before they decided to either watch the whole thing or click away.

There is some character development in *Nobody* but it is mostly about catharsis in bringing an action hero out of retirement and back into the fray, thereby enlivening him, and the satisfaction of seeing bad guys served their just desserts.

It is similar to the *John Wick* film series, starring Keanu Reeves as a former hit man brought out of retirement when assassins kill his dog. He's after revenge and thus becomes a target. These films are one fight scene after another, with little in the way of character development, except as a vehicle for more fight scenes. The links are such that the posters for *John Wick 2* and *Nobody* are nearly identical. For *John Wick 2*, we see Keanu Reeves's head against a black backdrop, surrounded by a few dozen guns pointed right at him, making a sort of violent halo around his face. For *Nobody*, we have the same setup, but with fists instead of guns surrounding Bob Odenkirk's visage. Liam Neeson has rejuvenated his career by specializing in such films, like *Taken*, in which he plays an ex-CIA and Green Beret whose daughter is kidnapped—the reason we watch is to see how he will whoop the bad guys and rescue her.

Action films have the burden of trying to constantly outdo themselves. set pieces should feel continuously more perilous, and bigger, with more special effects and a higher body count as the film goes on. It's very rare for a film to start with a spectacular scene and then follow it up with less dramatic ones. The ante is constantly being raised, which requires higher budgets and more creativity to make sure that we remain engaged. There has to be enough plot to drive the action. But the action is the reason we're watching. That does not mean that there are not very clever and thoughtful action films. Some of them, perhaps even the very best, those worth watching over and over again, are the ones that combine all these elements: character plot, suspense, but with plenty of action above all.

An example would be *The Matrix* series, which deals with interesting big ideas of the sort that you could discuss in a philosophy class, but the primary hook of which is the joyous, kung fu–style violence and a beautiful trendsetting aesthetic. There is enough "meat on the bone" of *The Matrix*

(2002) that it warrants rewatching, as you pick up on details that you missed on the first viewing. The rewatchability of films is a strong indicator of their quality (as opposed to "success," as many a mediocre film has been financially successful, even if it was critically panned). We'll watch almost anything once, but how many films would you happily watch multiple times?

Perhaps the best of all, in providing a complete action film that covers all the bases, is the Jason Bourne series starring Matt Damon (and later, Jeremy Renner). The series strikes a perfect balance of constant action with lots of twists and suspense while still including character development as the protagonist Jason Bourne tries to piece together elements of his past that he has completely forgotten. The Bourne movies bear watching over and over, as they are so well-written, directed, and edited. Paul Greengrass, the director of *The Bourne Supremacy* (2004), *The Bourne Ultimatum* (2007), and *Jason Bourne* (2016) took the series to its peak. He is a master at filming action fights and chases in which you always manage to know where the characters are in relation to each other, in time and space, which is hard to do with quick-cut action sequences. The series marks a level up from the films that inspired just about all espionage-style action movies: the James Bond franchise.

Figure 10.3 Matt Damon as Jason Bourne. *The Bourne Identity* (2002). Universal / Photofest © Universal.

From James Bond to Jason Bourne

Though some of them seem quaint and old-fashioned now, the James Bond film franchise established many norms of the action film genre. It popularized action-based spy movies. Spy movies have a long history, looking back to *Spione* (1928) by Fritz Lang or the Greta Garbo vehicle *Dishonored* (1931), numerous Hitchcock films, and more. But these usually were more geared toward suspense, with only periodic action. *From Russia with Love* (1963), starring Sean Connery as Bond, established the Cold War–era, West versus Russia spy story but packed it with frequent action scenes, which were its calling card and set up the Bond franchise for decades of sustained success.

Part of its appeal was how it raised the bar for action sequences. There had been periodic action tours de force, as in Hitchcock's *North by Northwest* (1959), which includes a famous sequence in which star Cary Grant is chased by an airplane that tries to swoop in and smash into him, as well as a literal **cliffhanger** in which a fight takes place atop Mount Rushmore, with Cary Grant fighting off the baddie and rescuing heroine Eva Marie Saint while trying to avoid plummeting to their deaths. The latter is a clever visual game. The origin of the term "cliffhanger," meaning a moment of high drama where the protagonist or his love interest is, literally or metaphorically, hanging from a cliff by his fingertips, with death staring him in the face and tension at a maximum, originated in the late nineteenth century. It was originally about serialized stories that were popular in newspapers and magazines of the time.

The integration of numerous cliffhanger moments (not just one at the climax) is a trope of action films, particularly in the Bond series. This can be accomplished simply with editing: a moment of tension, a villain approaching a victim with a weapon and murderous intent, for instance, and the editor cuts away to something else happening, leaving us wondering what happened. The tension, however, is not as great as it might be because of those "rules" of the action genre—at least the franchise series action films, in which we eagerly await the sequel because we're so drawn to the protagonist—in which the protagonist may only be injured but never killed. Bond caricatured this, hitting villains with every shot of his Beretta, while never sustaining serious injury (until the Daniel Craig–starring iteration, which made Bond grittier and darker).

Bond also established the cool hero. Heroes of past films were not necessarily to be admired. Some were timid and forced into action, others were drunks or depressed or otherwise imperfect—and more human. This is often found in film noir. However, Bond had no flaws, other than the fact that his machismo appears quite sexist and dated by our current standards. He is impeccably dressed, always has a perfect witty retort, and is never really frightened, even when strapped to a table as a laser beam moves its way toward slicing him in half, as in *Goldfinger* (1964). He has an arsenal of gadgets, provided by the inventor, Q, which likewise became a spy film tradition. He always beds the ladies, who cannot resist him, and he bests the bad guys. These may all sound commonplace for those used to more modern films, but Bond established the character type.

The films were also enthusiastically globetrotting, with Bond zipping from country to country, expanding the field of film to make the world its potential playground. The early Bond films coincided with the early days of transnational commercial flight and helped introduce audiences to exotic locations to which they, too, could conceivably travel.

In terms of format, Bond films all open with a bang, inevitably beginning with a chase that takes place before the credits even roll. Earlier we mentioned a chase down a mountain. In *The Spy Who Loved Me* (1977), one of the James Bond films starring Roger Moore, before the credits roll we see Bond being chased down a mountain on skis by various baddies in the Austrian Alps. Such an opening is guaranteed to hook the viewer, because we humans are drawn to mortal peril—even if we know, by the unwritten rules of action films, that the protagonist will not be killed (for otherwise we'd have a very short film, indeed).

Some of the most famous sequences have nothing to do with the plot really, they're quite literally just a fight or a chase. The opening scenes of Bond movies are usually unrelated to the plot of the film itself. It shows Bond being Bond—cool and slick while evading danger, establishing his character before we come to learn the actual adventure he'll go on for this film.

Bond helped establish the aforementioned trick of combining unnamed generic bad guys who will be killed in large quantities (without us worrying about them) while the protagonist miraculously escapes largely unscathed. The generic henchmen are disposable, but each film has one boss (occasionally more), who we anticipate as putting up a better fight. The boss bad guy must be dealt with one-on-one, outdueled by the protagonist—preferably just after providing some helpful exposition as to the nature of his nefarious plan. This became such a cliché in Bond films that it was successfully spoofed in Mike Myers's *Austin Powers* films (the first released in 1997), which even include a character named Basil Exposition.

The fact that these are clichés that we can expect and start to see in almost every action film does not detract from the appeal if the action is well directed. Thus, much of the pressure in action films is on the director (and the rarely highlighted editor), rather than the script or the actors.

The editing of these films is what keeps things exciting. Sometimes there are intentionally long sequences, but quick-cut edits tend to enhance our sense of urgency and can promote a pleasant confusion, which is strategic on the part of the director, cutting away at moments of high tension before returning to relieve that tension.

Editing has gotten ever more rapid, and sustained camerawork is rarer. If we watch a classic Bond film and then watch the new "JB" of spy movies, a film in the Jason Bourne series, we see the action genre leveled up in complexity, pace, tension, character development, and style. Bond doesn't develop as a character—each film was a sitcom-style free-floating adventure, always starting from the same point and without reference back to earlier adventures. This was changed when Daniel Craig took over the role of Bond. Bond was rethought to make new films in the series, removing the camp elements, making Bond tougher, more human, vengeful, and, importantly, considering the Craig series as one of cumulative adventures in a sequence. *Skyfall* (2012) is a more significant and deeper film than any of the previous twenty-two (there are twenty-five as of writing, running from 1962 to 2021). The Craig Bond films (which began with *Casino Royale* in 2006), took notes from the Bourne series, the first of which, *The Bourne Identity* (2002), had come out four years before. This is a masterclass in building tension and selectively relieving it by answering the questions raised, sometimes later in the film, sometimes putting off the answers to a future film in the series.

This is a writing technique: build tension by asking questions and intentionally delay the resolution of that tension by putting off the answer. If you see a film opening with, for example, a fresh scar bleeding on the protagonist's face, the implicit promise is that we will later learn how that scar got there. It is an example of "Chekhov's gun."

Chekhov's gun is a principle in storytelling that states that every element in a narrative should be necessary and serve a purpose. This principle is named after the Russian writer Anton Chekhov (1860–1904), who famously said, "If in the first act you have hung a pistol on the wall, then in the following one it should be fired. Otherwise, don't put it there."

In other words, Chekhov's gun suggests that anything mentioned in a story, whether it's a detail about a character, an object in a scene, or a seemingly inconsequential event, should be important to the story in some way. If it's not, it should be removed, because it will only distract the reader or viewer from the main plot. This principle is often used to create a sense of inevitability or surprise in a story, as details that may seem unimportant at first are revealed to have significant consequences later on.

In our example, the fresh scar must be referenced later in the film, and the implicit promise is that its relevance and origin will be revealed, though we may have to wait.

This is embodied in the opening scene, pre-credits (à la James Bond) of *Nobody*. The film opens with Bob Odenkirk, our protagonist, looking very beat up but still triumphant, smoking a cigarette in a police interrogation room, while he's being debriefed by two policemen. He unzips his jacket and takes a can of tuna fish and a can opener out of a pocket, opens the can, and lays it on the table in front of him. Then he takes a kitten out of his jacket and places it on the table so it can eat the tuna fish.

One of the policemen then asks the question that we, the audience, are likewise asking: "Who are you?" And because we know the name of the film, we can anticipate the response, though it's fun anyway. "Me? I'm nobody." The implicit deal is, if we watch the film, we'll see who he is and how he got to this rather surreal moment—a moment that would never have happened had not James Bond established so many of the rules of the action film genre.

Martial Arts

Kung fu movies, or more broadly martial arts movies, represent a subgenre of action that warrants its own discussion. As with the other subgenres mentioned, there is much crossover: there are martial arts used in fights in the Bourne movies, while there are car chases and gunplay in *The Matrix* series (which contains elements of action, sci-fi, and martial arts films all in one). But for our purposes, martial arts movies focus on the hero's empowerment and triumph over evil through mastery of the spiritual as well as physical practice of martial arts.

While storyline and character development play their roles in the best martial arts movies, the primary reason we tune in is for the elegant ass-whooping. Martial arts feel more meaningful, weighty, spiritual, and disciplined than your average street fight. They provide windows into the cultures that produced them (kung fu in China, karate in Japan, taekwondo in Korea). The choreography of the fight sequences is balletic, the athleticism of the fighters appears Olympian, and there is often a magical realism element to them.

The zenith of the art form may be *Crouching Tiger, Hidden Dragon* (2000), a beautiful film, with a gripping story and characters, which is built around epic fight sequences in which the fighters defy gravity and the laws of physics. Martial arts films can dip into fantasy, but most dance around the idea of magical realism—they are realistic, in plot and melee moves, until something lightly magical happens: a punch throws an adversary through a wall, a jump carries the leaper to the roof of a building, time stands still for a bullet or arrow to be nimbly dodged. This film is particularly apt to include because it stars Michelle Yeoh, who is among the biggest stars in martial arts. She is now a Hollywood stalwart (starring in the 2022 Academy Award–winning *Everything Everywhere All at Once*), but got her start in kung fu movies, with *Crouching Tiger, Hidden Dragon* as the film that launched her international acclaim.

Hong Kong was the hub for martial arts filmmaking before Hollywood joined in. Early stars of the genre include Jackie Chan (whose wonderful 1978 *Drunken Master* added comedy and slapstick to the mixture), Bruce Lee (the 1973 *Enter the Dragon*, Lee's final film, made the Chinatown-born San Franciscan a legend), and Jet Li (*Fist of Legend*, 1994). Their popularity led to American studios funding their own films, led by star Chuck Norris, a Bruce Lee student who played a villain in Lee's *Way of the Dragon* (1972) before becoming a protagonist of innumerable films, as well as a punchline of many a joke about his manliness and badassery (as in: "Chuck Norris doesn't read books. He stares them down until he gets the information he wants"). It was a novelty to feature actors who were trained to fight.

American films tend to ditch the philosophy and spiritual development angle, which makes for more butt-kicking and less operatic sophistication. In classic martial arts films, the moral hero, the one with good karma, will triumph over the skillful adversary who uses his or her abilities for evil. Qi, the spiritual vital energy that Chinese traditional medicine and thought believes flows through all living things, can be harnessed by skilled masters to preternatural effect. This is exemplified in *The Matrix*, when Neo (Keanu Reeves) suddenly finds himself, without particular effort, to be able to outduel numerous opponents, dodge bullets and, in the climax, come back from the dead.

These magical realism elements are a step toward fantasy and sci-fi, which we'll look at in the next chapter.

Chapter 11

Sci-Fi, Fantasy, and Superhero Films

Key Films

X-Men (2000)
Star Wars (1977, 1980, 1983)
The Lord of the Rings (2001–2003)
Harry Potter and the Sorcerer's Stone (2001)

If martial arts films as a subgenre of action were typified by elements of magical realism, the next larger genre includes films for which the magical, or technology-producing magic-like effects, are standard elements of the action. It is tempting to coin a phrase and call these "power films," because preternatural abilities are what distinguishes them from action, regardless of the origin or explanation for those powers. But they are traditionally divided into sci-fi, fantasy, and superhero films, though all of them involve superheroes, just not all in the mask-and-cape variety of comic book origin.

There are consistent elements across the three genres. The plots pit good against evil in a stark, black-and-white way. Good guys are almost exclusively good (with a crucial flaw, on which more later), while bad guys are completely bad (they might have an origin of their badness story that tugs at the heart just a bit, making us sympathetic but not excusing their choice to turn to the dark side). The crucial flaw in the good guys is a helpful addition because, traditionally, good guys were often less interesting than the baddies. For audiences, darkness is intriguing and the character depth of the backstory of how the villain turned villainous is more of a memorable draw than a vanilla, goody-two-shoes protagonist. Heroes need a little darkness, and villains need an element of sympathy, to be maximally engaging. This also helps them feel more like realistic, three-dimensional humans, for everyone has elements of darkness and light within them. A grounding in realism is helpful in genres for which everything else is unrealistic—these are films of spaceships and aliens, dragons and wizards.

Consider Superman as a hero. He's about as boring as they get, in personality terms, as he is good at all times. His powers are also so great that he is essentially invincible. Kryptonite is his only weakness, and thank goodness he has that, at least, because otherwise there's only so much action that's entertaining if there is zero risk to our hero. Batman, by contrast, has been far more popular since he feels more real: he has no magical powers, just Olympian physical abilities and a belt full of gadgets. We sympathize with him, even though he is mega-rich, because of his origin story, witnessing his parents' murder and vowing to fight criminals. Superman's gee-whiz attempts to hide his identity behind the front of Clark Kent, popping into telephone booths to rip off his civilian clothing and fly off as Superman, seem silly compared to Batman, who at least wears a mask to hide his identity as Bruce Wayne.

Superhero Films: *X-Men* (2000)

Films with origins in comic books form the core of the superhero film subgenre. They are a big business, with the Marvel and DC comic book universe optioning everything they can find in their repertoires to cash in. From 2002–2022, Marvel movies made billions. In just one series alone, *Avengers* movies—*The Avengers*, *Avengers: Age of Ultron*, *Avengers: Endgame*—made $1.3 billion, $1.15 billion, and $2.44 billion, respectively, worldwide. DC is noticeably less successful, with *Aquaman* (2018) making $335 million worldwide, while *Wonder Woman* (2017) bagged $410 million.

Superman was the first comic book hero to reach the big screen, via a 1941 animated serial, *The Mad Scientist*, that would screen before feature films in theaters. Batman followed shortly thereafter, with a similar eponymous serial debuting in 1943. The dates are not coincidental. The rise of comic book hero popularity coincided with World War II and the stark good-versus-evil narrative of it. Americans in particular looked for square-jawed, well-mannered good guys to kick the butts of their enemies from elsewhere, inspiring the real-life soldiers on the front.

Serials continued to be the way comic book characters made it to screens, but they did not leave too much of an impression. Campy TV series, like Adam West's *Batman* (1966–1968), were very lightweight fun but little more. It was in 1978, with the help of more advanced special effects, that the age of blockbusters began, with *Superman: The Movie* starring Christopher Reeve. It led to three sequels but was not matched until the *Batman* series began in 1989, the first installment directed by Tim Burton and starring Michael Keaton. This was far grittier, in keeping with the mean street violence of 1980s films like *Taxi Driver*. It took a superhero and placed him into a realistic, intimidating, criminal cityscape (Batman's Gotham is a very lightly disguised New York). Batman's popularity grew when Christopher Nolan took over as director for three films called "The Dark Knight Trilogy" (2005–2012).

The first of the *X-Men* series landed in 2000. The story of a secret school of "gifted" teenagers who feel alienated and misunderstood because they are "mutants," born with superpowers, resonated with real-life teens who, minus the superpowers, often struggled with how to fit in. It also showed film studios how a team of superheroes, each with their powers and backstory, could find a market of its own, with sequels as a team, and that this could then lead to spinoffs. The most popular of the X-Men, Wolverine, has his own series that is a great success.

Figure 11.1 Hugh Jackman, Patrick Stewart, Ian McKellen, et al. *X-Men* © 20th Century Fox. Screenshot captured by the authors.

The age of billion earners would not come until the 2000s, when the Marvel Cinematic Universe was established to churn out Marvel-based movies, beginning with *Iron Man* (2008). The film scripts added an element that was lacking in the comic books—making the protagonists very quirky, which proved a way to render them even more endearing. This was taken to an extreme with *Deadpool* (2016), where the hero is slightly mad due to an origin story trauma and so constantly quips humorously to the audience, breaking the fourth wall, aware that he is a superhero in a movie that we are watching.

Marvel and DC are at the fore, but other comic book companies have had films made from their material, including *The Watchmen* (2009) and *Hellboy* (2004). *The Watchmen* was born of a graphic novel, a literary genre that is comic-book-like but usually runs only for a single storyline in one volume (rather than an indefinite serial) and is meant for adult rather than youth readers. Graphic novels have proved a rich source to tap, with notable successes in *The Crow* (1994), *300* (2006), and *V for Vendetta* (2005).

The Crow is worth noting also as a hugely popular film soundtrack. This is not in the sense of music written for a film (the realm of Danny Elfman, Hans Zimmer, and John Williams, who seem to have penned almost all the most memorable classical scores for films of the past few decades), but in terms of soundtrack as mixtape.

The Crow featured original songs and covers by popular hard rock and metal bands—the soundtrack album sold 3.8 million copies, meaning it went triple platinum, and was number one on the US Billboard 200 chart. Perhaps in the streaming music era, when individual songs can be called upon to play at will, mixtapes and soundtracks like this one will no longer be so influential, but some films have become known as much or more for their soundtracks as for the film itself. *The Big Chill* (1983) is one such film, with a classic Motown soundtrack selling over six million copies in the United States alone.

In the streaming era, soundtracks seem less relevant but the strategic placement of individual songs within films or TV series is hugely influential. Looking back, "Stayin' Alive" by the Bee Gees is the resonant recollection of the film, *Saturday Night Fever* (1977), "I Will Always Love You" by Whitney Houston was the best thing about *The Bodyguard* (1994), and *The Gray Man* (2022) brought Mark Lindsay's 1970 song "Silver Bird" out of obscurity and made it a streaming hit.

Sci-Fi and *Star Wars* (1977, 1980, 1983)

The aforementioned composer John Williams was responsible for many of the epic blockbuster film scores of the 1980s and 1990s, working particularly closely with Stephen Spielberg and with George Lucas. His films include the *Star Wars* series, which must be given due credit for having broadened the popularity of the science fiction, or sci-fi, film genre, though it was hardly the first.

The roots of science fiction in cinema can be traced back to the silent film era. One of the earliest examples is the iconic 1902 French film, *A Trip* to the Moon (*Le voyage dans la Lune*) directed by Georges Méliès, which was discussed in the chapter on silent movies. This pioneering work showcased imaginative storytelling and groundbreaking special effects for its time, taking viewers on a fantastical journey to the moon—its most iconic image, a space rocket squishing into the eye of the "man-in-the-moon."

The genre gained further momentum during the 1950s and 1960s, often reflecting the societal fears and scientific advancements of the Cold War era. Films like *The Day the Earth Stood Still* (1951) and *War of the Worlds* (1953) explored themes of alien invasion and the consequences of humanity's actions. These films served as allegories for the anxieties surrounding nuclear weapons and the dangers of technological progress. *Them!* (1954) was a horror film involving giant ants made huge as a by-product of atomic testing. It was this same concern over radioactivity that drove the origin story of one of the most popular superhero comics (and then films): *Spider-Man* (the first comic book came out in 1962). Radioactivity on the one hand could make ants gigantic and fearsome, or could give a human spider powers!

The 1960s and 1970s witnessed a surge in science fiction films that pushed the boundaries of visual effects and storytelling. The anthology TV series *The Twilight Zone* (1959–1964) featured some radioactivity themes, and many of its episodes had sci-fi themes (often ending with a surprise twist). But it was the *Star Trek* (1966–1969) TV series that brought sci-fi to everyone's home and increased its popularity. It coincided with media excitement over the space race, with the moon landing on July 20, 1969. On the big screen, Stanley Kubrick's *2001: A Space Odyssey* (1968) revolutionized the genre with its epic scope, philosophical themes, and realistic depiction of space travel. It remains a benchmark for its technical achievements and thought-provoking narrative.

As special effects technology advanced, so too did the capability to make a big-screen cinematic spectacle particularly awe-inspiring for audiences. This grew more important with the ubiquity of television: you needed to give audiences a reason to go out to the cinema, rather than sit cozily at home and watch their small-screen TV.

The answer was in films that took full advantage of those expansive cinema screens and showed marvelous, awesome effects and details that a small screen simply couldn't show properly. The late 1970s and 1980s brought about a new wave of science fiction blockbusters that captured the imagination of a global audience. George Lucas's *Star Wars* franchise, launched in 1977, introduced a richly detailed universe of space operas, diverse characters, and groundbreaking visual effects.

Figure 11.2 Alec Guinness as Obi-Wan Kenobi. This continues a trend in casting prestigious A-level British actors in Sci-Fi and Fantasy films to lend an air of gravitas. *Star Wars* © Lucasfilm Ltd./ 20th Century Fox. Screenshot captured by the authors.

It's hard to overstate the influence of George Lucas's 1977 *Star Wars* film, as well as the other two he directed. *Star Wars* was a catalyst for the birth of the blockbuster era, fundamentally altering the way films were produced, marketed, and consumed. Before it, smaller, character-driven films dominated the industry. However, George Lucas's ambitious space opera shattered this mold, showcasing the potential for high-concept, effects-laden spectacles that resonated with audiences on an unprecedented scale. This success paved the way for the rise of summer blockbusters, creating a paradigm shift in Hollywood's approach to film production and distribution.

One of the most revolutionary aspects of *Star Wars* was its use of special effects. Industrial Light & Magic (ILM), the visual effects company founded by George Lucas, pioneered innovative techniques that brought the "galaxy far, far away" to life. From the jaw-dropping space battles to the lifelike aliens and futuristic landscapes, the film pushed the boundaries of what was thought possible in visual effects. The integration of practical effects and model work with cutting-edge technologies, such as motion control and computer-generated imagery (CGI), set new standards for realism and spectacle in filmmaking.

The enduring appeal of *Star Wars* can be attributed to its rich tapestry of

Figure 11.3 Peter Mayhew as Chewbacca, Carrie Fisher as Princess Leia, Anthony Daniels as C–3PO, Mark Hamill as Luke Skywalker, and Harrison Ford as Han Solo. *Star Wars* © Lucasfilm Ltd./ 20th Century Fox. Screenshot captured by the authors.

characters and mythological storytelling. The film introduced iconic figures like Luke Skywalker, Han Solo, Chewbacca, Yoda, Princess Leia, and villain Darth Vader, who quickly became cultural touchstones. These characters resonated with audiences, offering relatable archetypes and inspiring a new generation of fans. *Star Wars* presented a grand, interconnected universe complete with a complex mythology that extended beyond the confines of a single film, laying the foundation for a vast and immersive franchise that continues to expand to this day.

The format of the film crossed genres. It is firmly sci-fi, in that it takes place in the future and involves technology, space, and aliens, but it has Western elements (Han Solo is a gunslinging cowboy archetype, complete with a revolver in a side holster), fantasy aspects (Jedi knights are futuristic knights battling monsters with swords, even if those swords are laser light sabers), martial arts references (Luke becomes the protege of a sensei in Yoda and learns to control "the Force" which gives him magically abilities like telekinesis, a parallel to apprentices learning to control their *chi* in kung fu movies), and Wagnerian opera-like, with over-the-top plot elements like a son battling his lost father and a sister and brother who never knew each other reuniting.

The success of *Star Wars* paved the way for other iconic films like Ridley Scott's *Alien* (1979), a horror movie in space, and James Cameron's *The*

Terminator (1984), an action movie with a sci-fi premise, showcasing the genre's ability to blend action, adventure, and thought-provoking themes.

The 1990s and early 2000s witnessed a resurgence of science fiction films exploring virtual realities, dystopian futures, postapocalyptic hypothetical versions of Earth, and the ethical implications of technological advancements. The Wachowski siblings' *The Matrix* trilogy (1999–2003) pushed the boundaries of visual effects, a constant chorus with each new generation of sci-fi films—and also, as mentioned, combined sci-fi, action, and martial arts into a single franchise.

In recent years, science fiction films have continued to evolve and diversify. The Marvel Cinematic Universe has introduced a wealth of science fiction elements through superhero narratives, intergalactic battles, and alternate dimensions. Films like *Interstellar* (2014) and *Ex Machina* (2014) have explored the frontiers of space exploration and artificial intelligence, offering nuanced perspectives on humanity's place in the universe and the ethics of technological progress.

Science fiction films have become a prominent part of popular culture, offering entertainment, escapism, and thought-provoking ideas. They have not only entertained audiences but also acted as mirrors to society, reflecting our hopes, fears, and dreams. As technology advances and our understanding of the universe deepens, science fiction films will undoubtedly continue to captivate and inspire us with their imaginative visions of the future.

Fantasy and *The Lord of the Rings* Trilogy (2001–2003)

Fantasy as a genre is typified by an imagined Middle Ages in which magic and monsters were real. It placed on the screen stories inspired by medieval Arthurian romances, like *Sir Gawain and the Green Knight*, *Percival*, and *Lancelot* by poet Chrétien de Troyes (1160–1191) and later works like *Le Morte d'Arthur* by Thomas Malory (1485). In these tales, brave knights encounter fairies, wizards, superhuman enemies, and dragons, save maidens in distress, and embody Christian values of nobility and self-sacrifice.

Twentieth-century expansions of this genre look to Oxford professor J. R. R. Tolkien (1892–1973) as the godfather of modern fantasy, with his *The Hobbit* (1937) and *The Lord of the Rings* novels (1954–1955). These established some of the "rules" or archetypes of the fantasy world, including the many races within it and their attributes, like stocky, strong, warlike dwarves who live in mines and hate orcs and elegant, pale, nimble, pointy-eared elves. In the 1980s, the hugely popular analog roleplaying game, Dungeons & Dragons, allowed adolescents to create characters of the sort that might appear in a Tolkien novel and play as those characters, while a narrator (known as a Dungeon Master) walked them through a planned adventure, the fate of the characters a combination of their choice of actions, attributes and roles of multisided die. Computer games took over for pencil, paper, and dice and now roleplaying games are among the most popular of video game genres.

Such visually rich material seems an obvious choice for film, but it requires strong special effects to pull it off. We explore special effects in depth later in this chapter, but an early example was *King Kong* (1933), which used special effects to make the colossal gorilla seem like a living, endearing character. Early attempts can look dated today but wowed when they first came out. Ray Harryhausen was a British animator and special effects wizard who used stop-motion model animation, which he branded as Dynamation, to bring monsters to life on-screen. This began with *Mighty Joe Young* (1949), a *King Kong*–inspired film about another giant gorilla—it won an Academy Award for Best Visual Effects. His fantasy films, inspired by ancient mythology, included *The 7th Voyage of Sinbad* (1958) and *Jason and the Argonauts* (1963), the latter of which was particularly memorable for the monsters, including a hydra, a giant statue come to life, and a battle with seven animated skeletons. Stop-motion involves models, often made of clay, that are manipulated in tiny increments between each frame, to create the illusion of movement. This can include adjusting the position of limbs, changing facial expressions, or moving props. The animator must carefully control the movements to maintain consistency and smoothness throughout the animation. The frames are then sequenced and played back at a high frame rate to create fluid motion. Sound effects, music, and dialogue may be added in postproduction to enhance the overall experience. It is slow and painstaking but floored audiences when they first saw it in the 1950s.

This was also the only way to create cinematic monsters before Jim Henson, of *Muppets* and *Sesame Street* fame, applied his creativity in making elaborate and realistic puppets (some manipulated by an actor inside them, others by strings or by hand) to fantasy films, like *The Dark Crystal* (1982) and *Labyrinth* (1986) and with brief appearances in numerous others, like *The Princess Bride* (1987), a light romantic fantasy film with comic elements, for which Henson created the RUSs (rodents of unusual size)—giant rats that attack our hero. Henson also worked on *Star Wars*, responsible for creating Yoda (who was a rubber puppet), Chewbacca, and the Ewoks, among others.

Fantasy special effects eventually went from analog to digital, with computer-generated imagery (CGI) now the norm. In CGI animation, 3D models of characters, objects, and environments are created with 3D modeling software. These models are made up of polygons, which are connected to form the shape of the objects. The models can be created from scratch or based on concept art or real-life references (such as an actor wearing a special suit, with their movements tracked by digital cameras and then imported into the software, at which point they can be "drawn over" effectively, with animation mirroring the actor's movements). This is how Gollum, for instance, in the *Lord of the Rings* films, was created. The actor, Andy Serkis, was filmed wearing a special suit, and his movements were then animated by superimposing the 3D computer drawing of Gollum onto them. The result is that we see Gollum moving as Serkis had.

CGI has its roots in the late 1960s, but it made a splash in 1982 when it was put to good effect in a pair of blockbuster sci-fi films, *Star Trek II: The Wrath of Khan* and *Tron*. As computers got faster and more powerful, so too did the capabilities of CGI. Films like *Avatar* (2009) allowed human actors to act alongside giant blue aliens seamlessly.

Peter Jackson, the director of the *Lord of the Rings* trilogy (as well as a subsequent but much less good *Hobbit* trilogy), plunged viewers into the elaborate world of Middle Earth, much as Lucas had done with a "galaxy far, far away" in *Star Wars* three decades earlier. Jackson filmed all three movies at once, which was unusual (most sequels come only after the success of the first film). This saved costs, bringing together the cast and team just once and getting three films out of it, but it was one of the most expensive film projects ever at the time, with a budget of $281 million. It certainly paid off, with seventeen Academy Awards from thirty nominations, and with a box office gross of $2.99 billion.

One might imagine *Lord of the Rings* as a superhero team film set in the magical Middle Ages. The team sets off on an adventure to destroy the Ring of Power and stop the villain, Dark Lord Sauron, from regaining power and becoming unstoppable. Each member of the team, called the Fellowship of the Ring, has their own character traits and abilities that will come in handy as they battle orcs and monsters. The same themes that veined through Chretien de Troyes's twelfth-century Arthurian romances remain moving in these films, made nearly a thousand years later: self-sacrifice, the value of friendship, honor, and noble behavior. And a lot of swords and sorcery.

Figure 11.4 Ian McKellen as Gandalf, Elijah Wood as Frodo. *Lord of the Rings* © New Line Cinema. Screenshot captured by the authors.

One Film to Rule Them All: *Harry Potter* (2004)

The *Harry Potter* film series, based on the world-winning best-selling books by J. K. Rowling, combines elements of the three genres described in this chapter.

Harry is a social outcast, a "freak" and a "mutant" of sorts, like the X-Men, but instead of having a specific, narrow power, he is a wizard but just doesn't know it yet. Like the X-Men, he is recruited to a secret, special school where his powers develop under the tutorship of a sensei, Dumbledore. Thus we have superhero and martial arts tropes, but there are also Western elements (wizard duels, wand against wand instead of six-shooter at high noon), and knightly elements (the Order of the Phoenix). There are some sci-fi elements, though not the futuristic sort—instead, more of a steampunk variety. Steampunk is its own sub-subgenre, in which an imagined future or alternative present involves fantastical mechanical inventions that harken back to the Victorian era of early experiments with electricity and a lot of gears—a future in which computers and digitization never arrived to take the mechanics out of invention. And, of course, the *Harry Potter* films are mostly fantasy, with wizards at the core, battling dragons, monsters, and evil wizards. There's an unmistakable parallel with *Lord of the Rings* in which the main quest is to ensure that the primary evil (Sauron in *Lord of the Rings*, Voldemort in *Harry Potter*), who has been weakened, cannot return to full power. And those same Arthurian values are in place, but here set against the backdrop of children aging toward adulthood.

Figure 11.5 Daniel Radcliffe. *Harry Potter and the Sorcerer's Stone* © Warner Bros. Screenshot captured by the authors.

How Did They Do That?

King Kong in 1937 is one thing, but what about more realistic special effects? When watching *X-Men* with young children, they frequently ask the question: How did they do that? It's something that those of us who have grown up in the era of computer-generated special effects might take for granted. Comparing how special effects were done in the film *Star Wars* with those from *X-Men* will help explain the transition from mechanical and costume-based effects to the technology most often used today, CGI. All of this is generally referred to as video effects, or VFX.

The first *Star Wars* movie (confusingly subtitled *Episode IV: A New Hope*, since they would later make both sequels and prequels to it) was released in 1977 and revolutionized the film industry with its groundbreaking special effects. The film's director, George Lucas, worked with various teams, including a company he created, ILM, to develop these effects, which were largely based on mechanics, models, and costumes—analog tools. Many of the film's space battles and scenes on different planets were created using intricate miniatures and models. ILM built detailed models of spaceships, vehicles, and locations, which were then filmed using motion control techniques to simulate movement.

To help bring other planets to life, film sequences were shot on location in otherworldly geographies, like the deserts of Tunisia, and these were combined with **matte paintings**, handmade by artists and used as backgrounds for scenes. These paintings added depth and realism to the environments while allowing the filmmakers to depict larger and more complex settings. Thus, on the desert planet of Tatooine, you'd see the actor playing Luke Skywalker, Mark Hamill, filmed on location in Tunisia, but with some scenes set against a matte-painted backdrop.

Models and miniatures were also used, and shots of them were combined with the shots of the actors themselves. To blend images of the miniatures with those of the actors, **motion control technology** was used to create precise and repeatable camera movements. Each camera movement, setting, and position had to be precisely replicated so that the shots of the actors and those of the miniatures and models would fit perfectly together. This technology helped make the scenes appear seamless.

Costumes were supplemented by puppets and animatronics. Characters like the robots R2-D2, C-3PO, and various aliens were essentially puppets, manipulated by or worn by humans. R2-D2, the loveable robot that looks something like a rubbish bin, was played by an English actor, Kenny Baker, who was inside a model that he could manipulate from within, as well as by a remote-controlled animatronic. C-3PO, the golden anthropomorphic robot, was a costume worn by actor Anthony Daniels. Jabba the Hutt, the giant alien from *Return of the Jedi*, was a puppet so large and heavy that it weighed one ton, took three months to build, and cost half a million dollars. It took multiple puppeteers to manipulate.[1] Two puppeteers sat inside the body and head of Jabba, one manipulating each of the creature's arms. Two more puppeteers were beneath the creature, manipulating his torso and tail. Another was positioned inside Jabba's fat tail, while a final puppeteer used a fishing rod-like device to move the top of Jabba's head and his facial features.

In-camera effects were also used, techniques like rear projection and front projection helping to combine live-action footage with background imagery. This allowed characters to appear as if they were in various environments without the need for extensive postproduction work. This would be a key analog approach that was made far easier with CGI technology.

Other elements that had to be done in real-life, analog experiments before computers could take over, included what are called **practical special effects**: explosions, laser beams, and other effects were created using a combination of pyrotechnics and physical props.

Stop-motion animation was used for certain sequences, such as the chess game played by Chewbacca and R2-D2 on the *Millennium Falcon*. This involved moving physical objects frame by frame to create the illusion of movement. Famous stop-motion effects can be seen in the TV series *Shaun the Sheep* and in the 1960s epics with monsters animated by the aforementioned Ray Harryhausen such as the skeletal soldiers who come to life to fight Jason in *Jason and the Argonauts* (1963). These were made by physically manipulating models bit by bit, filming each new pose, and then stringing them together to make the movements appear natural and fluid.

Optical effects, like compositing multiple layers of footage, were used to combine different elements into a single shot. This technique allowed the filmmakers to create complex scenes with various elements interacting. Thus you might have actors in the foreground, but a matte painting in the background, plus a model of a spaceship flying across the middle ground, all combined into a single shot. These were augmented by specialized camera techniques, like motion blur and forced perspective, that made the scale and speed of spaceships more lifelike. The combination of these techniques, along with the creative vision of George Lucas and his team, resulted in the landmark special effects that captivated audiences and set new standards for the film industry. The success of these effects played a significant role in making *Star Wars* a cultural phenomenon and paved the way for advancements in visual effects in the years to come. This marked the apex of analog special effects, and other films would follow suit, building on what Lucas had done in *Star Wars* until computers were advanced and powerful enough to take over most of the workload, rendering midproduction effects far less necessary, and pushing the heavy lifting to postproduction.

It was only in the 1990s that computer technology became powerful enough to become the go-to means of creating special effects in film. The most common form is CGI: a catchall term for the technique of creating visual content using computer software. This could encompass anything from a feature-length animated film, like Disney's *Moana* (2016), entirely made with computer images, with actors merely there as voices, to actors wearing suits that track their movement so they can subsequently be animated over (as in Andy Serkis's performance as Smeagol in the *Lord of the Rings* trilogy, mentioned earlier), to computerized explosions, blood splatters, falling bodies, zooming spaceships and more added to traditional performances featuring human actors.

CGI involves generating images, animations, or visual effects that would be too difficult, expensive, or even impossible to create using traditional practical methods.

Let's take the film *X-Men* as an example to understand how CGI works in a movie. Before any CGI work begins, filmmakers create storyboards and previsualization sequences (**previs** in industry slang). Storyboards are drawings or digital sketches that outline key scenes and camera angles, while a previs is a rough digital representation of how those scenes will look in motion. This helps the director and CGI artists visualize the intended outcome.

In the case of *X-Men*, characters, environments, and objects that will be created using CGI need to be **modeled** in a digital 3D space. Artists use specialized software to create virtual 3D models of characters like Wolverine, Storm, and the mutant-filled environments.

Once the models are created, artists apply textures to give surfaces realistic appearances. These textures might include details like skin, clothing, metal, and more. **Texturing** is essential to make the CGI elements look convincing and blend with the live-action elements.

To animate the characters, a **rigging** process is performed. This involves creating a digital skeleton for the 3D models. This skeleton enables animators to manipulate the characters' movements in a way that resembles real-life motion.

Animators then use keyframe animation or motion-capture data to bring the characters to life. **Keyframe animation** involves setting key poses at specific frames and letting the software interpolate the movements in between. So Wolverine might pose in ten different ways, and the software will fill in the movements that connect those ten poses. **Motion capture** involves recording real actors' movements and transferring those movements to digital characters, as was done for Smeagol in *Lord of the Rings*.

Rendering is the process of turning the 3D models, textures, lighting, and animation data into final images or frames. It's a computationally intensive task that calculates how light interacts with surfaces, creating realistic shadows, reflections, and other visual effects. Modern CGI studios use powerful render farms to process these calculations efficiently. Rendering is the key to making something fake look real.

Once the CGI frames are rendered, they need to be integrated into the live-action footage. **Compositing** involves layering the CGI elements on top of the live-action footage, and adjusting their placement, lighting, and transparency to ensure they seamlessly interact with the real-world environment. This is when the computer image exists alongside the live action.

After compositing, various postprocessing techniques are applied to enhance the final visuals. These can include color correction, adding depth of field, adjusting contrast, etc. to create a cohesive and visually appealing look.

In the case of *X-Men*, CGI was used extensively for mutant powers, such as Storm's weather manipulation and in some shots Wolverine's retractable claws, as well as for larger-scale visual effects like explosions and fantastical settings.

The use of a **green screen** (though the color doesn't have to be green) is also key. Also known as chroma keying or blue screen (depending on the color used), it is a technique used in filmmaking and video production to combine live-action footage with computer-generated imagery (CGI) or other backgrounds. The basic idea behind a green screen is to shoot the main subject in front of a colored background (usually green or blue) that is later replaced with the desired CGI or background footage during the postproduction process. Assistants can be dressed entirely in green bodysuits, so that they, too, can be digitally "erased" in postproduction. To shoot the scene in *The Matrix* in which the hero, Neo, appears to hang in midair as he duels the bad guy, Agent Smith, both Neo and Agent Smith were suspended off the ground with wires.. This was a very early showcase for computer-generated visual effects, and it still looks modern today.

A blue screen was used for the climactic scene in *X-Men* in which the heroes try to stop Magneto's plot and wind up fighting atop the torch of the Statue of Liberty. The actors interacted on a stage floor meant to look like the exterior of the torch, but behind them was a blue floor and screen. In

Figure 11.6 Green Screen special effects. Keanu Reeves, Hugo Weaving. *The Matrix* (1999). Warner Bros. / Photofest © Warner Bros.

postproduction, a nighttime cityscape of New York replaced the blue color, so it appeared that the actors were high atop the statue.

The scene is set up with the main subject, actors, or objects, in front of a large, evenly lit green or blue background—in X-Men it was blue (the choice of green or blue depends on the colors that are least likely to appear on the subject being filmed, as this reduces the risk of color spill or bleeding onto the subject).

The live-action scene is then filmed or recorded. The goal is to capture the subject's actions and interactions as they would appear in the final scene. The green or blue background serves as a "placeholder" during the postproduction stage. That is when video editing software is used to replace the green or blue background with the desired CGI or background footage—in this case, the city harbor of New York as seen from on high at night. This process involves a technique called **chroma keying**, which involves selecting a specific color range (in this case blue) and making it "transparent" in the video editing software. This transparency allows the background (and bodysuit-wearing assistants) to be replaced with another layer of footage: the CGI background. The software identifies the selected color (e.g., blue) and removes all pixels within that color range, creating a "hole" in the video where the background used to be.

Once the green or blue background has been removed, the edited video layer (with the main subject, for instance, Wolverine fighting Sabretooth) can be composited or layered on top of another video or image layer (the CGI background of New York City). This process merges the two layers, creating the final composite shot.

The video editor can further fine-tune the composite by adjusting lighting, shadows, color balance, and other elements to ensure that the live-action subject looks well integrated into the CGI background.

By using this technique, filmmakers can create scenes that are physically impossible to shoot on location or too expensive to build as practical sets. It also allows for creative storytelling by placing characters in fantastical or fictional environments while maintaining a realistic look.

The answer to "how did they film that" these days is almost always "with CGI." This makes the possibilities infinite and the logistics far easier, though perhaps something is lost; the romance of the "olden days" hands-on analog world of puppets and miniatures.

Chapter 12

International Art House

Key Films

Bicycle Thieves (1948)
Seven Samurai (1954)
Nostalghia (1983)

The very idea of this chapter is stepping into a bear trap. How can we possibly cover "international" films in a single chapter, much less herd together films made anywhere outside of the North American vortex into a single category?

We are entirely aware that this is well-nigh impossible to do, or rather to do well. Still, there is something evoked when a North American film fan hears the term "international film" and that is what we're trying to crack open. A film made in Nigeria ("Nollywood" as it is sometimes called), a huge industry, producing some 1,500 films per year in around three hundred different languages, will differ considerably from one made in India ("Bollywood" films grossed over 172 billion Indian rupees, over $2 billion, in 2022).

We've mentioned a handful of international films already (French, Chinese, Japanese, Italian), and in the Movie Playlist in the back of the book we provide an extended list of classic international films for you to explore. Let us begin by stating that this chapter is an exercise in facilitating the understanding of what international film means, and how that understanding can be a useful guide to engage more deeply with such films. Rather than using international films we'll use "international art house," to specify the style of films that we wish to distinguish and analyze.

The Basic Distinction: Hollywood Style versus Art House Cinema

The term international film is often expanded to international art film (sometimes also called "art house cinema") and the knee-jerk understanding of what that describes is a good place to begin. There are many Hollywood-style films made outside of the United States, of course, but what people really mean when casually mentioning international films is that they are not in the Hollywood style. That somewhat awkward phrase is actually useful, in that it allows us to reprise some of the key features of Hollywood films, to set them against what people mean by international art cinema.

Hollywood Films

- A three-act structure with set things that "must" happen in each act.
- A linear approach to storytelling, rarely jumping around in time.
- Explain, show, provide exposition for what's happening rather than suggesting or implying.
- Until the 1960s, films were made on sets, not on location in the real world.
- Stories are wrapped up neatly at the end, little room for ambiguity.
- Each scene must propel the story forward—storytelling efficiency is paramount.
- Clear delineation between good guys and bad guys.
- Bigger is better—big explosions, car chases, outrageous can-you-believe-they-did-it moments tend to stand out, with each subsequent film trying to outdo previous ones.
- The stars must always look good and glamorous.
- The act of watching encourages feeling rather than thinking: emotional rather than cerebral.
- The auteur (a French term for the main creative force) is the producer more often than the director.

Art House Cinema

- Much lower budgets than Hollywood films, which require smaller-scale films and creative thinking.
- Filmed on location, for lack of elaborate studio sets.
- Sometimes use nonprofessional actors or lesser-known, for both authenticity and budgetary reasons.
- Plot is secondary to character and detail. Things don't have to happen or relatively little *needs* to happen to drive the interest: it could be a day in the life of an ordinary protagonist, for example.
- Editing tends to be far more leisurely than in Hollywood films, with fewer cuts, less jumping around.
- Storytelling can get creative, however, using flash-forwards or flashbacks;

it can sometimes challenge Hollywood-style films with faster cuts, that are intentionally jumpier and more disjointed.

- There is little active explaining or exposition to help the viewers understand what's going on—the emphasis is on suggesting or implying, and it's up to the viewer to connect the dots.
- May include intentionally confusing or puzzling elements that are not "explained away" by the end of the film.
- Requires thinking and engagement on the part of the viewer, not just passive entertainment.
- Often make a philosophical or political point, either explicitly or implicitly through the action of the story.
- Character-driven personal struggles are at the core, of individuals searching for their place in the world. This means that the antagonist may not be someone else, a villain, but an aspect of the protagonist themselves.
- Unhappy or ambiguous endings are acceptable—no need to tie up all loose ends happily.
- The director is the auteur, leading with their creative vision, rather than the studio or producer.
- Directorial style is often recognizable from film to film because the director is the master artist in the process.

The rare auteur directors in Hollywood, whose style is recognizable when you see the film, are almost all foreign (Ang Lee, Guillermo del Toro, Alfred Hitchcock, Christopher Nolan, Billy Wilder, Elia Kazan, Baz Luhrmann). There are fewer auteur American-born directors, like Frank Capra and Steven Spielberg, and those tend to be described as having "art house" or "European" sensibilities, like Martin Scorsese and Wes Anderson. Of course, there are crossovers, such as Ang Lee directing the Marvel superhero movie, *Hulk* (2003), and they are often particularly interesting because the director brings an art-house auteur approach to a Hollywood budget and expectations of action and superlatives. This can work brilliantly or less so, as seen in the headline "Ang Lee's Hulk Was Too Smart and Weird for Its Time," the title of an article in *GQ* magazine that is in praise of the film.[1] One of the reasons why it's useful to go into a film viewing experience with a bit of a priori knowledge is to temper expectations. If you're in the mood to sit back, throw down the popcorn and Junior Mints and be entertained Marvel-style, then the quirkier, more introspective *Hulk* might not be what you were hoping for. Likewise, you have to be in the mood for a film by Russian auteur Andrei Tarkovsky, a director beloved by other directors and film students, but whose work is slow, ponderous, deep, and more akin to watching a slideshow of beautiful imagery than watching a movie.

In short, Hollywood-style films tend to be simpler in structure and presentation, allowing the viewer to watch passively, to be entertained without having to "think" too much about what they are seeing. They move more quickly, forcing the viewer to be drawn in through action, tension, quick-cut edits, surprise. Many art house films include a scene in which someone slowly smokes a cigarette while staring out the window at the rain. Does this advance the plot or character development other than broadcasting a meditative state of ennui or deep introspection? Probably not. Such a scene would never make it into a Hollywood script—unless the cigarette was used as a weapon as a team of ninjas swooped in through the open window and ambushed the protagonist. Art house allows for such scenes as "pregnant pauses" full of meaning that allow the viewer to sort out what they've seen so far, without scrambling to keep up with the plot rocketing forward at Mach speed. Hollywood-style films are like karate, aggressive and driven, to the slow, meditative tai chi of international films.

Bicycle Thieves (Italy, 1948)

Neorealism, the film style that developed in Italy immediately after World War II, is best represented by the film *Bicycle Thieves* (*Ladri di biciclette*, in Italian; it was called *Bicycle Thief* when it was first released internationally. The plural is correct. There is more than one thief in this story).

In reaction to the superficiality of the "white telephone" films of fascist Italy (light comedies imitating Hollywood, expressing conservative values approved by the government), the postwar filmmakers endorsed the idea that a film should be as free of artifice as possible, minimizing the distance between reality and the story. They insisted on emotional honesty, simplicity, and hard truths, with an emphasis on the plight of workers in that economically distressed time.

That did not mean that the films were created casually. *Bicycle Thieves* took six months to be shaped by director Vittorio De Sica and his screenwriter Cesare Zavattini, from the novel of the same name, before filming could begin. They chose to film on the streets of Rome for a documentary feel, not to save money (the film had a generous budget of 100 million lire, and many crowd scenes requiring a large cast) and De Sica chose nonactors for the lead roles for their authenticity: their faces, how they held themselves. Antonio, the father, is played by Lamberto Maggiorani, who was a factory worker. The son, Bruno, was played by nine-year-old Enzo Staiola, who De Sica chose because of his expressive face, and his energetic walking.

Because this is a film where walking is important. The story is simple. Work is scarce and when Antonio is offered a job putting up movie posters he is overjoyed. But the job requires a bicycle and he has pawned his bicycle to put food on the table. His wife, Maria, gathers up their wedding sheets and brings them to the pawnshop. The pawnshop owner takes the carefully folded sheets and in a surreal moment we see him add them to a wall of shelves filled with sheets, reaching to the ceiling. An image that eloquently conveys the poverty and desperation of so many of these workers.

With the cash they redeem his bicycle. Antonio's son Bruno has been the breadwinner for the family working in a gas station, but now Antonio can resume his proper role. We see Bruno imitating his dad as they both get ready to go to work, picking up on his happy mood. Bruno notices that there is a dent in the bike and tells his father he should have complained, but Antonio brushes it off; he is just glad he has the bike and a job. In a classic Hollywood movie this detail might have become important later, perhaps helping them identify the missing bicycle—the famous Chekhov gun. But we never hear of it again. Instead, what it does show us is how observant and practical Bruno is. And how passively ineffective Antonio is.

The next day Antonio proudly goes to work. Putting up his first poster (of Rita Hayworth in the Hollywood film *Gilda*, a world away from postwar Italy), he leaves his bicycle leaning on the wall. A thief grabs it and rides away. Antonio gives chase but loses him. And so begins a day of frustration and lost hope for him and his son.

Antonio first reports the theft at the police station. When one policeman asks the other what is going on, the first says, "Nothing, just a stolen bicycle." But we know that this "nothing" means everything to Antonio and his family.

What follows is one disappointment after another. Antonio asks for help at the trade union hall. A search at Piazza Vittoria where stolen bicycles are sold is fruitless; the sellers are unsympathetic and challenge his right to look at their wares. Bruno is constantly looking up at his father, checking in on him and mirroring his mood. But Antonio is too preoccupied to notice, several times losing sight of Bruno and then in panic finding him again.

When they see the thief and chase him through the streets of Rome, his neighbors threaten Antonio: how dare he accuse him when he has no proof? Bruno runs to get a policeman, but when he comes, disperses the crowd, and does a cursory investigation of the boy's house, he tells Antonio that without witnesses there is nothing he can do. Everywhere he turns, Antonio finds indifference, hostility, and a social system that simply doesn't care.

Antonio suggests that they stop for a pizza, which he can't afford. Bruno lights up, he is hungry. The trattoria doesn't serve pizza so they order a mozzarella sandwich. At the next table, a well-off family is enjoying a feast and we see Bruno eyeing the boy at that table, and what he is eating—pasta, a real meal. Antonio tells him that you would have to earn a million lira a month to be able to eat like that. Antonio talks about how this job would have made everything okay for them and asks Bruno to do the math, how much they would have if he could work every day. Time and again we see how bright, sensible, and observant Bruno is, and how limited Antonio is. They enjoy their meal together.

They then wander toward the soccer stadium where a big match is ending. There are hundreds of bicycles parked outside. Bruno sits at the curb with Antonio, and then watches him staring at the bicycles, and then one in particular, leaning alone on a wall. Antonio tells Bruno to take the tram

Figure 12.1 Young Bruno is the moral center of this story. Bruno Staiola, Lamberto Maggiorani. Bicycle Thieves © Arthur Mayer and Joseph Burstyn Inc. Screenshot captured by the authors.

home, then walks to the bicycle and jumps on it to ride away. Just then the owner comes outside and begins to chase him, followed by a crowd.

They overtake Antonio, knock him to the ground, and begin to march him to the police. Bruno sees what is happening and runs to his father, crying. The bicycle owner, seeing Bruno at Antonio's side, says sarcastically, "You are a fine example for your son" and decides not to press charges. Antonio is humiliated, ashamed, and tearful. People are surging past, many on bicycles. Bruno looks up at his father lovingly and reaches up to take Antonio's hand. The moment is heartbreaking. They disappear into the crowd, and the movie ends.

This is powerful storytelling, beautiful and real. We are watching one story that could be thousands of stories. The transparency of feeling in Bruno's face is especially touching, but Antonio's moments of realization of what he almost had and what he has lost are moving as well. These nonactors are so inhabiting their roles that you almost can't call it acting.

The film magazine *Sight and Sound* did its first poll of international film in 1952. This film had such an impact that it was chosen as the greatest film of all time. *BBC Culture* in 2018 did a poll of the greatest foreign language films of all time. *Bicycle Thieves* came in at number two (number one was Kurosawa's *Seven Samurai*).

British versus American: *The Haunting* (1963) and *The Haunting* (1999)

Do British films count as international, for our purposes? They tend to split the difference between Hollywood and art house. Their budgets tend to be lower, the action more controlled, the characters more developed, the plots more intricate and thoughtful. Yet there are plenty of British blockbusters: the *Harry Potter* series, *The King's Speech* (2011), *Slumdog Millionaire* (2009), *Paddington* (2014), and *Four Weddings and a Funeral* (1994), to name but a few.

There are contrasting styles and cultural nuances portrayed in British and American films. From the eloquent dialogue and dry humor of British classics to the grandeur and spectacle of American blockbusters, these two distinct film industries have carved their own identities.

British cinema is renowned for its subtle storytelling, rich character development, and understated performances. British filmmakers have a penchant for delving into complex human emotions and social commentaries with a touch of dry wit and a less-is-more approach—think of it as a cinematic equivalent of artistic minimalism. What is the maximum that can be conveyed with a cool minimum of having things served to the audience on a platter? Works of directors like Carol Reed, Ken Loach, and Mike Leigh are known for their realistic portrayals of ordinary lives, tackling themes such as social class, societal norms, and political critique. Dialogue tends to take center stage rather than action, movement, and spectacle. Scripts are not vehicles for plot conveyance but are carefully crafted to highlight the nuances of interpersonal relationships and societal issues. The dialogue tends to be measured, with an emphasis on intelligent banter and clever wordplay. The British film industry also values the power of silence and subtle gestures, allowing viewers to read between the lines and derive deeper meaning from the narrative.

The use of natural lighting and subdued colors adds to the realism and authenticity of the storytelling, creating an immersive experience for the audience. British films tend to exhibit a distinct visual aesthetic, often capturing the atmospheric beauty of the countryside or the gritty urban landscapes. This means fewer films made on closed sets and less reliance on dazzling spectacle and special effects.

Contrast this to the spectacular escapism of much American cinema. Known for its grandeur, larger-than-life characters, and a focus on entertainment that has little to do with daily life (in fact, that helps you forget about the quotidian and, for ninety minutes or so, plunge into another world), American directors push the boundaries of filmmaking, showcasing their technical prowess and mastery of visual storytelling.

American films often feature high production values, elaborate set designs, and breathtaking special effects. From epic sci-fi blockbusters to action-packed superhero franchises, the American film industry thrives on delivering thrilling experiences and transporting audiences to fantastical realms. These films aim to entertain, offering viewers an "out" from reality and a chance to indulge in awe-inspiring visuals.

In terms of character portrayals, American cinema is known for its strong emphasis on individualism and the triumph of the human spirit. Many American films revolve around heroic narratives, where underdogs rise to overcome adversity and achieve their dreams. These narratives often celebrate the pursuit of success, reflecting the American ethos of ambition, self-determination, and the belief in endless possibilities. While British films often explore themes of social inequality, class divisions, and the quirks of British identity and confront uncomfortable truths, offering social critique and promoting introspection, American films tend to embody the American dream. This means highlighting individualism, ambition, and the pursuit of happiness. These films project American ideals onto the global stage, shaping international perceptions of the nation and its cultural values.

There is plenty of crossover, particularly when successful British directors move to Hollywood and find that their more artful sensibilities can be supported by American-sized budgets: Alfred Hitchcock, Christopher Nolan, Ridley Scott, Sam Mendes, David Lean, and Danny Boyle are a few who come to mind.

The contrast is particularly visible in American remakes of British films. Consider *The Haunting* (1963), directed by Robert Wise. This was a British black-and-white, artistic, and elegant film adaptation of the famous Shirley Jackson 1959 psychological horror novel, *The Haunting of Hill House*. This film was remade in America and released in 1999, and in 2018 the story was once again redone, now as an American television series.

The story follows Eleanor Vance, a psychologically fragile woman who joins a paranormal investigation led by Dr. Markway at Hill House, a mansion thought to be haunted.

Dr. Markway seeks to investigate the reported paranormal activity at Hill House and invites individuals to join his study. Among those present are Theodora (Theo), a psychic, and Eleanor, who experienced poltergeist occurrences during her childhood. Eleanor is also burdened by guilt over her recently deceased mother, having spent her adult life caring for her.

Upon arrival at Hill House, the group discovers the peculiar construction of the mansion, with askew angles, off-center perspectives, and doors that open and close on their own. The library features the dilapidated spiral staircase from which the previous owner hanged herself. On their first night, Eleanor and Theo are terrified by banging sounds against Theo's bedroom door and hear the echoing voice of a young girl.

Despite the fear, Eleanor develops a hesitant connection to Hill House. The next day, the group explores the house and discovers a chilling cold spot near the nursery. Another night of disturbances follows, and the words "Help Eleanor Come Home" are found scrawled on a wall in a chalky substance, deeply distressing Eleanor.

During the night, Theo joins Eleanor in her room, and they fall asleep together. Eleanor wakes up to the sounds of an indistinct male voice and a woman's laughter. Frightened, she asks Theo to hold her hand but soon feels a crushing grip. As Eleanor hears the cries of a young girl in pain, she confronts the source, shouting at whoever is causing harm. Theo wakes up to find Eleanor on the couch, realizing it wasn't her hand Eleanor held. This is one of the great scenes in film history, hugely creepy and effective without any action to speak of, just sounds.

The following day, Dr. Markway's skeptical wife, Grace, arrives at Hill House to warn him of a reporter who has discovered his investigation. Despite Eleanor's growing affection for Markway, unaware of his marital status, Grace insists on joining the group and demands a room in the nursery, despite her husband's warning of its likely connection to the disturbances. That night, the group experiences loud banging and an unseen force attempting to enter their living room, causing the door to bulge inward. The banging then moves toward the nursery, where sounds of destruction emerge. Eleanor rushes toward the nursery and discovers Grace missing.

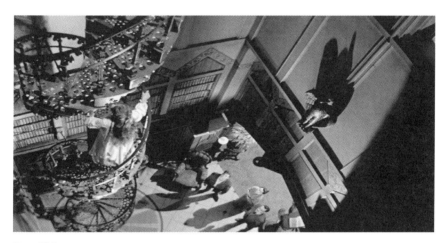

Figure 12.2 The dizzying height, the Dutch angle and looming shadows intensify the sense of dread. Julie Harris. *The Haunting* © MGM. Screenshot captured by authors.

The next morning, Eleanor's mental state deteriorates further as she climbs the decrepit spiral staircase in the library, with Markway following, attempting to coax her down. At the top, Eleanor catches a glimpse of Grace's face through a trapdoor. This is the only proper jump scare in the whole film. Startled, she nearly falls to her death but is rescued by Markway.

Growing alarmed by Eleanor's obsession with Hill House despite the danger, Markway insists she leave. Eleanor drives away, speeding toward the front gates. The steering wheel starts turning on its own, and Eleanor struggles to regain control before eventually succumbing to the unseen force.

Suddenly, a female figure appears and runs in front of the car, causing Eleanor to crash into a tree and die. Markway and the others arrive, only to discover that the figure is Grace, who claims the house deliberately kept her lost.

The British version was a critical success, with brilliant and understated use of atmosphere to evoke a growing, ever-creepier psychological horror. It relies on subtle scares, eerie cinematography, and a spooky vibe, assisted by the music and intentionally odd camera angles. Tension and fear are palpable, but there is hardly a jump scare in the film. There is no violence to speak of shown on-screen, and since it is in black and white, it lacks the vivid gore that is key to so many American horror films (though there have certainly been gory British horror films). The focus of the film is on psychological torment and the inner struggles of the characters. The *Guardian* listed this as the thirteenth-best horror film ever made, and it made Martin Scorsese's list, as well.

The American film is much more of a blunt instrument. It relies on special effects, jump scares, and intense full-color visuals to terrify. The scenes are not introspective but action-oriented, and the budget is in full view, with elaborate set designs, grand sequences, and remarkable special effects. The spectacle was there, and the director, Jan de Bont (of Dutch origin who showed his excellence in films like *Speed*) went too light on the aspects that made the original so brilliant. It was not well-reviewed, but it was a considerable financial success. Consider the box office vs budget for each film. The British version cost $1.05 million and grossed $1.02 million. A financial failure, whatever the reviewers and historians of film have to say about it. The American version cost $80 million to make—eighty times the cost of the British original—but made $180 million. More artistically inclined, perhaps even objectively "better" as a cultural product, does not necessarily (or even often) mean more successful.

Foreign versus American Remakes:
Seven Samurai (1954) and *The Magnificent Seven* (1960 and 2016)

Let us now compare a hugely successful international original, *Seven Samurai* (made in 1954 but released internationally in 1956), directed by Akira Kurosawa, considered among the greatest directors in film history, and a pair of American remakes.

Set in sixteenth-century feudal Japan, the story revolves around a small village plagued by frequent raids from a band of ruthless bandits. In

Figure 12.3 Toshirô Mifune,Yoshio Tsuchiya. *Seven Samurai* aka *Shichinin no samurai* (1954). Columbia Pictures / Photofest © Columbia Pictures.

desperation, the villagers seek the help of seven skilled and diverse samurai warriors to defend their village against the impending attack. The first third of the film, Act 1, follows the recruiting of the samurai. There is little action, other than some demonstrations of the abilities of the recruits and an opening scene that establishes the plight of the villagers.

Led by the wise and experienced Kambei, the samurai gradually form a bond with the villagers and begin preparing them for battle. They teach the villagers how to fight and fortify the village against the bandits. Each samurai brings his unique skills and personality to the group, creating a dynamic and engaging ensemble. This preparation for the climactic defense of the village covers Act 2.

As the film progresses, the samurai face various challenges and obstacles, both external and internal. They clash with the bandits in intense battles, showcasing their bravery and tactical prowess, but only toward the end, in Act 3. Amid the action, deep character development takes place, revealing the samurai's individual stories, fears, and motivations. The film also explores the complexities of honor, loyalty, sacrifice, and the contrast between the samurai's noble ideals and the harsh realities of their existence. The relationships that develop between the samurai, as well as their interactions with the villagers, provide a deeper understanding of their personalities and the moral dilemmas they face. They are shown as seven unique characters, with nothing generic or two-dimensional about them.

Seven Samurai climaxes with a battle between the samurai and the bandits, as the villagers fight alongside their defenders. This is withheld—we expect and indeed can't wait for an elaborate fight scene, and it doesn't disappoint. But it's delayed for so long that this can hardly be considered an action film—rather a character study and morality play that drives the audience along through the promise of action. The film delves into the human condition—it's as much about social class as anything else. The villagers want the samurai to save them, but they don't want anything to do with them beyond that, as samurai were considered of lower status than farmers. At the end of the film, a comment is made that only the farmers in the village won, not the samurai, who are packed off unheralded. Among the samurai we see the value of camaraderie and the sacrifices made in the pursuit of justice and protection, but the dynamic doesn't cross caste boundaries. There is action, but the fight scenes are controlled, as if movement were a valued commodity, which when one thinks about it, it is. We might be used to over-the-top, hacking, and twirling sword fights, but these are subtle, a step and a strike and they're over.

Seven Samurai has been listed among the best films ever made, by everything from Rotten Tomatoes to *Sight and Sound* to the British Film Institute. It is a masterwork of the cowriter and director, Kurosawa, and solidified the stardom of charismatic Toshiro Mifune, who had made his name in Kurosawa's 1950 *Rashomon*. It is part of a Japanese tradition called *jidaigeki*, period films taking place in historical times. These were hugely popular in Japan but found audiences beyond its borders. *Seven Samurai* is truly epic, in theme and to watch—it clocks in at three and a half hours! Despite critical praise, it only grossed $346,258 when it first came out. But its reputation remained strong, and a rerelease in 2002 grossed nearly a million.

The first remake, *The Magnificent Seven* (1960) shifts the story of a poor village recruiting samurai to defend them against bandits in sixteenth-century Japan to the nineteenth-century American Wild West. A poor Mexican village requires the same services and turns to gunslingers. In both cases, the heroes are motivated by the noble cause of defending the poor, the humble, the helpless. But they are also down on their luck and need the very modest money offered by the villagers.

Figure 12.4 Yul Brynner, Steve McQueen, Horst Bucholz, Charles Bronson, Robert Vaughn, Brad Dexter, James Coburn. *The Magnificent Seven* (1960). United Artists / Photofest © United Artists.

The format is the same, just now made American in setting and historical moment. The seven gunslingers in this ensemble cast are a who's who of future male stars. Yul Brynner was already a big star, but others like Steve McQueen, James Coburn, Charles Bronson, and Robert Vaughn were at the start of their careers. Eli Wallach as the bad guy steals the show with the standout performance, creating a charismatic, thoughtful, not-entirely-evil character; we learn later in the film that his own men, the bandits, are starving, so we understand his motivation and even feel a measure of sympathy for it. Director John Sturges gives us a higher body count but likewise is controlled in dosing out action. There are several rounds of the climactic battle, but the pace is steady, not what we expect from Hollywood (though this was 1960, a time with a much lower expected action quotient than in today's movies).

The producer Lou Morheim bought the rights to remake *Seven Samurai* for $2,500. This proved a shrewd move, because Yul Brynner's production company then bought those rights from him for $10,000 plus a 5 percent cut of the profits. Brynner, a Russian-born actor, originally planned to direct, with Anthony Quinn starring. But then John Sturges came in, and Brynner took the lead role.

The film was first released in the United States and earned *only* $2.25 million, which was considered a disappointment, particularly with the star power of the cast in mind. A *New York Times* review called it a "pallid, pretentious and overlong reflection of the Japanese original . . . don't expect anything like the ice-cold suspense, the superb juxtaposition of revealing human vignettes and especially the pile-driver tempo of the first *Seven*." While I'm not sure I agree that the three-and-a-half-hour original had a "pile-driver tempo," such an acclaimed film was certainly a hard act to follow. But then the film opened abroad. Italy, France, and the United Kingdom each sold more than seven million tickets, making it among the one hundred top-grossing films in the history of the latter two countries. In the Soviet Union, Brynner's homeland, sixty-seven million tickets sold, making it the most successful Hollywood film ever there. Overseas tickets amount to nearly ninety million sold–that's not $90 million, but ninety million tickets.

This was a big enough hit that three sequels and a TV series were made. It also inspired *The A-Team*, *Ocean's Eleven*, and *The Dirty Dozen*, action films about teams of misfit warriors played by an ensemble of stars. But that took some time, and it took international audiences to appreciate a Hollywood film that had more of a foreign film vibe.

That vibe is no longer present in the 2016 remake, which is a straight remake of *The Magnificent Seven* (not an adaptation, as the first had been of *Seven Samurai*). The ensemble of male stars included Denzel Washington, Chris Pratt, Ethan Hawke, and Vincent D'Onofrio. The director, Antoine Fuqua, is a modern action master, having shown his powers to create tension in the Washington and Hawke feature *Training Day* (2001), as well as *Shooter* (2007), *Olympus Has Fallen* (2013) and many more—this is a man who knows how to do action. He had a giant budget to work with, around $100 million, and the film grossed $167 million.

The plot introduces a frontier town that is terrorized by a mining tycoon. The townsfolk who were chased from their homes turn to a team of bounty hunters to come to their aid and reclaim it. The character names differ but their major features remain consistent with their equivalents in the original (Washington plays the Brynner character, Pratt plays the McQueen-like character). The concept remains, though instead of protecting a town and its people, the seven soldiers attack the town as it is occupied by the bad guys. What's upped is that action quotient and the body count. The violence is more graphic and tense—it's a very Hollywood remake of an original that was Hollywood-cum-international film. It is also far more diverse in terms of casting. The director, who is Black, noted that the original script and casting featured all white actors. The real Wild West of America was multicultural, with Black cowboys and Native Americans as well as immigrants from Asia. This led to a shift in casting, including Washington as the star, and a Korean actor (Byung-hun Lee), and an Indigenous actor (Martin Sensmeier).

The 2016 version takes the basic premise but turns it into a straight action film. There is much more tension, more fights, and a higher and bloodier body count, and it is gripping because action done well is gripping. But the characters are more caricatures, far less developed than in either previous version. *Seven Samurai* used three and a half hours to give generous time for the backstory of each of the seven samurai. These are three fine films: one an international classic, one a pure Hollywood action film, and one a bridge between the two.

A Single Ambiguous Action Defines the Film: Tarkovsky's *Nostalghia* (Russia, 1983)

The differences between American and British films are more subtle versions of the striking distinction between older, foreign language films and their American equivalents. Bigger-budget international films often feel more "Hollywood" as they seek to take in larger box offices and make money in international markets. This trend toward an "Americanization" of pop culture has been so often noted that it is now a term that doesn't require quotation marks surrounding it. Whether that's good or bad or a bit of both is not in discussion here, but it does mean that a foreign film like India's megahit *RRR* (2022), which with a budget of $72 million was one of the most expensive Indian films ever, earned $160 million worldwide, third-most in Indian film history, and had over fifty million viewers on Netflix alone, feels Hollywood even if the location and language are foreign. The international films that feel least American are those for which profit is not even truly a goal. Take the Slovenian film industry, for example. Only one film has ever made a profit there, and that was a super-low-budget slapstick comedy, *Pr'Hostar* (2016), filmed by a group of friends—it profited (earning just over $1 million) because it had almost no budget to earn back. In various interviews, Slovenian producers have expressed that they are not really chasing the box office. They are content with earning a salary out of the total film budget, in a country where all films are made via funding from the national Slovenian Film Center—earning profit from the film is not part of the equation. This, on the one hand, provides complete freedom not to cater to the bottom line. On the other hand, maybe there's something to be said for being held accountable for creating a product, even if it is an artwork, that will appeal enough to be financially successful.

There are so many foreign films that have found international success beyond the borders in which they were created that one can really speak of three categories. There are American, or American-style films. There are international films, like *The Seven Samurai*, that strike a balance, often hugely successful in their own nations, but also acclaimed and popular abroad, despite not trying to go Hollywood. And there are international, by which most mean art house, films which are "doing their own thing," not aiming to go Hollywood, but content to be works of art, often a passion project of the writer/director (these are most often distinct roles in Hollywood, sometimes with multiple screenwriters for any project), with entertainment and mass appeal not requisite parts of the equation.

Figure 12.5 Andrei Tarkovsky is renowned for surreal, haunting images like this shot of a roofless church blurred by snowfall. *Nostalghia* © Grange Communications Inc. Screenshot captured by the authors.

A Russian poet lies in the grass alongside a German shepherd dog. As the camera pulls away, we see that he is not in a sprawling field, but inside a ruined church. Then the camera pulls still farther back, and we see that the church is roofless, and cottony snow begins to fall within it.

The films of Russian director Andrei Tarkovsky (1932–1986) overflow with memorable, haunting images. He made only eight films during his career, but he is on the Mount Olympus of filmmakers. Tarkovsky is a filmmaker with a capital F. You will not find a *movie* in his oeuvre. His works are slow, puzzling, difficult to follow, and occasionally frustrating, depending on your mood and expectations. He is the poster boy for director-as-artist, beloved by film students, and dismissed by those who prefer to watch movies that merely entertain and permit them to watch passively. If you are not prepared to be an active viewer, to watch carefully and patiently, to untangle the riddle that Tarkovsky offers up to you, then you may grow confused or bored.

Tarkovsky's films can be appreciated by his many artistic references and the staggering beauty of his films. They are more like a series of tableaux vivant, even a slideshow, than a film in the traditional sense. *Nostalghia* is a film that you must settle into. Not much "happens" in terms of plot, and we are not privy to all that much in terms of character development, either. Dialogue is sparse and stilted.

What's left, you might ask? We are left with a series of situations, actions, and images that drive themselves into the mind.

Nostalghia follows the visit of a Russian poet and musician, Gorchakov, to the small Tuscan town of Bagno Vignoni, which is built around ancient hot springs, contained in a stone reservoir in the middle of the town. He is accompanied by Eugenia, a translator with long, curly hair. They first visit a church in which Eugenia watches a ritual involving a statue of the Virgin Mary, which is opened to release a flock of sparrows, in a chapel containing Piero della Francesca's famous *Madonna del Parto*, a painting to which women made pilgrimage if they had trouble conceiving. While wandering the town, they encounter Domenico, a local madman who once locked his family in their home for seven years. Many speculate on why he did this, and Gorchakov is intrigued. He tries to speak with Domenico, first via Eugenia, who is annoyed that Gorchakov expresses no interest in her physically. He eventually speaks with Domenico alone and is told that he must cross the hot springs with a candle, without it extinguishing—something Domenico is unable to do. Back in Rome and about to head home to Russia, Gorchakov learns that Domenico is in the city, acting strangely, and leading a demonstration. Domenico stands astride the statue of Marcus Aurelius on the Campidoglio, making bizarre proclamations before an audience of mentally disturbed citizens, before he calmly immolates himself to a soundtrack of Beethoven that fails to play properly. Gorchakov returns to Bagno Vignoni before Domenico's death, and slowly, achingly manages to cross the springs with the lit candle—at which point he collapses.

What stays with the viewer are the surreal sequences and images. A madman tells a Russian poet that he must cross a hot spring with a lit candle. It rains in someone's home. A church is flooded. It snows inside a church. A man immolates himself to a scratchy recording of Beethoven's *Ninth Symphony*, while astride the Equestrian Statue of Marcus Aurelius in Rome. A lot of people slowly smoke cigarettes and stare. *Nostalghia* is a film to ease into, but one which will pick at your brain for years to come. It asks you, the viewer, to *work*, and work hard, to figure out what is happening in the film and what it is actually about, because you come away with the certainty that the point Tarkovsky wishes to make is implied by what we see in the film but not actually visible there.

George Orwell's 1945 novel, *Animal Farm*, tells the story of a group of farm animals who rebel against their human farmer, hoping to create a society in which all animals can be free, happy, and live in a world of equality. It was not *actually* about farm animals but was a political fable about the Russian Revolution and Stalin (the farmer) betraying his people. We understand that *Nostalghia* is not actually about whether a poet can cross a reservoir with a lit candle. But we are also not overtly told what it is about. Hence the invitation to generations of film studies students to write essays trying to interpret it.

Lesser filmmakers might produce something utterly pretentious and off-putting using this same approach. Tarkovsky, the master, offers up a mystery. He paints moving Magrittes. Perhaps his legacy is best seen in the work of David Lynch, but Lynch volunteers that he has not conceived of a solution to the mysteries he throws on-screen, from *Twin Peaks* (1990) to *Mulholland Drive* (2001). In this way, Lynch is just like Magritte. The Belgian Surrealist painter designed intriguing, realistically-depicted, surrealistically-inspired paintings with evocative titles that prompt viewers to seek to solve the mystery that the paintings embody—but Magritte claimed that he never conceived of the solution.

Take his *Son of Man* (1964), a painting of a businessman in a bowler hat with an apple completely hiding his face. Showing this painting to art history students and asking them to interpret it, they'd get a good grade if they described the painting as about Original Sin, Adam, and the death of Jesus. But were you to ask Magritte, he would shrug his shoulders, refusing to answer, claiming that he didn't know, as he had never designed an answer to his visual riddles. He wanted to immerse viewers in a sense of mystery without resolution. For if the mystery is "solved," the viewer can set the picture aside, having "finished" with it. But if the mystery is present but refuses to be solved, then the desire to solve it remains, and the picture lives on. Lynch subscribes to the Magritte School of Mystery. Tarkovsky, on the other hand, has very specific things in mind. He just doesn't want to hand them to you—he wants you to have to work for them.

The film offers more questions than answers. Does Gorchakov die at the end, or merely collapse from the effort? Why did Domenico lock himself and his family away for seven years? What are we to make of the patch of white on Gorchakov's hair? Or the German shepherd who appears as the companion and pet of everyone in the film, whether they are in black-and-white flashbacks to Russia or in color in Italy? Would the film be any good, if all of these questions were neatly answered? Or if a team of ninjas swooped in to snatch away the lit candle just as Gorchakov reached the end of the reservoir?

There is a time, place, and mood for art house cinema, and dips into the world of international films provide beautiful, moving, thought-provoking views into world cultures. These views outward are ultimately introspective glances within, since the human experience is remarkably similar, regardless of where we might have been born or choose to live.

Just know what you're getting into. Some nights you want swooping ninjas, some nights smoking philosophers.

The Movie Playlist

Here you can find a curated "menu" of movies that we do not discuss in our chapters. The films mentioned in the chapters are ones we consider the most exemplary of the ideas we wish to convey, and are also, honestly, the best of the best. But there are so many other great movies out there, and you will find them here, in playlists by genre that we hope will inspire more popcorn evenings.

Silent Movies
Modern Times (1936)
The Great Dictator (1940)
Seven Chances (1925)
The General (1926)
Lulu
Pandora's Box (1929)
The Show Off (1926)
Wings (1927)
Faust (1926)
Napoleon (1927)
Battleship Potemkin (1925)
The Thief of Bagdad (1924)

Classic Hollywood
The Best Years of Our Lives (1946)
Only Angels Have Wings (1939)
Ninotchka (1939)
The Grapes of Wrath (1940)
Sunset Boulevard (1950)
Snow White and the Seven Dwarfs (1937)
Lawrence of Arabia (1962)
Gone with the Wind (1939)
Dinner at Eight (1934)
All About Eve (1950)
Now, Voyager (1942)

The Western
High Noon (1952)
Shane (1953)
She Wore a Yellow Ribbon (1949)
Cat Ballou (1965)
True Grit (1969, 2010)
The Treasure of the Sierra Madre (1948)
The Ox-Bow Incident (1943)
Hud (1963)
Bad Day at Black Rock (1955)

Destry Rides Again 1939)
Johnny Guitar (1954)
Winchester 73 (1950)

Film Noir
In a Lonely Place (1950)
Sweet Smell of Success (1957)
The Lady from Shanghai (1947)
High Sierra (1941)
The Asphalt Jungle (1950)
The Killers (1946)
A Kiss before Dying (1956)
The Big Heat (1953)
Kiss Me Deadly (1955)
This Gun for Hire (1942)
The Woman in the Window (1944)
The Blue Dahlia (1946)

Comedy
Romantic
Moonstruck (1987)
Arthur (1981)
The Goodbye Girl (1977)
Roman Holiday (1953)
Annie Hall (1977)
Amelie (2001)
Sleepless in Seattle (1993)
A Touch of Class (1973)
The Apartment (1960)
The Graduate (1967)
The Philadelphia Story (1940)
Enough Said (2013)

Farce/Slapstick
The In-Laws (1979)
Bananas (1971)
What's New Pussycat? (1965)

A Day at the Races (1937)
Horse Feathers (1932)
The Naked Gun (1988)
National Lampoon's Animal House (1978)
The Blues Brothers (1980)
The Court Jester (1956)
The Nutty Professor (1963)
Ghostbusters (1984)
A Shot in the Dark (Pink Panther) (1964)

Screwball
Twentieth Century (1934)
The Front Page (1931)
His Girl Friday (1940)
The Awful Truth (1937)
Ball of Fire (1941)
A Fish Called Wanda (1988)
Bananas (1971)
Arsenic and Old Lace (1944)
Local Hero (1983)
What About Bob? (1991)
The Thin Man (1934)
The Producers (1967)

Satire/Parody
Blazing Saddles (1974)
The Miracle at Morgan's Creek (1944)
Adam's Rib (1949)
Hopscotch (1980)
This Is Spinal Tap (1984)
Monty Python's Life of Brian (1979)
Monty Python and the Holy Grail (1975)
Young Frankenstein (1974)
Shaun of the Dead (2004)
Sons of the Desert (1933)
Way Out West (1936)
Born Yesterday (1951)

Worldly
Tootsie (1982)
The Odd Couple (1968)
Lost in Yonkers (1993)
As Good As It Gets (1997)
Grosse Point Blank (1997)
Eternal Sunshine of the Spotless Mind (2004)
The General (1926)
The Heartbreak Kid (1972)
American Graffiti (1973)

Shampoo (1975)
To Be or Not to Be (1942)
Diner (1982)

Musicals
Follow the Fleet (1936)
Shall We Dance (1937)
On the Town (1949)
The Sound of Music (1965)
An American in Paris (1951)
That's Entertainment (1974)
All That Jazz (1979)
Funny Face (1957)
Rocky Horror Picture Show (1975)
Show Boat (1936)
Help! (1965)
Matilda (2022)

Suspense
Rear Window (1954)
North by Northwest (1959)
Notorious (1946)
The Silence of the Lambs (1991)
The Conversation (1974)
Se7en (1995)
Blow Out (1981)
The Usual Suspects (1995)
Drive (2011)
The Hurt Locker (2009)
All the President's Men (1976)
One False Move (1992)

Horror
A Quiet Place (2018)
The Fly (1986)
Poltergeist (1982)
Saint Maude (2019)
The Last House on the Left (1972)
The Sixth Sense (1999)
Dr. Jekyll and Mr. Hyde (1931)
The Innocents (1961)
Suspiria (1977)
Evil Dead II (1987)
The Wicker Man (1973)
Jaws (1975)

Action
Raiders of the Lost Ark (1981)

The Fugitive (1993)
From Russia with Love (1963)
Skyfall (2012)
Oldboy (2003)
Terminator (1984)
Mission: Impossible—Dead Reckoning Part
    One (2023)
No Country for Old Men (2007)
The Bourne Supremacy (2004)
Day of the Jackal (1973)
The Russia House (1990)
The Gray Man (2022)

Sci-Fi, Fantasy, and Superhero Films
Sci-Fi
Star Wars (1977)
Star Wars: The Empire Strikes Back (1980)
Star Wars: The Return of the Jedi (1983)
Star Trek (2009)
Interstellar (2014)
Back to the Future (1985)
Aliens (1986)
Wall-E (2008)
Close Encounter of the Third Kind (1977)
E.T. the Extra-Terrestrial (1982)
Gravity (2013)
Forbidden Planet (1956)
Pacific Rim (2013)

Fantasy
The Princess Bride (1987)
Pirates of the Caribbean (2003)
Groundhog Day (1993)
The Green Mile (1999)
Beauty and the Beast (1991)
Stairway to Heaven (1946)
Enchanted (2007)
Frozen (2013)
Big (1988)
How to Train Your Dragon (2010)
Time Bandits (1981)
Highlander (1986)

Superheroes
Superman (1978)
The Dark Knight (2008)
Guardians of the Galaxy (2014)
Iron Man (2008)
Avengers: Endgame (2019)
Spider-Man (2002)
Black Panther (2018)
Sin City (2005)
Wonder Woman (2017)
Nimona (2023)
Hellboy (2004)
The Old Guard (2020)

International Art Films
In these films, the director's sensibility defines them. For this reason, we are listing them by director. We are also breaking our rule of twelve to give you a more complete selection. Note that European convention is that only the first word in a title is capitalized, the rest are all lowercase. The films are listed with their original language titles, with occasional exceptions when the English title is better known.

France
Jean Renoir
La bête humaine (1938)
La règle du jeu (1939)

Marcel Carné
Le jour se lève (1939)
Les enfants du paradis (1945)

René Clair
A nous la liberté (1931)

François Truffaut
    Les quatre cents coups (1959)
Jules and Jim (1962)
Day for Night (1973)
The Bride Wore Black (1968)

Jean-Luc Godard
À bout de souffle (1960)
Alphaville (1965)
Une femme mariée (1964)

Eric Rohmer
Ma nuit chez Maud (1969)
Claire's Knee (1970)

Jean-Pierre Melville
Le cercle rouge (1970)
Le samourai (1987)
Bob le flambeur (1956)

Italy
Luchino Visconti
Ossessione (1943)

Roberto Rossellini
Roma città aperta (1945)

Vittorio De Sica
Umberto D (1952)
La ciociara (1960)

Luchino Visconti
Rocco e i suoi fratelli (1960)
The Leopard (1963)
Death in Venice (1971)

Federico Fellini
La strada (1954)
La dolce vita (1960)
8 ½ (1963)
Amarcord (1973)

Michelangelo Antonioni
L'avventura (1960)
L'eclisse (1962)
Blow-Up (1966)

Pier Paolo Pasolini
Edipo re (1967)
Il Decameron (1971)
Salo o le 120 giornate di Sodoma (1976)

Lina Wertmuller
The Seduction of Mimi (1972)
Swept Away (1975)
Seven Beauties (1976)

Sergio Leone
A Fistful of Dollars (1964)

The Good, The Bad, and the Ugly (1968)
Once Upon a Time in America (1984)

Dario Argento
L'uccello dalle piume di cristallo (1970)

Giuseppe Tornatore
Cinema paradiso (1988)

Roberto Benigni
La vita e bella (1997)

Paolo Sorrentino
La grande bellezza (2013)

Spain
Luis Buñuel
Los olvidados (1950)
Viridiana (1961)
Belle de jour (1967)
The Discreet Charm of the Bourgeoisie (1972)

Pedro Almodóvar
Mujeres al borde de un ataque de "nervios"
    (1988)
All about My Mother (1999)

India
Satyajit Ray
Pather Panchali (1955)

Shah Rukh Khan
Kuch Kuch Hota Hai (1998)
Om Shanti Om (2007)

S. S. Rajamouli
RRR (2022)

Japan
Akira Kurasawa
Rashomon (1950)
High and Low (1963)
Throne of Blood (1957)
Ran (1985)

Yasujio Ozu
Tokyo Story (1953)

Masaki Kobayashi
Kaidan (1964)

Hiroshi Teshigahara
Woman of the Dunes (1964)

Juzo Itami
Tampopo (1985)
A Taxing Woman (1987)

Ishiro Honda
Godzilla (1954)

Hideo Nakata
Ringu (1998)
Dark Water (2002)

Katsuhiro Otomo
Akira (1988)

Hayao Miyazaki
Princess Mononoke (1997)
Spirited Away (2001)

Australia
Peter Weir
Picnic at Hanging Rock (1975)

Gillian Armstrong
My Brilliant Career (1979)

George Miller
Mad Max (1979)
Happy Feet (2006)
Mad Max: Fury Road (2015)

Baz Luhrmann
Strictly Ballroom (1992)
Romeo and Juliet (1996)
Elvis (2022)

Sweden
Ingmar Bergman
The Virgin Spring (1960)
Wild Strawberries (1957)
Smiles of a Summer Night (1955)
The Seventh Seal (1957)
Through a Glass Darkly (1961)

Fanny and Alexander (1982)

(Ex)Yugoslavia
Jože Gale
Kekec (1951)

France Štiglic
Dolina miru (1956)

Slobodan Sijan
Ko to tamo peva (1980)

Danis Tanovic
No Man's Land (2001)

Žiga Virc
Houston, We Have a Problem (2016)

Russia
Andrei Tarkovsky
Stalker (1979)
Zerkalo (1975)
Solyaris (1972)

Aleksandr Sokurov
Russian Ark (2002)

Denmark
Carl Dreyer
The Passion of Joan of Arc (1928)
Vampyr (1932)

Lars von Trier
Breaking the Waves (1996)
Dogville (2003)
Dancer in the Dark (2000)
Melancholia (2011)
Nymphomania 1 and 2 (2013)

Behind-the-Scenes Movie Job Titles

This short glossary covers some of the most arcane-sounding jobs listed in the credits of any film, to help you differentiate your Key Grips from your Best Boys.

Armorer, or Pyro Technician

The person responsible for the handling, maintenance, and safety of all weapons and explosives used in a movie.

Best Boy

The best boy (a term used for females, too) is the second-in-command for any job, often the chief assistant to the **gaffer**. More specifically, the Best Boy can be the head electrician, controlling the distribution of the power required for the lights.

Body Double

Someone who takes the place of an actor or actress either because they do not want to expose their bodies, or because they are not able, or do not want to do the stunt required, and whose body type is similar to the person they stand in for. This could be for a scene involving nudity or a potentially dangerous stunt.

Boom Operators

Operators of the boom microphone, which is a microphone attached to a long pole that hangs just out of view of the camera in a scene. Holding the boom for a long take and following the actors' movements without the microphone intruding on the scene can require significant physical endurance.

Dialogue Coach

Helps a performer's speech pattern fit the character they are playing, making their accent or how they pronounce words more authentic to the story. See the song "Moses Supposes" from *Singin' in the Rain* for a charming parody of dialogue coaching.

Director of Photography (or DOP)

The person responsible for capturing the film images for every scene, especially controlling the lighting, focus, framing, and camera movement, creating the visual look of the movie (following the director's vision).

Dolly Grip

A grip responsible for the dolly, which is a small truck that moves along tracks and holds the camera, the person running the camera and often the director.

Foley Artist

In postproduction (after the filming, when the film is edited and all the elements assembled), they create important incidental sound effects, such as footsteps, a door hinge creaking, the sound of a bag being opened, or birds in the trees. They can be very creative coming up with ingenious ways for creating effective sounds, hence, being called "artist."

Gaffer

The person in charge of the electrical equipment, especially the lighting, and who works closely with the director of photography.

Grip

The person who positions the lighting and other equipment on the set.

Key Grip

The person in charge of all the groups of grips. They work with the best boy and the gaffer to set up the camera and lighting equipment to the best advantage for each shot.

Matte Artist
The person who creates the artwork for a background image in a shot, such as a cityscape.

Prop Master
The person responsible for finding and organizing all the props (objects that are part of a scene and can be moved easily, such as guns, lamps, phones, or kitchenware) used in a film.

Storyboard Artist
The person who creates a series of drawings or sketches early in the preparation for the movie, each of which represents a different camera setup. Usually made under the director's instruction, these drawings will serve as a guide throughout filming.

Wrangler
The person responsible for controlling all the animals used in a movie as well as any items that need sorting. A new use of the term is **data wrangler**, who organizes the digital materials used for editing the movie.

Recommended Reading

This is not an academic book, so we have not included a traditional bibliography. Instead, we offer this list of twelve recommended authors to read if you'd like to continue your exploration of film beyond our "twelve-hour" offering.

Bassinger, Jean, and Sam Wasson. *Hollywood: The Oral History*. HarperCollins, 2022.

Bogdanovich, Peter. *Who the Devil Made It: Conversations with the Legendary Film Directors*. Ballantine Books, 1998.

———. *Who the Hell's in It: Conversations with Hollywood's Legendary Actors*. Ballantine Books, 2005.

Bordwell, David, Kirsten Thompson, and Jeff Smith. *Film Art: An Introduction*, 12th ed. McGraw-Hill, 2020.

Charney, James. *Madness at the Movies*. Johns Hopkins University Press, 2023.

Clover, Carol J. *Men, Women, and Chainsaws: Gender in the Modern Horror Film*. Princeton University Press, 1993.

Ebert, Roger. *The Great Movies*. Vols. 1–4. Broadway Books, 2002–2020.

Gabler, Neal. *An Empire of Their Own: How the Jews Invented Hollywood*. Anchor Press, 1989.

Kael, Pauline. *The Age of Movies: Selected Writings*. Library of America, 2016.

Lumet, Sidney. *Making Movies*. Alfred Knopf, 1995.

Rosenblum, Ralph. *When the Shooting Stops . . . the Cutting Begins*. Da Capo, 1996.

Schulberg, Budd. *Moving Pictures, Memories of a Hollywood Prince*. Ivan R Dee, 2003.

Thomson, David. *The New Biographical Dictionary of Film*, 6th ed. Alfred Knopf, 2014.

Notes

Chapter 2

1   Lillian Gish with Ann Pinchot, *The Movies, Mr. Griffith, and Me* (Prentice-Hall, 1969), 116.
2   Roger Ebert, *Great Movies II* (Broadway Books, 2005), 107.
3   Charles Chaplin, *My Autobiography* (Penguin Classic, new edition), 2000, 145.
4   Roger Ebert, Great Movies: "The Films of Buster Keaton," November 10, 2002, https://www.rogerebert.com/reviews/great-movie-the-films-of-buster-keaton.
5   Francois Truffaut and Alfred Hitchcock, *Hitchcock/Truffaut* (Simon & Schuster, 1984), 44.

Chapter 3

1   Ben Hecht, *A Child of the Century* (Simon & Schuster, 1954), 466.
2   Ingrid Bergman, interview with Michael Parkinson, *Talking Pictures*, BBC Two, 1973, video, 4:31–4:57, https://youtu.be/SQIRTr4Pohg.

Chapter 5

1   Steven Soderbergh and Roger Deakins, *On Chinatown*, Cinematographers on Cinematography, https://youtu.be/TqblVWWvY-A?si=_jkebjEpkgqCA2Y-.

Chapter 6

1   Stephen Follows, "Genre Trends in Global Film Production," https://stephenfollows.com/genre-trends-global-film-production/.
2   "Comedy," Online Dictionary of Etymology, https://www.etymonline.com/word/comedy.
3   Bellevue College, https://www2.bellevuecollege.edu/artshum/materials/drama/Hoffman/101SIXARISTOAPLAYspro3.asp.
4   The first scripted reference to this is from George Axelrod's stage play, *Will Success Spoil Rock Hunter?* (1955).

5   As noted in the *Empire* magazine online edition, https://www.empireonline.com/movies/features/best-comedy-movies/, May 19, 2023; and "The 100 Greatest Comedies of All Time," https://www.bbc.com/culture/article/20170821-the-100-greatest-comedies-of-all-time.
6   Denis Hollier and R. Howard Bloch, eds., *A New History of French Literature* (Harvard University Press, 1994), p. 126.
7   Bilge Ebiri, "On AFI Top 100," *New York* (February 26, 2014).

Chapter 8

1   Alfred Hitchcock on Mastering Cinematic Tension, American Film Institute, accessed September 1, 2023, https://youtu.be/DPFsuc_M_3E?si=hDp1PS8I6IRaWy h.

Chapter 10

1   Martin Brigg, "Here's Why the *Bullitt* Car Chase Scene Was So Influential," in *Carbuzz*, October 29, 2017, https://carbuzz.com/news/here-s-why-the-bullitt-car-chase-scene-was-so-influential.

Chapter 11

1   George Lucas commentary, *Star Wars Episode VI: Return of the Jedi*, Special Edition, directed by Richard Marquand (DVD, Twentieth Century Fox, 2004).

Chapter 12

1   Jake Kring-Schreifels, "Ang Lee's *Hulk* Was Too Smart and Weird for Its Time," *GQ*, June 20, 2023, https://www.gq.com/story/hulk-ang-lee-2003-film-twenty-years-later.

Index of Feature Films

About the Authors

Taking the first class in film history offered at Columbia College inspired **Dr. James Charney**'s love of movies. He became the very definition of an amateur: a self-taught lover of film, film history, and film craft. His day job as a child and family psychiatrist, teaching at the Yale School of Medicine, led him to develop a popular seminar for seniors at Yale College called *Madness at the Movies*, exploring how mental illness is portrayed in commercial films. He has given talks on film history and taught courses and workshops based on the Yale seminar at the American University in Rome, Arcadia University in Rome, the University of Ljubljana in Slovenia, and the Yale Alumni College, and it is the basis of his first book, *Madness at the Movies*, published in January 2023 by Johns Hopkins University Press. He and his wife, Diane, spend half the year in New Haven, Connecticut, where he continues to teach in the Medical School at Yale, and half the year at their home in Umbria, Italy, to be near their son, Noah, his wife, and their two daughters who all share a passion for the movies.

Dr. Noah Charney is the internationally best-selling author of more than a dozen books, translated into fourteen languages, including *The Collector of Lives: Giorgio Vasari and the Invention of Art*, which was nominated for the 2017 Pulitzer Prize in Biography, and *Museum of Lost Art*, which was the finalist for the 2018 Digital Book World Award. He is a professor of art history specializing in art crime and has taught for Yale University, Brown University, American University of Rome, and University of Ljubljana. He is the founder of ARCA, the Association for Research into Crimes against Art, a groundbreaking research group (www.artcrimeresearch.org), and teaches their annual summer-long postgraduate program in Art Crime and Cultural Heritage Protection. He writes regularly for dozens of major magazines and newspapers, including *The Guardian, Washington Post, Observer*, and *The Art Newspaper*. He is also a TV and radio presenter for BBC and elsewhere and an award-winning podcast host. He lives in Slovenia with his wife, children, and their hairless dog, Hubert van Eyck. Learn more at www.noahcharney.com.